CONTENTS

JIM CLARK'S D-TYPE
THE WHOLE STORY OF TKF 9

58

50

68

30

CONTINUED →

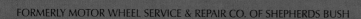

JAGUAR
THE COMPLETE STORY

EDITORIAL OFFICE
Dennis Publishing, 4 Tower Court,
Irchester Road, Wollaston,
Northants NN29 7PJ, UK
Tel: +44 (0)20 7907 6585
Fax: +44 (0)1933 663367
Email: info@octane-magazine.com
or eds@evo.co.uk
Websites: www.octane-magazine.com
or www.evo.co.uk

ADVERTISING OFFICE
Octane Media Advertising Dept,
19 Highfield Lane,
Maidenhead, Berkshire SL6 3AN, UK
Tel: +44 (0)1628 510080.
Fax: +44 (0)1628 510090
Email: ads@octane-magazine.com

Co-editors	David Lillywhite and Peter Tomalin
Designer	Robert Hefferon
Production editor	Glen Waddington
Sub-editor	Sarah Bradley
Publishing assistant	Alex Lowit
Advertising director	Sanjay Seetanah
Advertising sales	Rob Schulp
Advertising production	Anisha Mogra
Publishing director	Geoff Love
Magbook manager	Dharmesh Mistry
Associate publisher	Nicola Bates
Newstrade director	David Barker
Managing director	Ian Westwood
Group finance director	Ian Leggett
COO	Brett Reynolds
CEO	James Tye
Chairman	Felix Dennis

Jaguar: The Complete Story is published under
licence from Dennis Publishing Limited, United
Kingdom. All rights in the licensed material
belong to Felix Dennis, Octane Media
or Dennis Publishing and may not be
reproduced, whether in whole or in part,
without their prior written consent.
Octane is a registered trademark.

Repro by Octane Repro
Printed by BGP, Bicester, UK
Distribution Seymour, 2 East Poultry Avenue,
London EC1A 9PT. Tel: +44 (0)20 7429 4000

WELCOME

Jaguar just gets better and better

WHAT A TIME it's been for Jaguar. It's a company that seems to be riding high lately, with class-leading models in its current range, exciting prototypes up its corporate sleeve and, of course, a history of classics that is becoming ever more appreciated worldwide.

The 50th anniversary of the E-type was The Big One in the classic world recently, with show-stealing displays at Goodwood Festival of Speed and Revival, the Geneva motor show, Pebble Beach concours and many more.

And then there have also been the reveals of the frankly amazing C-X75 hybrid concept car and the gorgeous C-X16 production concept, the long-awaited release of the 2.2-litre diesel version of the XF, the launch of the XKR-S (the fastest-ever roadgoing Jaguar) and the facelift of the XK. Meanwhile the top-of-the-range XJ has continued to attract rave reviews.

What a marque! And what a collection of features from *Octane* and *Evo* magazines over the years that the marque has prompted – the best of which are included in this, the heavily revised second edition of *Jaguar: The Complete Story*. We hope you enjoy it.

DAVID LILLYWHITE EDITOR @Octane_magazine

CONTRIBUTORS

ROBERT COUCHER
XK140 owner Robert drives the Eagle Lightweight Speedster. The ultimate E-type? Read his verdict, beginning on p138.

PHILIP PORTER
The whirlwind behind the XK Club, E-type Club and so many Jaguar books, Philip reports here on the ten greatest ever E-types, p114.

JOHN SIMISTER
John was lucky enough to help with the restoration of the XJ13, and then to test drive it – a rare privilege. See p144.

ROWAN ATKINSON
The world-famous actor is also a dedicated historic racer. Here he describes a drive at the Goodwood Revival, p68.

DEREK BELL
He's best known for winning Le Mans five times, but Derek appreciates his Jaguars, and loved racing a MkI. See p74.

JAGUAR TODAY

THE PRIDE OF LYONS IS ENJOYING THE MOST SUCCESSFUL PERIOD IN ITS HISTORY... EVER

Words: Keith Adams

PRODUCT-LED RECOVERY. A phrase used a lot by former BL chairman Michael Edwardes when explaining how he was going to take the company from the strife-torn 1970s and into the '80s. And we all know what happened next. But now Jaguar – once the prestige division within BL – is undergoing its own product-led recovery. And the signs are rather more promising.

Its recent ownership history has been far from straightforward. Since it left BL behind in 1984, Jaguar remained an independent PLC until 1989, when Ford picked up the company (following a tug-of-war with General Motors) for £1.6bn. Under Ford, Jaguar modernised and grew: its factories were gutted, model lines renewed, and quality improved along the way.

In 2000, Ford purchased Land Rover from BMW (in a post-Rover fire-sale), reuniting the two former BL bedfellows. But in 2007, and after countless billions of dollars of investment in the UK, Ford made public its desire to sell Jaguar Land Rover. Tata Motors emerged as the preferred bidder and, in June 2008, the sale of Jaguar Land Rover to the Indian company was completed for £1.7bn.

It was a marriage that worked well from the outset. Chairman Ratan Tata is passionate about cars, and made it →

Above
Jaguar's C-X75 concept car was unveiled to an awed reception at the 2010 Paris motor show. Supercar looks, hybrid drivetrain – with a micro-turbine twist.

Right and below
You can expect a
production version of
the C-X16 concept car
in 2013. It steals much
of its style from the
E-type, yet extends the
design language first
seen on the XF.

clear from the beginning that he would be leading Jaguar into a new era of success. At the time of the takeover the XK had been on sale a couple of years, and the XF had been unveiled at the previous year's Frankfurt motor show – a waiting list for it soon built up.

Jaguar's future model development was clear for all to see, but the new and existing models in the range jarred. On the new front are XK and XF – and on the retro side of the fence lay the X-type and XJ, both of which harked back to the earlier days of Ford's ownership, and a time when Jaguar had been reluctant to let go of the styling themes of the 1960s and '70s. Dealing with the XJ was straightforward. Under the olde-worlde skin of the X350 was an extremely advanced lightweight aluminium saloon. Project X351 – the new-era XJ – was already underway. And Tata was happy to commit it to production.

The X-type, on the other hand, caused more of a dilemma. It may not have generated serious volumes or been a commercial threat to the BMW 3-series and Audi A4, but it generated volume for the company's Halewood factory. However, there was an alternative strategy, which would see Jaguar abandon the X-type. Many within Jaguar wanted an entry-level sports car – something to fight the Porsche Cayman – and a car like this could be developed in the vacuum left by the X-type.

Tata signed-off the sports car project. It was an obvious decision to take. Jaguar Land Rover's concerns about Halewood – the X-type's assembly plant – would subsequently be alleviated. The factory also builds the Freelander and its upmarket counterpart, the Range Rover Evoque. It's hoped that the latter especially will more than take up the slack at Halewood since the departure of the X-type.

In July 2009, Jaguar's new-age triumvirate was completed with the arrival of the Ian Callum-styled XJ. The new car was a massive evolutionary leap from its predecessor, developing the design themes that first appeared in the XF. The new limousine was offered in two wheelbases, with a 5.0-litre petrol V8 in supercharged or naturally aspirated form, and a 3.0-litre twin-turbo diesel V6. Thanks to relatively light weight compared with the German opposition (aluminium construction typically shaves 200kg from the kerbweight) and taut handling, the new car feels considerably more agile than its 5m-plus length would have you expect.

Buyers liked it too. As with the XF, the XJ immediately started posting sales increases over its predecessor. In 2010, the first year of the new-generation threesome of big cats, Jaguar Land Rover posted an increase in retail sales of 19%. The strongest performances were in the UK, United States and China – traditionally seen as the most conservative markets, and ones that might have been expected to struggle to accept Ian Callum's new design language.

For Jaguar alone, the 2010 books balanced 2009. This was an astonishing performance considering the loss of the 'volume' X-type and the delayed introduction of the XJ, which only really started making an impact during the summer months. Jaguar's top five markets emerged as the UK, United States, Germany, China and Italy which, when combined, equated to 74% of sales for the year. The rise of the XF continued globally throughout 2010 with a rise of 8%, but the new star was definitely the XJ.

This growth carried on into 2011. Jaguar continued its slew of positive numbers – China up 6%, Korea up 29, Russia up 70%, Germany up 49% and Japan up 34%. The XF's rise continued but, once again, it's the XJ that's driving Jaguar's volume upwards. And it's making huge amounts of money, too – Jaguar Land Rover's pre-tax profits were £1.1bn in the financial year ending 31 March 2011, up from £14.6m the previous year.

2011 also saw the arrival of the revised XK and facelifted XF, bringing them closer in style to the XJ. And now the XF is set to balloon in sales, as finally a low-emission 2.2-litre four-cylinder turbodiesel has been installed. It's this car that will go toe-to-toe with the big-selling Audi A6 TDI and BMW 520d, and should mean the addition of the XF to many more fleet managers' purchasing lists.

So what about the future? In terms of production sites, both Halewood and Castle Bromwich remain open for business (after the company's U-turn on its decision to close the latter), and Tata has confirmed fresh investment in the UK with the announcement that it's to open a new facility to manufacture low-emission engines near Wolverhampton in the West Midlands.

The new engine facility follows the Hams Hall Mini production plant to become the second substantial new factory of its type in the UK in the 21st century. The British government said it would support JLR's project through the Grant for Business Investment scheme, which provides up to £10 million. The engine manufacturing facility is expected to create up to 750 highly-skilled engineering and manufacturing posts at JLR, along with thousands more highly-skilled manufacturing jobs, and will be part of JLR's plans to invest £1.5 billion per year for the next five years.

And what of the sports car that Ratan Tata signed-off back in 2008? Jaguar has desperately wanted to build such a car since the mid-1990s

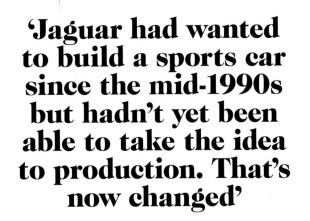

'Jaguar had wanted to build a sports car since the mid-1990s but hadn't yet been able to take the idea to production. That's now changed'

has never yet been in the position to take the idea to production. That's now changed, and Jaguar has been busily working on a new £55,000-70,000 sports car to take on the Porsche Cayman. We've seen the results of that hard work – in concept form – at the 2011 Frankfurt motor show, with the unveiling of the sensational C-X16. And you can find out more about it on page 214.

Be in no doubt that the C-X16 will be hitting the marketplace in production form in 2013. The concept's supercharged V6 produces 375bhp and 332lb ft, and is based on the impressive modular AJ-V8 engine. In the concept car, it's combined with a 95bhp electric power pack to deliver hugely impressive performance as well as just 165g/km of CO_2 emissions.

But it's the C-X16's styling that will dominate your first impressions – unlike the XK, XF and especially XJ, which moved forward the marque's design language by breaking with the past, the more organic C-X16 is instantly recognisable as a Jaguar, even if it looks ultra-modern. Design boss Ian Callum says it is 'an evolution of the design ethos of past Jaguars,' but adds that 'it defines an agenda for a future of dramatic, innovative sports cars'. And this is what makes the C-X16 so exciting. What we're looking at is Jaguar's new sports car – arguably its first since the Jaguar E-type Series 1 – in near-production form.

Jaguar's confidence and ambition for the future goes beyond even this. Consider that it confirmed the C-X75 concept is heading for production. Anyone who visited the 2010 Paris motor show will never forget seeing the sleek car for the first time – it's a Jaguar through-and-through, looking incredibly modern yet with clear styling links back to the ill-fated (and beautiful) XJ13 sports racing car.

The Jaguar C-X75 will become the British marque's most advanced offering ever, with performance on a par with the fastest production cars on the market, but using hybrid technology that promises to deliver CO_2 emissions of less than 99g/km and a 200mph maximum speed. It is currently being developed in association with Williams Grand Prix Engineering Ltd/Williams F1, which is providing engineering expertise in areas including aerodynamics, carbon-composite manufacture, and hybrid technologies. The C-X75's chassis will be made of carbonfibre to create an incredibly light yet strong structure.

The car in production form is coming together incredibly quickly – thanks to Formula 1-style working practices. Jaguar continues to develop the use of the micro-turbine technology that was showcased in the original C-X75 concept and, just to show it means business, Tata has taken a significant stake in Bladon Jets, and will develop this very advanced technology as a medium-term aspiration to play a part in Jaguars of the future. Only 250 examples will be built, each costing between £700,000 and £900,000 depending on market and local taxes.

Since the launch of the new-generation XK in 2006, Jaguar's transformation has been astonishing. The arrival of the XF and XJ has cemented the company's position at the pinnacle of the luxury-car sector, proving that British can still be best. Until 2006, sales were sliding as Jaguar found itself stuck in a retro timewarp – but ever since the arrival of the XK, the most remarkable product-led recovery has been taking place.

These are exciting times for Jaguar, which under young and ambitious management hopes to take over the world – and who would bet against that happening now?　*End*

'The XF and new XJ have cemented Jaguar's position at the pinnacle of the luxury car sector'

Clockwise from above
The current trio: XF, XJ and XK (from left); XJ's tail styling caused controversy at launch and still divides opinion; XF cabin marks a departure from the timber-laden interiors of previous Jaguar saloons.

Jaguar BEGINNINGS

The success of Jaguar from the humblest of starts was led by one man, William Lyons

WORDS: DAVID LILLYWHITE

'Lyons learned early on how to appeal to the car-buying public'

THERE HAVE BEEN COUNTLESS talented individuals involved in the success of Jaguar. But its direction and image were down to one man, William Lyons, who started out with the company that became Jaguar before he was 21, and continued until retirement at 71, in 1972.

William Lyons, later Sir, learned early on how to appeal to the car-buying public, but it was as a young motorcycle enthusiast (pictured in 1920 on the previous spread) that he made his first shrewd move: spotting the potential in a business run by one William Walmsley, who was building sidecars and fitting them to reconditioned motorcycles. It was a good product let down by poor business skills, and Lyons homed in on it.

He formed the Swallow Sidecar Company in 1922 with a bank overdraft of £1000, found basic premises in Blackpool and started to build the sidecars in partnership with Walmsley. The sidecars, made in aluminium, were among the most stylish around – something that Lyons realised was crucial in appealing to the potential buyer.

Unfortunately for Lyons and Walmsley, the strong between-the-wars sidecar market was obliterated by the introduction of the Austin Seven, which brought motoring to the masses with its low purchase price, reliability, ease of driving and modest running costs.

It was at this point that Lyons displayed the shrewd thinking that would define his management of Jaguar over the years: he understood the mentality of potential buyers, and set about creating a car that would be affordable and yet appealing to those who saw themselves as a cut →

Above
Lyons shows off the 1955 Le Mans–winning D-type on March 1956 tour of the Browns Lane, Coventry factory.

**Clockwise
from above**
The E-type cemented the
Jaguar legend; Lyons
with VW boss Kurt Lotz;
C-type moved Jaguar into
major motorsport
success; but it all started
with neat aluminium
sidecars built by Swallow.

above the typical Austin Seven owner. He created a stylish two-seater aluminium body mounted on the proven Austin Seven chassis and negotiated the first of many deals with Bertie Henly, of the successful dealership Henlys, to supply 500 cars.

The Austin Seven Swallow genuinely looked special, with neat lines and a polished radiator cowl, allowing its owners to live out the fantasy that they actually weren't too badly affected by the economic hardship of the 1920s and early '30s, and instead keep up appearances among their peers. But at £175, or £185 with a hinged hardtop, the model was only about £10 more than a typical standard Seven.

Such was the Swallow's success that the company introduced a sedan variant, swiftly followed by a larger vehicle built on the Morris Cowley chassis.

By the time of the 1929 London Motor Show, the firm was exhibiting new models based on the Fiat Tipo 509A, the Swift Ten and the Standard Big Nine. The largest, the Standard Swallow, was to prove especially important, for it offered relatively extravagant styling and a range of colours that were genuinely daring and extrovert for the era.

Actually, though, Lyons felt restricted by the use of other manufacturers' chassis. Yet he was well aware that the industry at the time was littered with failed auto makers, so he decided to stick with Standard running gear on a Swallow-design platform and new body. And so the SS I and SS II sports coupés were

born, in summer 1931. Lyons' obsession with building cars that were low to the ground made for a sleek-looking machine, with an outrageously long bonnet that prompted one newspaper report to claim that the new model had the look of a £1000 car – and yet it was just £310.

Lyons had used simple tricks to make the SS models stand out from their more mundane (but similarly priced) rivals. Engines were mounted further back in the chassis than was normal practice at the time, and front leaf springs were mounted alongside the motor, for the lowest ride possible. The flagship SS I was the one that everyone hankered after, but the smaller, cheaper SS II was cleverly styled to bask in the SS I's reflected glory – and it sold strongly.

In 1933, Lyons demonstrated another trick that he would go on to use again and again to maximum effect: the use of his cars in motorsport. The new Tourer version of the SS I became the first of the breed to take part in a serious competitive event, with three entered into the tough and prestigious Alpine Trial. Success over the following years did much to enhance the SS name.

William Walmsley, however, had lost interest and left the company in 1934, leaving Lyons to go it alone with his ambitions to improve the quality of his cars. His first steps were to appoint a chief engineer, William Heynes, and expert engine design consultant Harry Weslake. Meanwhile, the SS I Airline sedan and the SS 90 models were born, and the range was becoming

comprehensive and classy enough to warrant a new, more appropriate name. Jaguar. But the company was still named SS, and the cars were known as 'SS Jaguars'.

With engines tweaked by Weslake and Heynes, the SS 90 was developed into the wonderfully stylish and sporting SS 100, now the most legendary of the pre-World War Two models. Of course, its run was cut short by the conflict, during which the Jaguar plant was turned to war production, but it was during wartime firewatch shifts on the roof of the factory that Heynes sketched out the initial designs for the engine that would move the cars and the company into a new era. The motor became known as the XK, a 160bhp (higher later) six-cylinder twin-overhead-cam design first introduced to the public in a two-seater sports car, the XK120.

The XK120's swooping looks, stunning performance and success in motorsport, in particular at Le Mans (from 1950) made it and subsequent models a great success. From this grew C-type and D-type racing cars, the E-type and later the XK8 and XKR, plus a long line of sleek sedans and coupés that survived poor management and quality control (mostly after Lyons' retirement) to evolve into the current XK and XF ranges. Incredibly, the XK engine lasted right up until 1994, but it's the legacy of Sir William Lyons, to produce sporty, distinctive cars that punch above their weight in terms of price, that provides the link from 1922 to the present day. **End**

'Lyons had used simple tricks to make the SS models stand out from their mundane rivals'

JWS 353

THE LEGEND BEGINS

A memorable day behind the wheels of a Le Mans
XK120 and Ecurie Ecosse C-type shows why Jaguar's
iconic designs redefined the post-war sports car

WORDS: PETER MORGAN // PHOTOGRAPHY: MICHAEL BAILIE

Above and facing page
XK120 'AEN 546', en route
to 11th at Le Mans in 1951,
and as it is today.

I'M HURTLING ALONG in top at what seems like an incredible speed. The 3.4-litre straight-six is settled into an easy gallop and the big Smiths tacho needle is pointing to 3500rpm with the sureness of Big Ben announcing mid-day. Beyond the radiant Flag Metallic Blue bonnet the long straight stretches ahead, and I'm in seventh heaven.

An icy blast numbs my face, but I hunch down further into the cockpit and savour the warmth that is wafting over my legs like a comforting blanket.

Behind me, a golden rooster tail of fallen autumnal leaves defines the course of this car, like an arrow-straight contrail in a brilliant blue sky. Is there really anything better in life than driving a C-type Jaguar on a sunny winter's day?

All that is good and great in Britain's motor-racing heritage is defined in this car. It is the Establishment – an early 1950s statement on motor sport's future by a generation who, just ten years before, had engineered Spitfires and Hurricanes.

It almost goes with the calibre of the car that it is quite tricky to drive, and you need a sympathetic touch to handle the engine and the sometimes recalcitrant gearbox. But after a few laps of the test track I'm doing OK, and enjoying this glorious celebration of 'the way it was'.

For a moment, I can picture being a part of the weekend's sport in France. I grin at the thought of the drivers' Champagne-induced headaches the day after victory at La Sarthe (twice, in 1951 and 1953), and their victorious blast back to Coventry.

I double-declutch and downshift to third, just for the sake of hearing again the crisp report of this seemingly unburstable engine, casting another glance around the gauges to check the Ts and Ps. And then I look at the speedo. I'm

> '**On sunny days at Goodwood, it's easy to forget what the danger and hardship of driving them was really like**'

barely doing 80mph! Suddenly, I don't feel so cock-sure of myself after all. A voice in my head tells me to try turning off the sun, throw in a blustery rain shower and double my speed. And I imagine that it's the darkest, coldest time of the night on the loneliest place in racing – the three-and-a-tad miles of the Ligne Droit des Hunaudières.

The big Lucas headlamps, which looked so impressive in the pits, now project two hopelessly inadequate fingers of yellow light barely 30 or 40 yards ahead. And the only thing I can see in the rain-lashed beams is the strobing dashed line in the centre of the road. I'm exhausted, wet and cold, but my life depends on what my straining eyes can pick out of the murk ahead – that first glimmer of a slow red tail-light that, if I don't see and pass, could kill me.

Today, when we see cars like this on sunny summer days at Goodwood, it's easy to forget what the danger and hardship of driving them was really like. Of course, for a generation which had survived so much, that was part of the thrill. But let's not kid ourselves today that winning in these cars was easy. Look past the oil-smudged faces of drivers like Whitehead, Walker, Hamilton and Rolt, and their eyes show a satisfaction in knowing they have tested themselves, not just their cars, to their limits. Their smiles are the smiles of men who appreciate the joy of just being alive.

The C-type was Jaguar's first Le Mans winner. A product of a wartime dream to build, first, a world-beating engine and then, in a resurgent world of motorsport, a car that could put the Jaguar name at the top of every driver's most-wanted list.

The straight-six that William Lyons' team developed is one of the great automobile engines of all time. Called the XK, the long-legged 3.4-litre had an alloy head with double overhead camshafts and initially produced a →

1951 JAGUAR XK120

ENGINE
3442cc, dohc in-line six, two SU carburettors
POWER
160bhp @ 5000rpm
TORQUE
195lb ft @ 2500rpm
TRANSMISSION
Four-speed manual, rear-wheel drive
SUSPENSION
Front: ind, via wishbones and torsion bars, telescopic dampers, anti-roll bar. Rear: live axle, semi-elliptic springs, lever-arm dampers
BRAKES
Drums all round
WEIGHT
1321kg (2912lb)
PERFORMANCE
Top speed 125-132mph
VALUE
Cost new £1263
Value now c£200,000

1952 C-TYPE

ENGINE
3442cc, dohc in-line six,
two SU carburettors
POWER
200bhp @ 5800rpm
TORQUE
220lb ft @ 3900rpm
TRANSMISSION
Four-speed manual,
rear-wheel drive
SUSPENSION
Front: ind, via wishbones
and torsion bars,
telescopic dampers,
anti-roll bar.
Rear: live axle suspended
on trailing links,
transverse torsion
bar, Panhard rod,
telescopic dampers
BRAKES
Originally drums all round
WEIGHT
1016kg (2240lb)
PERFORMANCE
Top speed c150mph
VALUE
Cost new £2327
Value now c£800,000

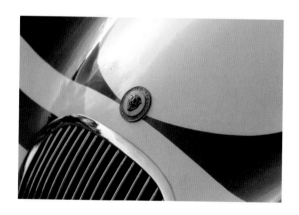

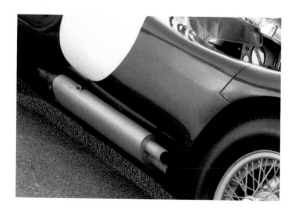

Below
Ian Stewart takes
the chequered flag in
XKC006's first race:
Jersey, 1952.

maximum power of 160bhp. And when they realised they had no suitable car that would fully demonstrate the performance of their new engine, the men at Jaguar built a new chassis.

At the 1948 Motor Show, the new XK120 was a sensation. The '120' stood for the model's maximum speed – a remarkable figure for a production car at that time. To silence sceptics, Jaguar took a car to a stretch of motorway at Jabbeke in Belgium and recorded no less than 126mph. And with the windscreen removed, the test team achieved 133mph!

Nevertheless, Jaguar didn't expect a car like the 120 to sell that strongly: it planned to make just 200, aiming them at the competition world. But once the word was out the XK120 did indeed sell like fresh, hot cakes.

Meanwhile, the competition successes began to build. The first major victory came in the Dundrod Tourist Trophy, when a promising youngster named Stirling Moss discovered the new car's rich potential.

The initial steps on the international stage were taken with an exploratory visit to Le Mans in 1950. Success eluded the three specially prepared XKs, but many lessons were learned. Jaguar's engineers knew that what they really needed was a purpose-built racing car.

At Le Mans in 1951, the team turned out with the new XK120C – which quickly became known to all as the C-type. It was lighter and more slippery than the production car, and it proved to be a winning formula. Although two of the three factory cars retired, the Peters Whitehead and Walker claimed victory.

A second and far more emphatic victory at Le Mans would follow in 1953. By this time the 24 Hours had taken on very significant importance

'Fast laps are all about accepting that the hard Dunlop racing tyres work best when they are sliding'

for any manufacturer hoping to appeal to the burgeoning world sports car market. The opposition was stiff, and included competitive entries from Ferrari, Alfa Romeo and Cunningham.

Nonetheless, what tipped the balance for the C-types was not only the solid reliability of the XK engine but a perfect unfair advantage in the form of Dunlop's new disc brake. For lap after fade-free lap the C-types were able to leave their braking into the sharp Mulsanne corner much later than the other, drum-braked, cars.

Major Tony Rolt and Duncan Hamilton won that year's race at an average speed of nearly 106mph, with the Moss/Walker car second, and Whitehead and Ian Stewart fourth. The C-type passed into motor racing legend and the Jaguar XK became the sports car every driver coveted.

The Pastel Green example featured here finished 11th at Le Mans in 1951, the highest-placed XK120, in the hands of Bob Lawrie and Ivan Waller. They averaged over 84mph for the 24 hours and completed 1992 miles to the finish – 265 miles behind the winning C-type. The story goes that the more accomplished Waller drove fully 18 hours himself.

Current owner Guy Broad's family has known this car, on and off, since the early 1970s. Despite its factory preparation for the 1951 24 Hours, he says that there are no really significant differences between this and a regular production example – including a typical 160bhp from the engine. But there are many fascinating details that set it apart.

The bonnet has three neat circles cut into it, giving teasing glimpses of the highly polished twin-cam head. The openings allowed faster oil and water top-ups and helped cool the engine bay. I also note the delicate hollow copper beading finishing the rear wheelarches, which on the production car →

would have been covered by fully enclosed spats. And perhaps recalling a lost 1930s zest for life are the delicate swirls of the fast fuel filler and the streamlined, bowled lenses of the special Marchal headlamps.

Factory prepping for the 1951 race gave this car a huge 40-gallon fuel tank (the same size as the C-type's) and wire wheels – the latter an option that did not become available on the production cars until the following year. This XK doesn't, though, have disc brakes. These were available only after 1953, and its successive owners have resisted the temptation to customise this otherwise largely original 1951 example.

'On' rather than 'in' seems to be the appropriate description for how you occupy the well-finished cockpit. The simply trimmed bucket seats have both driver and passenger sitting out in the airstream in period style.

Starting is a matter of twisting the ignition key and pressing the button. Some energetic pumping of the accelerator coaxes petrol from the twin SUs into the cylinders and, seemingly in its own good time, the big six rumbles into life.

The slow-acting four-speed gearbox could be described as the Achilles' heel of the early XKs, but the clutch action is weighted well and there's a mechanical thumbwheel device on this car for blocking accidental selection

> ## 'The six-cylinder's free-revving spirit must have been a revelation to those brought up on a diet of Bentleys'

of reverse gear. There is synchromesh – theoretically – but I find the only way I can get a clean downshift is to double declutch and use a generous boot of throttle to spin the engine up.

Nevertheless, the XK120 is as docile as a lamb – and a beauty to drive. It pulls well from as little as 1500rpm and has a wonderful hard edge to its exhaust above 2500. The acceleration is brisk, and I love it all the more because I'm so close to the engine's noise and, of course, to nature.

The six-cylinder's free-revving spirit must have been a revelation to those brought up on a diet of slow-turning Bentleys. Front torsion bar independent suspension means the ride is also far more confident than that of pre-war British sports cars.

Nevertheless, after some 15 minutes behind the wheel, I'm getting tired. At low speeds the steering is monumentally heavy (by today's standards), and to haul this car through the tighter corners demands a lot of effort. When I stop, I'm cold enough that my speech is slurring, my arms are aching and my legs feel like jelly. I'm wondering what Messrs Lawrie and Waller did for stamina.

So it is with some trepidation that I clamber into the compact cockpit of the C-type. All around me are bare aluminium sheet and the sturdy tubes of the spaceframe chassis. A set of spare spark plugs wait for their moment →

'What tipped the balance for the C-type was not only the solid reliability of the XK engine but a perfect unfair advantage in the form of Dunlop's new disc brake'

Above
Owner-driver
Bob Lawrie stands
proudly with his
XK, Le Mans '51.

JWS 353

C-type is lighter, more powerful and faster than XK – but they're both wonderful to drive.

by my right elbow and, like the whole of the dashboard area, the outsized Bakelite steering wheel is finished in a functional black.

While the engine retained its original 3442cc capacity it was given a higher compression ratio, higher-lift camshafts, larger exhaust valves and bigger carburettors, lifting the maximum power to between 220 and 230bhp. A lighter, stiffer spaceframe replaced the XK120's very conventional twin box-section chassis. There were torsion bars front and rear (the 120 has leaf springs on the rear), and a rack and pinion replaced the less precise recirculating ball steering.

This is a car for life's players, and few would dispute that this one has played in a few important games. By 1952, the C-type had established itself as the next step up for successful XK120 drivers. After a promising first season in 1951, this was the path taken by Ecurie Ecosse team owner David Murray. The team's first C-type was this car, chassis XKC006, initially purchased and driven by Ian Stewart in July 1952.

Stewart drove the brand new JWS 353, resplendent in British Racing Green, straight from the factory to the Jersey road races and won, first time out. Subsequently, Stewart took wins at Charterhall and Crimond, and followed Moss and Hamilton home third at Turnberry. He was first in the Wakefield Trophy at the Curragh and later at Castle Combe. Perhaps one of the more satisfying wins came once more at Charterhall, where he set fastest lap to Stirling Moss in XKC005 and Roy Salvadori's Ferrari.

For 1953, the car was painted in the Ecosse team's Flag Metallic Blue colours, with white recognition stripes on the front. Future Le Mans winner Ninian Sanderson drove the car to sixth place in that year's Goodwood Easter Handicap, while Stewart himself continued with a consistent string of wins and placings.

The C-type was sold to Hans Davids in Holland at the end of the year. The Dutch driver won at Spa and Zandvoort before selling it on to Bryan Corser of Shrewsbury. The car later went to the USA and only came back to

'At low speeds there is a feeling that the car is like a coiled spring – an athlete walking to the startline'

the UK in 1974, when Lynx Engineering restored it for owner Bill Lake. Even before I start the engine, this feels like a well-sorted racer. My body is tucked away deep inside that aerodynamic body and the controls fall to hand and foot without effort. Maybe the importance of reducing the driver's fatigue levels was more understood by 1953.

Nevertheless, at low speeds there is a feeling that the car is like a coiled spring, an athlete walking to the startline. And when I press the throttle hard, the engine note takes on a glorious-sounding roar and the Jag forces its way forward.

Guy Broad had told me earlier that the only way to drive these cars half decently was to hang out their tails and steer them on the throttle. Fast laps are all about cornering balance and accepting that the hard Dunlop Racing tyres work best when they are sliding.

With the Ecosse example conservatively valued at around £800,000 by auctioneer Christie's, I wasn't about to test that theory, but I could certainly admire the level of car control that drivers took for granted back in the 1950s.

I marvel at the difference between the 120's drum brakes and the discs of this C-type. I can imagine the likes of Rolt and Hamilton positively grinning like Cheshire cats as they flew past the red cars going over the brow into Mulsanne.

There were only 54 C-types built and, to quote the late Andrew Whyte in his definitive volume *Jaguar, the Sports Racing and Works Competition Cars to 1953*, 'an authentic C-type is a thing of great value'.

That value is based on more than just rarity or aesthetics. There's also a priceless worth that can be sensed only behind the steering wheel. It's in the cockpit, with the tacho needle edging round the dial, that you also grasp the quality of the people who drove these cars. **End**

THANKS TO Christie's (www.christies.com) and Guy Broad Parts (www.guybroad.co.uk), and to Aviation Leathercraft/Moto-Lita Ltd (www.flying-jacket.com, www.moto-lita.co.uk) for the period clothing.

JAGUAR XK

More than six decades after the arrival of the
XK range, marque expert and founder of The
XK Club Philip Porter describes why these
cars created such a stir – and still do

PHOTOGRAPHY: MICHAEL BAILIE

OVER 60 YEARS AGO, in 1948, the Jaguar XK120 Super Sports Open Two-Seater took London's Earls Court Show and the motoring world by storm. Combining performance that had previously been enjoyed only by racing cars and a few examples of rarefied exotica with ultra-modern styling and relative sophistication, the XK120 really was a landmark.

The XK burst into a very grey world that was still recovering from the ravages of World War Two, and which served only to heighten the drama of the car's entrance. Famously intended just as a testbed for the new engine that had been designed for a fresh range of saloons, the sensational new sports car inspired an overwhelming clamour – in spite of some scepticism about its claimed performance. The Jaguar stuttered into production over the 1949-'50 period, in the process switching from the initial aluminium and ash frame construction to pressed steel panels.

With 'Export Or Die' the dictat from Government, the 120 led the way into America, both symbolically and commercially. The stars of Hollywood embraced the Jag-wah. An unambiguous demonstration of the car's genuine performance in front of the press at Jabbeke in Belgium and a fairytale win in the model's first race at Silverstone (admittedly against some pretty average opposition) only served to lengthen the order books. A tentative entry at Le Mans nearly resulted in unexpected glory. →

'The XK120 was a real wind-in-the-hair machine, yet it proved that sports cars did not need to be for masochists only'

JAGUAR XK120 OPEN TWO-SEATER

ENGINE
3442cc in-line dohc six, iron block, alloy head, twin SU carburettors
POWER
160bhp @ 5000rpm
TORQUE
195lb ft @ 2500rpm
TRANSMISSION
Four-speed manual, rear-wheel drive
SUSPENSION
Front: independent via wishbone and torsion bar, anti-roll bar, lever-arm dampers. Rear: live axle, semi-elliptics, lever-arm dampers
BRAKES
Hydraulic drums
PERFORMANCE
0-60mph 10sec
Top speed 124mph

A very young man who had impressed everyone vastly in little motorcycle-engined single-seater racers was looking to make the step up and make the crucial breakthrough. He managed to borrow one of the six works-prepared 120s (Jaguar was not amused) and, with a masterly display in appalling conditions, Stirling Moss took a brilliant victory in the classic Tourist Trophy.

Combine all this with record-breaking and Ian Appleyard's unprecedented success in international rallying with another of the six (NUB 120), and the 120 could do no wrong. What was its secret? The heart of the car was the new twin-overhead-cam engine that William Lyons had the courage to put into production. Believed to be too complex for a road car, the motor, with its hemispherical aluminium head, gave excellent performance, terrific torque and, above all, had massive reserves for future development. One of the greatest engines of all time, it would remain in production for almost 40 years and power everything from world-beating sports racers to silent executive saloons, from tanks to the equally sensational E-type.

The 120 Roadster, as the Open Two-Seater became known, was a traditional sports car in some senses and radically different in others. It had a rudimentary soft-top, crude sidescreens and standard seats that were something of a joke when cornering hard. It was a real wind-in-the-hair machine, of the type beloved pre-war. Yet it shocked some of those diehards because it had

'boulevard' suspension. With a massively over-engineered chassis, inherited from the new Mark V saloon, and suspension that was rather soft by traditional standards, the 120 found a wider audience and proved that sports cars did not need to be for masochists only. And if anyone said that the XK was a softy, just look at what it achieved in motor sport, where there are no compromises.

Having said that, the 120 was far from perfect. The brakes had not kept pace with the increased level of performance, an area Jaguar needed to address. Some felt the position of the steering wheel as it was presented to the driver, and its heaviness, were truck-like. Lights were marginal for the virtually unheard-of performance. The gearbox was slow and agricultural, even if it was very tough. In general, the car was no lightweight from behind the wheel.

The XK120 gave the Jaguar marque what today we would call the 'halo effect'. The new Mark VII saloon basked in the reflected glory of its sporting sibling, and victory at Le Mans with a competition version of the XK120, the C-type, brought untold publicity for the little British company, putting it on the map worldwide.

Great car though the 120 was, it could not be considered that practical in climates less friendly than California, and Jaguar responded with the introduction of the XK120 Fixed Head Coupé in 1951. The styling was another Lyons masterpiece: although he had simply crafted a roof onto the basic →

Below and right
First of the XKs, this particular 120 is in fact the very first steel-bodied Roadster produced.

'XK140 Coupés were given two rear seats that could be occupied by children or by fully-grown pygmies'

1955 JAGUAR XK140 DROP HEAD COUPÉ

ENGINE
3442cc in-line dohc six, iron block, alloy head, twin SU carburettors
POWER
190bhp @ 5500rpm
(this car SE spec: 210bhp @ 5750rpm)
TORQUE
210lb ft @ 2500rpm
(213lb ft @ 4000rpm)
TRANSMISSION
Four-speed manual (SE spec with overdrive), rear-wheel drive
SUSPENSION
Front: independent via wishbone and torsion bar, anti-roll bar, telescopic dampers. Rear: live axle, semi-elliptics, telescopic dampers
BRAKES
Hydraulic drums
PERFORMANCE
0-60mph 11sec
Top speed 129mph

Roadster shape, no-one could have known it was as simple as that. Highly revered today, the FHC had definite undertones of Jean Bugatti's work and is pure sculpture.

The new Coupé was actually a very different animal to its stablemate in a number of ways. It was, if you like, a tamed Jaguar. Gone was the devil-may-care character of the Roadster and instead here was a car that was highly sophisticated. It combined the essence of the performance with pre-war levels of opulence. The luxury of wind-up windows was complemented by the decadence of a veneered dashboard and door cappings.

While rather more practical than the Roadster, the Coupé's interior space was actually at more of a premium and its boot space very similar. But for these compromises, the 120 FHC would have been a true Grand Tourer. It was, though, a fabulous long-distance car for those who travelled light!

It was announced as being for export only, and it seems you had to be someone to obtain a right-hand-drive example; with less than 200 built, these are exceedingly rare cars today. The list of original owners includes Ecurie Ecosse racer Ian Stewart; Neville Duke, the famous test pilot; 'Gentleman' Jack Sears, who raced his; Jack Hallay, who rallied his; and Sir Jackie's brother, the late Jim Stewart, who drove for Ecosse and the Works.

The Roadster and Fixed Head represented two extremes. There was room for

388 XUE

yet another version that bridged the two, a car that had the FHC's sophistication but could also offer open-air motoring. The solution was what the Americans called a convertible and what Jaguar christened the Drop Head Coupé (DHC). Aping the opulence of the FHC with its interior fittings, it was graced with a luxurious, fully-lined, folding top. Once again the model found favour in the vital US market, and gave Jaguar superlative coverage of the higher-performance sports car sector.

As with all Lyons's models, the XKs were incredible value for money, which further fuelled demand. This was achieved by relatively long production runs, by saving money on sophisticated tooling and, unfortunately, by compromising on quality in certain areas. By 1954 it was time to 'refresh' the XK range, and also address some of the slight shortcomings. The result was the evolutionary XK140.

The 140 essentially retained the 120's style, and the Coupé interiors were the areas most altered; both these models were given two seats in the rear that could be occupied by children or fully-grown pygmies. Today they are used by most owners for extra luggage and such like, and are thus rather more practical. To achieve the extra space, the batteries, which had previously enjoyed the privilege of being adjacent to the interior, were demoted to positions under the front wings. →

Below and right
The XK140 was mechanically better than the 120, but full-width bumpers did nothing for looks.

Externally, the DHC model was little changed in terms of overall shape. The FHC, though, came in for rather more radical surgery. To potentially house one's little horrors in the back, the roofline was extended rearwards, making this model easily distinguishable. Furthermore, the front footwells were lengthened either side of the engine and the screen moved forward. All of this added up to considerably more generous interior space and better suited those 120 FHC owners who tended to suffer from claustrophobia.

Mechanically, the 140s were given the uprated engines that had previously been offered in Special Equipment versions of the 120. The brakes were improved a little, too. Handling was assisted by moving the engine forward and swapping the ancient lever-arm rear shockers for telescopic chaps. A rack-and-pinion set-up made the steering lighter, and the generous provision of a UJ in the column altered the angle of the wheel.

Externally, there were some detailed but very obvious changes. To save money the delicate grille of soldered, fluted vanes was replaced by a rather crude cast replica. The trade commission at the British Embassy in Washington had highlighted in a report that the imported UK cars were inadequately protected front and rear from the vast and seriously heavy Detroit sedans. Hence the 140 was blessed with 'proper' bumpers, as opposed to the ornaments on the 120, but these did little for the aesthetics.

Below and left
For comfort and power, the XK150 is by far the best of the range, yet the shape isn't as sensuous.

The Roadster model, still known as the Open Two-Seater (OTS), shared most of these changes apart from the provision of the 'nipper seats' and remained delightfully selfish. This variant was really intended for the warmer climes of the world, and almost all were exported. They proved, like the other models, to be extremely successful for Jaguar and Britain.

Retrospectively, at least, views have diverged on whether the 140 was an improvement or not. Traditionalists felt it had gone soft, and preferred the more he-man character of the 120. Others found the 140 considerably more pleasant to drive.

The 140 had evolved and, in parallel, the competition world had moved on; it was no longer possible to turn up with your 120, pump up the tyres, remove the spare and enjoy a hearty club race. Jaguar had itself played a part in that progression with the C-type, which had been designed as a dedicated sports racing car: a rather new breed of animal. Hence the 140s did not sample, or enjoy, the same level of competition activity as their predecessors, which perhaps helps account for their softer image.

By 1957, the XK range needed an injection of updating to keep Jaguar at the forefront of sports car design. With the ludicrously small team of engineers having devoted most of their time to designing and developing the new 'small' saloon range and the fabulous D-types, which followed the C-type's two Le →

**1960 JAGUAR
XK150 3.8S
FIXED HEAD
COUPÉ**

ENGINE
3781cc in-line dohc six,
iron block, alloy head,
three SU carburettors
POWER
265bhp @ 5500rpm
TORQUE
260lb ft @ 4000rpm
TRANSMISSION
Four-speed manual
plus overdrive,
rear-wheel drive
SUSPENSION
Front: independent via
wishbone and torsion
bar, anti-roll bar,
telescopic dampers.
Rear: live axle, semi-
elliptics, telescopic
dampers
BRAKES
Dunlop discs
PERFORMANCE
0-60mph 7.6sec
Top speed 136mph

'Disc brakes gave the XK150 technical credibility and, apart from the low-volume Jensen, a feature the competition lacked'

Above
Three iterations of XK: three very different characters, each one highly desirable to today's collectors.

'The XK150 has been better revered in recent years as the ultimate example of the XK range'

Mans victories with three more, Jaguar was unable to introduce a completely new sports car at this stage.

Modernised in many ways, the 150 was the ultimate iteration of the XK theme and itself would sire various versions. The big step forward for the 150 was the adoption of disc brakes, which Jaguar had developed with Dunlop and used very effectively on the later Cs and the Ds. This feature gave the 150 technical credibility and, apart from the very low-volume Jensen, a feature the competition lacked. A new B-type cylinder head increased power, which had progressed from the 120's 180bhp to the 140's 190bhp, to 210bhp.

Visually, the 150 was far more changed than the 140 had been over the 120. The old two-piece flat windscreen was looking very dated now and it was replaced by a wraparound one-piece item. The dramatic fall and rise of the wing line was considerably straightened and the cabin widened. This was achieved by putting the doors on a diet; the slimmer versions benefited the interior space considerably. Initially launched in Fixed Head and Drop Head Coupé form only, the range was augmented in late 1958 by the OTS.

Coincident with the launch of the 150 roadster, Jaguar made an additional 'S' version available for the Coupé models in early '59. With a so-called straight-port head and triple two-inch SUs, power was raised to a claimed 250bhp. The horsepower race was on in the States, and to compete Jaguar added XK engines enlarged from 3.4 to 3.8 litres, and offered an S variant of the 3.8 which, supposedly, produced 265bhp (actually much nearer 200bhp!). There were thus 12 different XK150s available before production tailed off in late 1960, in readiness for the launch of the E-type.

The XK150 has probably been better revered in more recent years, when it could be judged as a stand-alone car rather than compared alongside its peers in period. The concept was, not surprisingly, ageing by the end of the decade, but it was the ultimate example of the incredible XK range. *End*

Thanks to Derek Hood of JD Classics for the loan of these magnificent Jaguar XKs. www.jdclassics.co.uk, +44 (0)1621 879579.

BREWING UP TROUBLE

Jaguar's long-tail Le Mans C-types were a rare failure at a time when the company was enjoying motor sport success. So why has an enthusiast now recreated one?

WORDS: TONY DRON // ACTION PHOTOGRAPHY: PAUL HARMER

Above
Tony Brown's superb replica of a 'low drag' C-type, one of three cars entered for the 1952 Le Mans 24 Hours (top right).

THE NAME KETTLE has been unfairly blackened in Jaguar's history. So says Norman Dewis, the legendary factory test driver. In 1952, when the works cars failed ignominiously at Le Mans, everything was rapidly hushed up. Those cars could have won, they should have won, but all three engines boiled immediately on the Mulsanne straight. Nobody was blamed then but, gradually, the joke went round: it was asking for trouble to put a man called Kettle in charge of cooling. Roy Kettle, poor chap, surely suffered.

That catastrophic overheating took the Jaguar team by surprise. It was attributed initially to the hastily constructed aerodynamic bodies. Frantic work was done, such as cutting alternate louvres from the bonnets to increase airflow. Spotlights inside the radiator grille of each car were removed. The plumbing was changed where possible… but they still all failed.

The real problem, soon discovered back at the factory, did indeed lie in the plumbing of the cooling system. It differed from that of the standard C-type because the streamlined bodies were lower at the front. A remote radiator header tank, as used successfully by BRM in Formula One, was specified and, yes, the job of drawing this fell to Mr Kettle.

Defending Roy Kettle, Norman told me: 'He was a good man on cooling systems and this was not his fault. He was rushed into it ➔

Right and far right
The real thing at the Browns Lane factory; Rolt/Hamilton car on the ramp at Le Mans for scrutineering.

Above and left
Rolt/Hamilton car no.18 clearly in trouble near Tertre Rouge; Dron gives replica its head at Goodwood.

and there was no testing.' Norman explained that all it needed was two simple changes: a larger-diameter hose from the radiator to the header tank, and a different water pump pulley to run the impeller at a higher speed. Had there been time to test it, those answers would have been found quickly and, in all probability, Jaguar would have won the 1952 Le Mans 24 Hours.

The disaster had been set in motion by a famous telegram which Stirling Moss, quite correctly, sent to Jaguar boss William Lyons. Driving a works C-type in the 1952 Mille Miglia, with Norman as passenger, Moss had been astonished when a works Mercedes-Benz sailed past them on a long straight. His telegram – 'Must have more speed at Le Mans' – had an immediate, dramatic effect.

Jaguar designer Malcolm Sayer was one of the first people to apply scientific principles to automotive aerodynamics. He had already prepared a range of such improvements for the C-type, as shown in diagrams dated March 19, 1952, and seen in Philip Porter's book *Jaguar Sports Racing Cars*. Taking the drag of the standard body as being 100%, Sayer had conducted wind tunnel tests on models. The best of these, a new body with an extended nose and tail, created a relative drag of only 79%.

Receiving Stirling's telegram, the Jaguar top brass decided to make three such aerodynamic bodies for Le Mans. The Mille Miglia fell in the first week in May. The cars would have to be at Le Mans for scrutineering several days before the 24 Hours, due to start at 4pm on June 15. It was too much to ask.

Norman, still in Italy sorting things out after the Mille Miglia, was unaware of developments. To his mind, the Le Mans cars were already prepared, tested and ready to go. By the time he got

back to Coventry, however, the modifications had been done. He was unhappy. After all, he had been in that C-type when the Mercedes went past and he took a different view. He would have argued to stick with the standard cars, but it was too late for that.

In practice at Le Mans, the engines overheated immediately, doing what would turn out to be fatal damage. After practice, the cars of Stirling Moss/Peter Walker and Hamilton/Rolt were modified to carry the standard C-type cooling system, with its taller radiator. The sleek bonnets were panel-bashed hurriedly to suit. The third car, that of Peter Whitehead/Ian Stewart, retained the remote header tank for the race, but all three were doomed. Two were damaged too badly before the race even started. The one surviving engine, in the Moss/Walker entry, was wrecked when a broken piece of timing chain tensioner jammed open the oil pressure relief valve. How unlucky can you get?

Although the low-drag bodies came under suspicion, at least one journalist hinted at the truth. Rodney Walkerley, sports editor of *The Motor*, wrote: 'There was worry in practice on account of heating, due, it was thought, to moving the water header tanks to a position behind the engine…'

The painful fact, it was later realised, was that the standard C-types would have been fast enough to win at Le Mans in 1952 anyway. The fastest lap of Le Mans by a standard C-type, set during the 1951 race at an average of 105.24mph, was not beaten by the winning Mercedes-Benz cars during the race in 1952, although it was bettered by Ascari's works Ferrari that year. It clocked a new record lap, 107.38mph, but retired early with clutch failure.

Back in Coventry afterwards, William Lyons was anxious to →

'Was it not asking for trouble to put
a man called Kettle in charge of cooling?
Poor Roy surely suffered'

Right and far right
Whitehead/Stewart car
no.19 and Moss/Walker
no.17; a shot taken in
the Jaguar workshop, in a
side street in Le Mans.

Above and left
Rolt/Hamilton car
in the classic 'ear
of corn' formation
before the start; superbly
recreated cockpit.

erase all trace of the episode as soon as possible. Those bodies were not to be seen again. Once more in standard trim, the same three cars ran in the Goodwood Nine Hours that August.

People climb mountains, they say, 'because they are there'. Building an accurate copy of the works Jaguar C-type, XKC 002, which ran as car number 19 in the 1952 Le Mans 24 Hours, was as hard as climbing a mountain. However, in this case Jaguar enthusiast Tony Brown set about the task because he thought it should be there but it wasn't.

This obsession began back in 2002. Well aware that Jaguar had won the Le Mans 24 Hours in 1951 and 1953 with the C-type, and again in 1955, 1956 and 1957 with the D-type, Brown looked more closely at what had happened in 1952. He spent a couple of years researching this and discovered that, at 100mph, the '52 works cars required over 20% less power to push them through the air. He searched for every contemporary photograph before deciding to recreate 002, as driven by Whitehead/Stewart at Le Mans that year.

There is some confusion over the chassis numbers of the three Le Mans Jaguars of 1952. Respected publications disagree, but Philip Porter's book is correct and Norman's own biography, *Norman Dewis of Jaguar*, written by Paul Skilleter, is conspicuously accurate. All we need to know is this: everybody agrees that the Whitehead/Stewart 1952 Le Mans car was 002 and that is what Tony Brown elected to recreate, accurately and precisely 'down to the last detail'.

A suitable chassis number was found from an appropriate donor car, a totally wrecked standard XK120. A recognised C-type chassis specialist, Andy Thomas of Classic Chassis, produced a perfect copy of 002 as a rolling chassis. It then went

to classic Jaguar expert Chris Keith-Lucas for the even trickier job of recreating the aerodynamic body from scratch and producing a working motor car. Nobody is better qualified for such a task than Chris, whose Sussex-based company CKL Developments Ltd, run with business partner Melvin Floyd, is world-famous.

This was 'anorak territory' of the finest order, with many months spent referring to photographs in order to construct dimensionally accurate bucks for the body, made by hand from the correct grade of aluminium alloy. The 3.4-litre engine was rebuilt to 1952 Le Mans specification, giving 210bhp at 5800rpm.

Close attention was paid to every tiny detail, including the paint colour and composition so that the look would be neither too matt nor too shiny. The green Rexine-type seat upholstery is correct as well as being more comfortable than absorbent leather for 24 hours of changeable weather in an open car.

It would have been daft to replicate the original plumbing. Work continues there, with high-speed experiments needed to prove that this problem has been solved. The car won't be much use if it still boils at top speed. Adopting the successful modifications Norman Dewis tested after Le Mans in 1952 might be a good start. One good thing to come out of that '52 disaster, Norman told me, was that Bill Heynes, Jaguar's engineering director, decreed that from then on nothing would be run in competition until it had been tested thoroughly and approved by Dewis first.

When I drove this amazing recreation at the Goodwood circuit on England's south coast, the aerodynamic C-type felt, initially at least, like the standard C-type works racing cars that I know well. Then, through the chicane, I pushed harder and a →

'After receiving Stirling's telegram,
Jaguar top brass decided to make three
aerodynamic bodies for Le Mans'

Right and far right
New alloy body was painstakingly made by CKL Developments, who shaped panels on an English wheel.

Above and left
Body was built up on a lattice of metal strips, working from period photos – no blueprints survive.

big difference emerged as the tail swung out very readily. It was quite easy to control but there was definitely too much oversteer. The car needed a great armful of opposite lock, rapidly applied, to prevent it from spinning. I mentioned this afterwards to Norman, who said: 'Yes, oversteer was a big problem with the aerodynamic cars, and even worse on full tanks with 36 gallons on board.'

Tony Brown's car appears to be an accurate reproduction of the original in every respect. This fault, caused by considerable extra weight extending behind the rear axle and acting as a pendulum even with a nearly empty tank, needs to be kept in perspective. It would have presented little difficulty to racing drivers of the calibre employed by Jaguar in those days. They could drive round it, as we say.

Equally, they would have coped with the rumoured high-speed instability of the 1952 Le Mans C-types, caused by aerodynamic lift at the rear.

The 1952 Le Mans race was run at a hot pace but Stirling Moss was able to climb through the pack and run with the quick cars, holding a strong second place after one lap. No problem for a top man there then, and there's no doubt that Sayer's aerodynamic bodies did raise the C-type's top speed – but who knows by how much? There was that significant technical difference at 100mph but it's frustrating not to know how much faster they were. Such tests can now be conducted but it will take a faster circuit than Goodwood, some miles of straight running being required.

For that matter, how quick was a standard C-type anyway? The respectable authorities, loyal Jaguar enthusiasts to a man, will all tell you that these cars were good for 155mph-plus. This

does seem debatable. Norman Dewis took 012 to Belgium late in 1952 for *The Motor* magazine, whose editor went on to an extended Continental tour. Part of the test included measuring the maximum speed on the famous motorway at Jabbeke, closed for the occasion. In heavy rain, Norman bravely drove alone to record a mean top speed of 143.711mph.

This clearly stung the Jaguar people. When the road test appeared in the magazine, the news pages also carried a lengthy explanation of how the bad weather had compromised the figure. One suspects Jaguar's PR department was behind the final comment: 'It is possible that the car touched about 155mph, which the Jaguar company considers to be a speed obtainable by the production version of the 120C under more suitable conditions.'

Jaguar fans won't like this, but I don't believe the production cars were ever that quick and I have seen no proof that the specially prepared and slightly more powerful works racing cars were either. Norman Dewis was back at Jabbeke with 012 in April 1953. In good weather, and fitted with a 214bhp engine, it recorded a 'disappointing' 147.662mph for the flying mile. Significantly, engineers then removed the standard front end and repeated the test with one of the 1952 Le Mans long-nose bonnets. The rear bodywork remained standard. The long nose alone gave no improvement and that was the last time any part of the 1952 aerodynamic C-type was seen. That result suggests that it was the extended rear which really made the aerodynamic difference, whatever that difference might have been, but C-type top speed remains a rich area for emotionally charged debate.

As for the looks, Sayer was trying to put function before ➔

'There's no doubt that Sayer's aerodynamic bodies did raise the C-type's top speed – but by how much?'

form. Look at the very front of the aerodynamic C-type: the faired-in headlights are smaller than those of the early D-types but the basic shape is identical. The rear end, which was more critical in the quest to reduce drag and relatively successful in that respect, seems to recall the flowing, elegant lines of 1930s thinking. In producing this design, Malcolm Sayer did not follow the theories of Professor Kamm, already in the public domain in 1952, which produced sharply chopped tails and a more futuristic style.

A Cunningham, its enclosed body designed by Kamm, led the first lap at Le Mans in 1952, the aerodynamics obviously proving effective despite its huge proportions. Perhaps Sayer felt his way was better, or possibly there wasn't enough time – but then again it could be that William Lyons, more conscious of styling, ruled out Kamm's theories on aesthetic grounds. We can only guess about that, yet reliable reports state that Lyons didn't like the look of the 1952 works cars, either. When they failed, he saw to it that those back ends were never seen again.

Until today, that is. I suppose some people will ask whether this should have been done at all. To my mind, we should remind ourselves that 1952 at Le Mans was only a regrettable blip in an otherwise glorious age of Jaguar racing, but this superb

1952 LE MANS JAGUAR C-TYPE

ENGINE
3442cc straight-six, cast-iron block, alloy head, twin SU H8 carbs
POWER
210bhp @ 5800rpm
TORQUE
232ft lb @ N/A
TRANSMISSION
Four-speed manual, rear-wheel drive
SUSPENSION
Front: independent by double wishbones, torsion bars. Rear: live axle, trailing arms, torsion bars
BRAKES
Twin-leading-shoe drums all round
PERFORMANCE
Top speed 150mph (claimed)
0-60mph c8.1sec
WEIGHT
940kg for standard C-type; 1952 version not recorded but would be heavier

reconstruction enables us to see and experience again one missing part of that great story. Meanwhile, we can debate whether 002's 1952 Le Mans body has been copied accurately.

Norman says it has been beautifully constructed but wonders whether it might be a few inches too wide across the back. On the other hand, Ian Stewart emailed Tony Brown recently, saying: 'No.19 looks magnificent and you must be delighted with the outcome. The car is far better finished than the original as I remember it, despite being an entirely faithful duplicate, and is certainly the best recreation of any Jaguar. Every last detail is spot-on, even down to the space in the door where I stuffed my "refreshments" at the start of the race – lemon drops; a lifelong addiction! Having been told to take it easy at the outset, I thought I might as well stock up. I can't remember the quantity, but I got through the lot in about two laps – must have been the adrenalin or something…'

Perhaps at some point the opportunity may arise for us to finally discover how good the aerodynamic C-type really is on a modern-day sports car circuit. Meanwhile, let's try to give Roy Kettle a break. Unfortunately, the joke is just too good. They are, for ever more, 'The Kettle Cars'. *End*

'This superb C-type reconstruction enables us to see and experience again one missing part of that great Jaguar racing story'

Heritage

JAGUAR PARTS — supplying parts for a legend

Heritage Jaguar Parts was founded after discovering a previously undiscovered treasure trove of rare original Jaguar parts dating back to the early 1950's

Over **10,000** components are 'new old stock' covering the Jaguar XK, E-type and saloon range from the 1950's 60's and 70's. Many of which are still in their original packaging

Please E-mail your wish-list or a photo of what you are looking for, **jason@heritagejaguarparts.com** or telephone Jason with your requirements on **01924 430818**

www.heritagejaguarparts.com
Ebay id : heritage-jaguar-parts-ltd

IT SEEMED LIKE a great idea at the time... from the comfort of a cosy restaurant with a number of glasses of claret under the belt. 'Those Bentley Boys had a go at a train in the 1930s and beat it, so why don't we have a crack at a train as well? What is the best one to race? Of course, the Orient-Express. We'll murder it!'

Jonathan Turner, 44, is annoyingly good looking and successful. In the oil business (Gulf and Bayford), he has recently been collecting a number of important British sports and racing cars. He has done the arduous Peking to Paris twice. His Bentley was the first pre-war car home in 1997, and in '07 his Itala broke its camshaft in the Gobi desert. Undeterred, Turner trucked to Siberia to pick up another engine from a 30-year-old Russian motor, fitted it to the 1907 machine and continued on his way to Paris.

Having recently purchased this magnificent Ecurie Ecosse D-type – chassis number XKD603, one of 11 works long-nose jobs and sourced by specialist dealer Andrew Hall – he is intent on using the Jaguar hard and fast. The car was driven by Mike Hawthorn at Silverstone, and came →

THE EXPRESS WAY TO VENICE

Join *Octane* in an epic high-speed battle across Europe as we race in a Jaguar D-type from London to Venice against the legendary Orient-Express

WORDS: ROBERT COUCHER // PHOTOGRAPHY: THEO LIASI & DAVID BARZILAY

'We drop in and see how Moss is getting on after his accident. He's as energetic and enthusiastic as ever, peering over the balcony to look at the Jag'

second at Le Mans in '57 in the hands of Sanderson and Lawrence. Rightfully regarded as one of the most original and desirable works long-nose D-types in existence, it has authentic mechanicals, leather interior and largely original paintwork, and is sympathetically maintained by David Brazell Engineering.

The D is garaged at Gregor Fisken's dealership in London's Kensington the Wednesday night before the off, where Turner and I meet up to have a look around the old racing car. Only now does it dawn on me that this is going to be no walk in the park. Have you ever sat in the passenger seat of a D-type? Neither have I until now. There is a hole cut into the top of the aluminium bodywork, seemingly in a grudging manner, and a small seat is inserted in compliance with the rules of Le Mans.

The exhaust runs directly below the passenger footwell and seat, so there is virtually no legroom and a lot of heat. Fisken looks at me trying to get comfortable below the vestigial Perspex windscreen and mutters: 'Glad I'm not going to be sitting in there for 36 straight hours.'

Jonathan Turner, breezy and positive as ever, suggests I find some sort of matting to prevent my shoes from melting. So that night I pack my wife's

yoga sheepskin rug into my luggage along with various caps, goggles, gloves and a wax jacket. Turns out the sheepskin works well.

On Thursday 29 April we point the D-type Jaguar towards Victoria Station, but on the way we take a detour to Shepherd Street in Mayfair to drop in and see how Sir Stirling Moss is getting on after his awful lift-shaft accident. He is as energetic and enthusiastic as ever, peering over the balcony to look at the Jaguar. We go up to his bedroom for a chat and he immediately fires off questions about the D.

Turner tells him it was fitted with a works 3.75-litre engine, and Moss retorts this is wrong as they never ran that engine at Le Mans. A £20 bet is wagered and wife Susie Moss goes and collects Stirling's bound cuttings, dated 1956 and '57. The results indicate that Moss is correct in one way, because this particular car ran with a 3.4-litre engine (it was later changed for Monza), although another model did run with the 3.75-litre unit. Parting with £20 really grates Turner; he's a Yorkshireman, you understand. At Victoria, Health 'n' Safety decrees that we cannot park the D-type on the platform alongside the British Pullman, so we pull up outside on the main

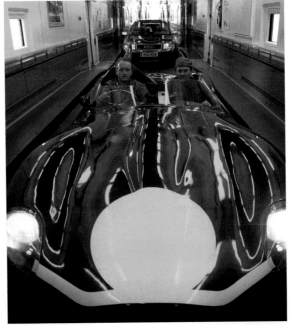

LONDON
DAY 1 10:40
DEPARTURE 5 MINS

DOVER ○   CALAIS

PARIS ○

concourse. The noise of the car's straight-through exhaust system gets the attention of commuters and soon we are swamped by photographers. I say, we are rather famous!

Then a blond fellow, slim as a whippet, wanders into view. The snappers start barging each other for position and shots. Ah, it's Ronan Keating from pop band Boyzone, so we remain totally non-famous. Keating jumps into the D and revs the engine with glee as numerous other passengers from the Orient-Express come out to look at the car and to wonder why we are doing this. So am I, as it starts to drizzle. At 10.40am the train pulls out of the station and Jonathan fires up the D.

We set off towards Folkestone but don't take the congested route suggested; in order to spare the Jaguar we opt instead for the A3 out to the M25. As the car is fitted with a TrackaPhone locating device, those watching our progress via a BlackBerry on the train think we have already gone the wrong way and sense that we stand no chance of beating them to Venice.

The Italian city, some 1740km (1044 miles) distant, begins to seem a long way off as the D-type canters down the motorway to the coast. There we cross the Channel via the Eurotunnel

with the Orient-Express passengers in fully stocked luxury coaches, and drive to Calais station to meet the Venice-Simplon-Orient-Express. What a magnificent train it is. The coaches are elaborate and beautifully trimmed. They were found and bought up from all over Europe by James Sherwood, scion of the Orient-Express Hotels group, and beautifully restored to immaculate condition.

Obviously very proud of their special train, the Italian staff show us around the carriages. Goodness, it is luxurious and comfortable, with three restaurants and an entire carriage devoted to a Champagne bar and lounging area complete with piano. Typically, Turner opens the lid and plays a few bars perfectly.

At 4.36pm, the whistle sounds and the Orient-Express starts to pull out of the station. With no Health 'n' Safety nannies to worry about, Jonathan guns the Jaguar and wheelspins it down the platform next to the train, careful to avoid the stationmaster and furniture! The race is on. A camera team in a Range Rover wants to film us leaving Calais, so we follow them and their sat-nav. Of course, the device takes us in totally the wrong direction along the E402, and Turner

→

'I snick the car up through the gearbox, and soon we are galloping along at speed. It feels like a long-legged horse – a true thoroughbred'

explodes: 'Bloody sat-nav is useless! Use maps. They don't lie!' Being a top-notch navigator he's right, so I unfurl the old map of France and figure out how to get us onto the correct Autoroute.

With such a long way to drive we opt not to follow the train around Paris but to go straight to Reims. We had been hoping to drop in and visit Moët & Chandon managing director Jean Berchon, who is a keen classic car collector. Fortunately he is on his way to Monte Carlo for the Monaco Historique, so we avoid the temptation of a glass of his champoo. At Reims we cut off the Autoroute and on to the D913. Filling up with (lots!) of petrol, Jonathan suggests I drive the next stint. It would be a pleasure.

The driver's seat in the D feels fabulously comfortable after the cramped and hot passenger perch. All that lovely legroom! You sit low in the car and its voluptuous bodywork wraps around you. The engine fires up with a rasp and the racing clutch pushes down with surprising ease. The delicate gearshift engages first and the Jaguar springs off the mark. Quickly getting to know the car I snick it up through the close-ratio box, and soon we are galloping along at speed. It feels like a long-legged horse – a true thoroughbred.

The steering is superbly alive and incredibly light, the disc brakes are super-sharp and

powerful, and the independent front suspension feels soft and pliable, soaking up the bumps and undulations. The well-located solid rear axle is free of hop, although the low-slung exhaust does ground over severe bumps. Weighing just 980kg the D is a pure racing machine, but it is adept at effortlessly gobbling up long road miles.

Spearing through the open French countryside at dusk, the sun settling on the far horizon, in a willing works D-type Jaguar, is a memory that will stay with me forever. The moment is made even more poignant as we race past cemeteries with rows and rows of carefully tended gravestones of all the young men sacrificed in the First World War. Approaching Verdun we pull over to pay our respects, and Jonathan quietly notes: 'It's humbling to be enjoying ourselves so

much at this place.' I feel it as well, because the nearby Delville Wood was scene of the battle where the volunteers from my native South Africa were massacred. It was described as 'the bloodiest battle of hell of 1916' with 80% losses.

Chastened, we continue our way into Verdun, a beautiful town bathed in orange light. Coming across the attractive Café Le Boucher du Quai at 10.30pm, we park the D slap outside and Turner marches in and persuades the chef to fire up his cooling oven. The most delicious steak frites and salad is served along with ice-cold Coca Cola and strong coffee. I don't care how much lobster is being guzzled on the train – this turns out to be a superb supper.

At the start, Jonathan's gorgeous wife Karen had told me to keep an eye on him and not encourage him to drive too fast. So I feel rather silly when, motoring quickly through the dark towards Metz, a French police car comes tearing up behind with all its lights going and pulls me over. Six gendarmes climb out looking menacing, with cropped hair, dark blue fatigues and weapons. Then another police van arrives and I have visions of a cold and unfriendly cell.

We produce licences and papers, and Turner starts his patter. It becomes evident that we have not actually been caught speeding, and he is soon conversing in broken French about how the Jaguar had competed at Le Mans. The police soften and allow us to take snaps of them with the car, before shaking our hands and bidding us *bonne chance*.

The long drive continues east to Strasbourg and down to Mulhouse. Coming into Switzerland at about 5am, rain starts to pelt down – just as the customs officials inform us we need to purchase →

Below
Orient-Express passes through stunning mountain scenery as it speeds across Europe.

Above
Duo battles across the Continent – at one point running side-by-side in the Brenner Pass (inset centre).

REIMS ◯

STRASBOURG ◯

MULHOUSE ◯

BASEL ◯

INNSBRUCK ◯

IN PURSUIT OF PERFECTION

THE BEACHAM XK 150 V8 S

THE BEACHAM E TYPE V8 S

THE BEACHAM XK 150 V8 S

AFTER 46 YEARS TECHNOLOGY EVOLVES TO MEET WITH ICONIC STYLING

In the history of motor vehicle manufacture only Beacham have taken 46 year old designs and redeveloped them with sympathetic synergy of the best of the old and the best of new Jaguar motors and technology. Produced in very small numbers the Beacham E type, XK 150 and MK2 V8 represent unique hand built works of motoring art under which are cars with true heart, classic styling, performance and safety features which combine to place them ahead of many modern high performance cars.

Beacham also restore to original factory specifications. Restorations are also offered for Aston Martin, Daimler, Rolls Royce and Bentley.

For further information and ordering:

BEACHAM INDEPENDENT JAGUAR SPECIALISTS LTD. NEW ZEALAND

BEACHAM JAGUAR

ph +64 274735432 | fax +64 6 878 8056 | greg@beacham-jaguar.co.nz | www.beacham-jaguar.co.nz

ON BOARD
THE SIMPLON-ORIENT-EXPRESS

'WHY ON EARTH is a racing car sitting outside Victoria?' The question came from a blonde whose partner was wrestling with two very large suitcases. 'It's racing us to Venice,' answered her escort. 'Don't be silly, darling. Things like that don't happen,' she replied.

Well, of course, he was right! Jonathan Turner and *Octane* editor Robert Coucher were in the D-type's driving seat and about to be flagged off by the Italian Consul General Uberto Vanni d'Archirafi and pop star Ronan Keating on a challenge reminiscent of the great car versus train races of the '30s.

Train passengers were about to be involved in a battle that had taken months of planning. They joined the British Pullman at Victoria for its run to the coast, and then transferred to luxury coaches for their Eurotunnel journey to Calais, where they met the Venice-Simplon-Orient-Express.

Octane set up operations in a couchette in carriage K, where a steady stream of passengers checked in to see who was in the lead. Thanks to TrackaPhone, we were able to tell them. A small tracking device in the carriage monitored the train, another in the D-type monitored the car. A BlackBerry plotted each and showed us where they were. Turner and Coucher kept in touch by text, telling us they'd stopped for steak frites. We told them we had dined on Brittany lobster!

As dawn broke, the passengers wanted to know who was in the lead. The D-type was, but our positions changed many times. We got a real thrill on the Brenner Pass when the car ran alongside us, and again in Italy when railway line and motorway converged.

The result was very tight! Passengers were hoping the train would win – yet with 20 minutes to go we heard the Jag was already in Venice. Some people had probably lost a bit of money, but everyone in the bar car cheered and toasted the D-type with Champagne in true Orient-Express style.   **David Barzilay**

Left and below
Victory – and relief – as epic journey ends in Venice for Turner, Coucher and venerable D-type.

VERONA   **VENICE**

'We rocket along the causeway and onto the island, arriving 20 minutes before the train. What an incredible car the Jag is, and what a great race'

a motorway pass for €40. This is the low point. Jonathan's goggles steam up and we can barely see where we are going over the screen. Just as we think about stopping, the rain relents and dawn breaks. Immediately we feel better.

Our objective is the town of Unterterzen on Lake Walensee for a photo op of the train coming past. We arrive first and wave at the passengers as the Orient-Express hisses by. Chuffed that we have beaten the train to the first rendezvous, we race off towards Liechtenstein and into Austria. As we feel we are well ahead, we take a detour to enjoy a drive up the Arlberg Pass.

That's when the Austrian police arrive and issue us with a €120 fine for not having an Austrian motorway pass. Annoying, because the border guards had waved us through and, unlike the Swiss, did not tell us we need a pass. And here we are thinking Austria is part of the EU. A blatant stitch-up.

This set-back delays us, so I have to really push the D-type hard up the Brenner Pass, which is again a fantastic blast. In blazing sunshine we catch the train in Belzano and get some great

pictures running alongside it towards Trento. Jonathan does the final hot slog to Padova, and soon Venice comes into view. We rocket along the final causeway and onto the island, arriving just 20 minutes before the train.

Feeling exhausted and exhilarated after 36 hours of non-stop driving, we have completed the race – and won! XKD603 has beaten the fabled Orient-Express, and Jonathan Turner and I have enjoyed a tremendous motoring adventure. I am impressed by his driving: firm but gentle, treating the car with the respect it deserves. But the real hero is the magnificent Ecurie Ecosse long-nose works D-type Jaguar that performed with effortless but searing ability. What an incredible machine. And what a great race!   *End*

THANKS TO: Anna Nash and Stephen Lock of the Venice-Simplon-Orient-Express; Phil Derry and Martin Worth of TrackaPhone; John Keefe, Gael Guesdon and Catherine Cleall-Harding of Eurotunnel; Tony O'Keefe of Jaguar Cars; Land Rover; Jaguar Italia; the Italian Tourist Board in London; the Italian Consul General; Motor Sport Unit, Bristol Film Studios; Jonathan Turner; David Barzilay.

WHITE LIGHTNING

THE STORY OF TKF 9 – JIM CLARK'S D-TYPE JAGUAR

What started out green, changed to white, back to green and is now white again?
The answer is D-type Jaguar chassis number XKD517, best known as the 'Border
Reivers, Jim Clark D-type', which has been rebuilt to a stunning standard

SOME YEARS AGO I was in conversation with noted collector and historic racer Neil Corner, who has always selected the best cars available to him. At one time he owned an ex-Ecurie Ecosse D-type (and loved the car), but eventually it was sold to help buy the farmhouse in which he now lives. He explained at the time that his son Nigel was not really interested in his cars, but then, after the D-type was sold, Nigel became more of an enthusiast than his father. The one car he longed for was a D-type, and as Neil sadly remarked: 'There are only about three D-type Jaguars worth buying, and they are all owned by people unlikely to sell them.' One of these was the Border Reivers car. Nigel was to wait many years before it eventually came into his hands.

Back in 1956, Coventry Jaguar distributor Henlys had a customer for XKD517, a 41-year-old motor trader from Liverpool called Gilbert 'Gillie' Tyrer who had been a regular post-war racer. He was an early agent for Frazer Nash cars and built a Special using a BMW 328 sports car with the wings sawn off. He then got his hands on one of the streamlined 1940 Mille Miglia BMWs, and this helped make him one of the most successful north of England sports car drivers in the 1950s.

Gillie first dipped his toe in the Jaguar pond when he bought XKC038, one of the 1953 C-type factory cars built for Le Mans. It did not actually race at La Sarthe that year as it was the reserve, and it was then prepared

for a planned visit by Jag to the Mexican Road Race, but this never took place. Obviously Gillie was now bitten by the Jaguar bug and made plans to get himself a D-type – hence the Henlys order placed by Tyrer's garage, Litherland Motors.

Model XKD517 was a straightforward short-nose customer car and was one of three D-types handled by Henlys around that time. It had sold XKD515 to Col. Ronnie Hoare of Maranello Concessionaires and XKD518 to Peter Blond – the only D-type originally painted in red. The Tyrer model was fitted with engine number E2026-9 and the colour was described as Pastel Green rather than British Racing Green.

Tyrer actually did very little with the car save recording 131.58mph in it at the Chester Motor Club's Queensferry Sprint, before it was sold on to his friend Alex McMillan, who owned the Futura Rubber Company. Again, the Jaguar was used mainly for club race meetings for the rest of the year.

At the end of the 1956 racing season the D-type was offered for sale by McMillan. He was approached by Bud Murkett, whose family owned the Jaguar dealership for the Bedford and Peterborough area. The plan was that Bud's nephew, Tony Murkett, would race the car in the 1957 season.

The short-nose D-type might have been a relatively easy vehicle to drive, but when you got it up to racing speeds it needed considerable

skill to handle. Tony Murkett found this out the hard way: he had a big accident on the Silverstone Club Circuit and, on the advice of the insurance company, it was decided that someone else should race the car. Bud Murkett remembered that a local farmer friend, Charles Taylor, had a son who was a racing driver and asked if he would like to contest the D-type. The son was Henry Taylor, and the car virtually took him out of British club racing and into International events.

Henry Taylor was born in 1932 in Bedfordshire. He was mad about cars and started rallying, but found it boring. At the age of 22 he bought his first racing car, a MkIV Cooper 500 with a Vincent 500cc vee-twin, which was not exactly the most competitive engine.

Then his father stepped in and told him that if he was serious about racing he should have the right equipment, and so Henry bought Bob Gerard's MkVIII Cooper and told his dad he could probably get a secondhand JAP engine for £30. However, his father insisted that they buy two brand-new JAP units, which Vic Martin tuned for them. In 1955 Henry had 52 wins in all sorts of events, but changed the JAP engine for a Norton and became Autosport Champion. Another season in 500s led to the offer to drive the D-type. Up to that time he had driven only little 500s and now he was in a big sports car: 'I loved the D-type and found it very easy to drive, particularly with the tail out – and I was a tail-out kind of driver.'

His first race with the car was the British Empire Trophy at Oulton Park, which was run in three heats and a final. Here he was up against →

Far left and above
Gilbert 'Gillie' Tyrer, the D-type's first owner; farmer's son Henry Taylor at Silverstone, duelling with Sears' Lister-Bristol.

'THIS WAS THE FIRST SPORTS CAR TO LAP ANY CIRCUIT IN BRITAIN AT AN AVERAGE SPEED OF OVER 100MPH
– JIM CLARK WAS ON HIS WAY UP!'

Britain's top drivers, including Archie Scott Brown and Roy Salvadori, and acquitted himself well, finishing eighth overall. This was despite a little incident at the notorious Cascades corner.

'I arrived much too fast in the wet,' Henry explained. 'I spun the car and it shot off the road. I was conscious of the Oulton Park lake coming towards me fast, but managed to stop the D from going into the water on a small patch of grass almost exactly the size of the D-type.'

At the end of the race Henry returned to the paddock damp, but warm from the heat in the cockpit, only to find his wife Peggy and mechanic Ray Lane soaking wet and blue with the cold.

'I took one look at them and realised it would be awful to try and push the car back into the transporter, so I suggested they get into that and drive it back and I would drive the D-type home to Bedford. I left the circuit, turned on to the A5 and drove it all the way back on my set of Dunlop green spot tyres, which were pretty good in the wet.'

His first International was the Nürburgring 1000km race on 26 May, 1957, when the Murkett Brothers entered the car for Henry Taylor and Archie Scott Brown. This was also scheduled to be Archie Scott Brown's first continental race. Archie was quickest of all the D-types in practice, ahead of the Ecurie Ecosse cars, but he did not get a chance to race the car, as Henry crashed heavily on the fourth lap and hit a tree. He had better luck at Spa, where he finished third overall in the sports car race that supported the Belgian Grand Prix. It was a wet event and Henry, who was always good in the rain, initially led the all-conquering factory Aston Martin DBR1s of Brooks and Salvadori.

Henry took another eighth place in the Sussex Trophy at Goodwood, and had one or two other runs in the car before his best performance of the year at Goodwood on 28 September. Here he was lined up with people like Jack Brabham in the new Tojeiro-Jaguar and Archie Scott Brown in the Lister-Jaguar. Henry managed to hold off a determined Roy Salvadori in a factory Lotus Eleven and take third place, but what pleased him most was defeating Duncan Hamilton in another D-type.

By now the season was coming to an end, and the Murkett Brothers had no intention of keeping the D-type. Word of this got to Scotland, where Jock McBain was keen to get the Border Reivers team back into serious motor racing. Egged on by the enthusiastic Ian Scott Watson, they made the decision to buy the D-type from the Murketts and run it in 1958 with regular BR driver Jimmy Somervail and newcomer Jim Clark. Clark had raced nothing more powerful than Scott Watson's Porsche 1600 Super, so a test day was booked at Charterhall, their local

circuit, and the potential drivers turned up. Ian Scott Watson was one such racer but found that on the main straight it was difficult to see through his glasses, as the wind affected his eyesight. Then Jimmy Somervail went out and lapped quickly with the car, but it was Jim Clark who was the most impressive. He sat down, relaxed, and drove to perfection.

Although Jimmy Somervail was to race the car on a couple of occasions in 1958 he, like the gentleman he remained to his death in June 2011, announced that he'd retire from motor racing because Jim Clark was clearly a driver of great ability who could make best use of the D-type.

Scott Watson now set to work organising a programme for Border Reivers, and it so happened the first race meeting of the 1958 season was almost on their doorstep, at Full Sutton in North Yorkshire. This ex-US Air Force airfield was used for the first time on 5 April, 1958.

The next problem was how to get the D-type to Full Sutton. Jim Clark suggested his own farm lorry, which he kept parked out in a barn. Although April, it was still very cold in the Borders and so the D-type was loaded on the truck on the Friday evening for an early start the next morning. Jim looked outside at the weather and decided to empty the radiator of the lorry just in case it froze overnight. Unfortunately, unknown to Jim, his farm manager had the same idea and later he also turned the tap underneath the radiator – only what he was doing was actually closing the empty radiator!

Next morning Jim was up bright and early, went to the barn, 'closed' the tap and filled up the radiator with water. However, all the liquid ran out of the bottom onto some straw, so he didn't hear it. After he had put what he thought was enough water into the radiator, he prepared to leave. The lorry travelled about three miles before the engine seized due to overheating. There was nothing else to do but unload the D-type.

Jim wrapped himself up in a heavy jacket and scarf, and then drove the car down the A1 to Full Sutton. At this meeting he not only won the sports car race but set the initial lap record for the circuit at over 100mph. This was the first sports car to lap any racing circuit in Britain at an average speed of more than 100mph – Clark was on his way up!

Remember, too, that Jim had only ever ran five races in his life before that day. On the Sunday morning he decided to get up early and drive the D-type back up the A1 to Chirnside. I remember him telling me how quick the D-type was – and on that road journey back he was in for another surprise. Around eight o'clock in the morning, on a section of dual-carriageway, Jim couldn't believe his eyes when he saw another →

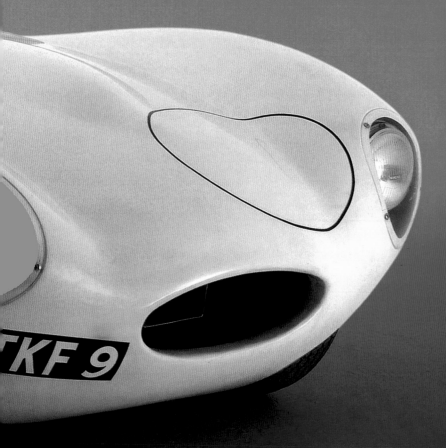

'SPA WAS FAST AND HERE WAS CLARK, FACED WITH THIS DAUNTING CIRCUIT IN ONLY HIS FOURTH RACE IN THE D-TYPE'

'JIM COULDN'T BELIEVE HIS EYES WHEN HE SAW ANOTHER D-TYPE COMING DOWN THE OPPOSITE CARRIAGEWAY TOWARDS HIM'

D-type coming down the opposite carriageway towards him. Both drivers braked hard and had a chat. The other D-type was owned by Sir Robert Ropner, who was a great friend of Bill Lyons of Jaguar and who had already owned a C-type but was now exercising his road-registered D-type.

Following the Full Sutton success Ian Scott Watson was spinning like a top, with big plans for the team. He announced that Border Reivers had been given an entry for the Spa 1000km race the following month and that they would go there...

Spa was fast in those days, and here was Clark faced with this daunting circuit in only his fourth race with the D-type. At the track, veteran British driver Jack Fairman took pity on Jim and drove him round the circuit in a rented Volkswagen Beetle to show him the corners. Clark was overawed when Fairman told him the speed at which he would have to take some of those corners, but rose to the challenge. His first shock came when the race leader, Masten Gregory in the Ecurie Ecosse Lister-Jaguar, passed him. A week later, when he told me of the experience, he was still in awe of the speed Gregory was going and opined that he thought he would never be able to drive as fast as that (sic).

Clark was to finish eighth in that race, but the accident in the same event, which cost Archie Scott Brown his life, stayed with him for the rest of his life. From that moment, he hated the circuit. Indeed, many years later he remarked: 'Why is it that I love Monaco and have never won the Monaco Grand Prix, but I hate Spa and have won it four times...?'

Jim had many wins with the car, and on one occasion at Charterhall the young Duke of Kent visited the track as a guest of Jock McBain, who ran Border Reivers. Jock drove the Duke round the track a couple of times and then the royal took the wheel, so becoming probably the only Duke to test a D-type Jaguar on a race circuit.

When the season ended Clark had logged a remarkable 12 wins out of the 20 races he contested TKF 9 for Border Reivers. The team sold the D-type and bought a Lister-Jaguar for 1959 – and by now Jim had come under the spell of Colin Chapman.

The man who bought XKD517 was Alan Ensoll, an enthusiast from the north of England, who also owned an ex-Ecurie Ecosse C-type Jaguar. His plan was to convert the D-type into a full road car, but he never completed the job. When the makers of the film *The Green Helmet* were looking for racing sports cars Alan loaned the D-type to them. Then he sold it to Irishman Bob Duncan, who had seen the model during the making of the film and later raced it at Kirkistown. It then returned to the mainland in the hands of Bryan Corser. Corser was the founder of the Loton Park hillclimb, and he used the D-type as his course car. By now the Jaguar had been painted green, and it was to remain green until the present owner bought it in 2006.

Corser sold XKD517 to American Jaguar collector Walter Hill, but Hill kept the car in England in the hands of Martin Morris and did not take it back to the States; he felt it added nothing to his already impressive collection of Jaguars.

Eventually, in 1979, Hill sold the D-type to former Chevron racing driver and Devonian estate agent Willie Tuckett. Willie had first seen the car at Martin Morris's workshops and said that if it ever came up for sale he would like to buy it. Willie met Walter Hill at the Rembrandt Hotel in London, where Hill personally gave him the bill of sale. At the time Henry Taylor also wanted to buy the D-type as a souvenir of his early racing days, but Willie Tuckett beat him to the punch. As a result, Taylor had a replica of TKF 9 made and used it on a number of touring events.

Tuckett raced XKD517 on many occasions in historic events, ran it on many motoring tours and thoroughly enjoyed it. During Willie's tenure the car had a heavy racing accident at Silverstone, and Martin Morris made a new bonnet section but retained the damaged original.

Tuckett won the Coy's '50s sports car race at the Nürburgring in 1990 and in 1995 finished third in the 1000km event at the same venue, sharing the car with his friend David Piper. His last race with it was the Magny Cours Historic in 1999.

Meanwhile Nigel Corner, who had by now carved a name for himself in historic racing, had been badgering his friend Adrian Hamilton about this D-type. In turn, Hamilton urged Willie Tuckett to sell the car, but the deal all hinged on Corner selling his Lightweight E-type Jaguar. Once this was sold, the way was clear to buy TKF 9. Nigel used it for a number of historic tours but his wife Harriet found it uncomfortable to travel in. During this time Corner added a tailfin to the car, something it had never had, and replaced the original gearbox. Eventually he sold the D-type to the present owner early in 2006. The car was then sent to Chris Keith-Lucas at CKL Developments for a very sympathetic rebuild. The tailfin was removed and Chris was able to retain the integrity of the bodywork with the minimum amount of new metal, including the replacement of the original nose, easily recognisable by the domed rivets from a hasty Border Reivers repair.

Also, the original gearbox has been totally rebuilt and TKF 9 has once again returned to the creamy-white of the Murkett Brothers/Border Reivers days, with the latter's original logo of a Border Reiver on his horse – taken from a statue in Hawick in the Scottish Borders.

Today XKD517 looks exactly as it did the first time I saw it in pristine condition in the paddock at Oulton Park more than 50 years ago. Enthusiasts can be assured that the car is in very good hands, with an owner who wants to preserve it as one of the finest D-type Jaguars in the world. **End**

THANKS TO all at historic Jaguar and racing specialist CKL Developments in East Sussex, www.ckldevelopments.co.uk +44 (0)1424 870600.

'THE TAILFIN WAS REMOVED AND CHRIS WAS ABLE TO RETAIN THE INTEGRITY OF THE BODYWORK WITH THE MINIMUM OF NEW METAL'

Below
Repairing and refitting the original bonnet, seemingly crumpled beyond repair, returned the D-type to Clark-era specification.

Rowan goes forth...

...and finishes sixth on aggregate in his Jaguar MkVII.
Here's how he acted as both Pro and Am driver at the Goodwood Revival

PHOTOGRAPHY: JEFF BLOXHAM, JOHN COLLEY, STEVE HAVELOCK, MIKE JOHNSON   WORDS: ROWAN ATKINSON

I'VE WRITTEN SO MUCH about this funny old car over the years, that I shrink from opining any more on the subject. *Octane* aficionados might remember me wibbling on in various columns about its restoration, the agony over its colour choice and its failure to appear on the Tour Auto, so if those readers want to skip the opening paragraphs, I will understand completely. However, I should perhaps recap the basics for any Johnny-cum-Latelys to the *Octane* fold.

This is a 1952 Jaguar MkVII, a car of which, four years prior to writing this, I hadn't even heard. It's a big, fat, Bentley-sized object built by Jaguar on a stretched XK120 chassis with a 3.4-litre version of the XK engine. It may look rather grand but it was never that expensive, just one of those Jaguar saloons of the 1950s and 1960s which represented remarkable value for money. They all exuded more than a hint of Flash Cash from a Diana Dors/East End/Great Train Robbery kind of world, but the MkVII was nevertheless a quite outstanding sports saloon for its day and Jaguar raced it from the very first year of production.

The big annual event of the era was the Silverstone Production Car Race, and the MkVII's victory in the event of 1952 was the first of no less than five consecutive victories. I can hear some of you chortling when I point out that its closest rivals were the Austin Westminster and the Daimler Conquest, but I don't think that takes much away from William Lyons' achievement with the MkVII. It dominated those races because it had an excellent chassis allied to a fabulous engine in the XK unit.

It enjoyed success not only as a racing saloon. Even more astonishing for a vehicle of this weight and size was its prowess as a rally car, culminating in its most improbable achievement: an outright win on the Monte Carlo Rally of 1956. I've tried to form a picture in my mind of this leviathan slithering down ice-laden Alpine passes, but I'm afraid the image remains fuzzy and ill-defined.

In 1954, Jaguar began to experiment with the manufacture of light alloy body panels for the MkVII in an attempt to ensure its continued dominance of racing and rallying. The racing department took Sir William Lyons' personal car, an early steel MkVII of 1952, and replaced its body with an entire structure pressed from magnesium alloy.

This model was intended to be one of the Jaguar entries for the Production Car race of 1954 but, for whatever reason, it never appeared. A partly-alloy car did win the 1955 race in the capable hands of Mike Hawthorn, though. Once

Below
Jaguar MkVII has serious presence on the starting grid, making it hard to creep up on other drivers and catch them unawares.

'The racing department took Sir William Lyons' personal car, an early steel MkVII, and replaced its body with an entire structure pressed from magnesium alloy'

the MkI Jaguar was introduced in 1956, (don't ask me to explain the mathematical incongruity of the marque's numbering!) the MkVII's competition days were over and that original one-off Works car, constructed entirely of magnesium but never raced, was dumped at the back of the Racing Department with yellow crosses all over it indicating its 'scrapped' status.

It was then spotted by young Jaguar PR director and occasional racing driver Bob Berry. He bought it for £250, fitted pre-production versions of the then-innovative disc brakes and what he described as a 'wet-sump D-type engine' and took it racing. He competed in it for only a year before selling off all the D-type bits and reverting to the then-new 3.8-litre road powerplant.

In 1963, Berry sold it to dental student Christopher Sturridge, in whose family the car remained for nearly 40 years. I then bought and restored it, and drove it at the Goodwood Revival meeting.

It was intended that I should drive the car in the St Mary's Trophy for 1950s saloons (a 30-car grid), sharing with Sir Stirling Moss, the blissful symmetry of his involvement being that not only did he win the first race of any kind staged at Goodwood in 1948, he was also the man who

gave the MkVII its first win in that Production Car race of 1952. Sadly, he was having back trouble and was unable to drive at that particular Revival. However, he did attend the meeting as a spectator – I don't think you could keep him away from Goodwood if you nailed his feet to the floor.

At Goodwood, the St Mary's Trophy had the 'Pro-Am' driver structure of earlier years but consisted now of two races, one for the old Pros on Saturday and another for the amateur owners on the Sunday morning. Overall result was to be the aggregate of the two, but the cloud of disappointment surrounding Sir Stirling's absence had a modest silver lining for me viz, I got to do two races instead of one.

And so, deputising for El Maestro, I presented myself at the Old Pros' drivers' briefing before qualifying on Friday in some extremely exalted company. Derek Bell, Tiff Needell, Patrick Tambay, Gerry Marshall, Perry McCarthy, Rene Arnoux and Dickie Attwood were amongst them. There were also others who may have been Pro but were not remotely old: Audi sports car star Allan McNish and young hotshoe Nelson Piquet Junior, for instance.

Because of a bit of a *faux pas* by my preparation bods, my car turned up sporting the wrong tyres and so I set off for qualifying on an enforced spanking new set of Dunlops. Still, →

MODIFIED JAGUAR MKVII

ENGINE
3781cc, six-cylinder, twin overhead cam, three twin-choke Webers
POWER
260bhp @ 5500rpm
TORQUE
270lb ft @ 3500rpm
TRANSMISSION
Four-speed manual
SUSPENSION
Front: wishbones, torsion bars and hydraulic dampers. Rear: semi-elliptic leaf springs and hydraulic dampers
BRAKES
Servo-assist, discs
TOP SPEED
135mph (est)
VALUE
£55,000

the length of the practice session (25 minutes) seemed to give me ample time to scrub the new rubber in for a few laps, come into the pits for a look round by the mechanics and then go out for some times.

Big mistake. The first of a few throughout the weekend which showed the considerable gulf between the Pro and the Am. My thinking was totally Am. Initially things went to plan: the tyres had no grip at first, but were nicely warmed and scrubbed by my pit-stop and I set off for some hot laps. Half a tepid lap later, red flags came out. A car broken down in the wrong place, meeting running late, end of qualifying session. Aaargh!

Amateur, you see. A Pro would have thought: 'You never know how long a session is going to last. As soon as the tyres are able, give them hell and get some good times under your belt. Only then should you think about dropping into the pits for a cup of tea and a cream puff.'

I qualified 15th, pretty poor I thought, with a lap time of 1min 55sec. Tiff Needell in another (steel) MkVII was around 1.50. But the session for the owners' race went much better: tyres were good, we ran less fuel, I'd gained confidence and the times came tumbling down. I managed a 1.49 and qualified ninth: altogether more pleasing.

Although knocking six seconds off might seem impressive, I think that again it was only revealing of the amateur within

and how slow I am to build up confidence in both a car and a track. At the totally delightful Goodwood cricket match on Thursday, I was discussing with the writer Doug Nye the differences between a proper racing driver and an enthusiast. He then asked whether I could remember my lap times from the last time I raced the MkVII at Goodwood. I confessed that I couldn't. 'Enthusiast!' he cried, jabbing an accusing finger at me like Hercule Poirot. And he was so right.

Knowing the margin by which my times had improved, it was with some optimism that I formed up for the Pros' race on a beautifully sunny Saturday afternoon. My grid position was in the midst of a number of smaller but less powerful cars (Standard Ten, Riley 1.5) that I thought were probably better at cornering than accelerating. And so it turned out to be. I made a good start at the drop of the Union Jack and had gained several places at the end of the first lap. I then lost one or two as a couple of smaller cars made up for their start line laggardness, but things seemed to go well until the engine in Jackie Oliver's Austin A35 had a bit of a turn and dropped oil at Lavant.

The entry to this double right-hander just before the main straight is always a tad greasy, but Jackie's extra lubrication made a little off-piste exploration inevitable. I managed to avoid the gravel trap, so my spin wasn't too time-consuming. But there was more Extra Virgin Oliver Oil at the end of the

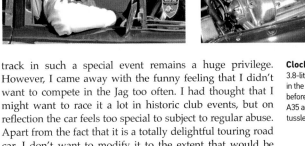

Clockwise from above
3.8-litre XK engine was fitted in the early 1960s; the calm before the racing storm; A35 and MkI enjoy race-long tussle; following racing line.

straight and I drove like a wuss through those areas until race end. I did finish ninth, though, just behind Tiff and Mike Salmon in the other two MkVIIs.

Sunday dawned, another blissful but even hotter day for the Am race. In this, I made a blistering start, exploiting the Jag's grunt and gaining several places. I was feeling a trifle smug and, of course, it's always at moments like these that the race is stopped. A Ford Zodiac had rolled at Madgwick (in a suitably gentle, balletic fashion) and we had a restart. Scheisse! as Austin Powers would say.

Did OK on the restart, but those in front were ready for me this time and it's never easy to take people unawares in a MkVII. After a lot of give and take, I settled into a comfy seventh and things felt pretty good until the last lap, when heck if I didn't spin in exactly the same place as the first race but without any excuse or explanation this time, other than that I am a cack-handed wally.

I know that a Pro wouldn't have done it, simply because he would have known he was on the last lap and not taken any chances. Ditsy old me hadn't a clue what lap I was on; I just drive until someone says 'stop'. So I finished tenth, three positions shy of where I could have been but with an aggregate position of sixth. Which, all things considered, felt like a good result.

It was a great weekend, as Goodwood always is. The Jag went really well, and being allowed to race at such a special

track in such a special event remains a huge privilege. However, I came away with the funny feeling that I didn't want to compete in the Jag too often. I had thought that I might want to race it a lot in historic club events, but on reflection the car feels too special to subject to regular abuse. Apart from the fact that it is a totally delightful touring road car, I don't want to modify it to the extent that would be necessary to keep it competitive in historic racing. It may be modified as MkVIIs go, yet all its modifications essentially were carried out before 1961 and I'm not inclined to drag it screaming into the 21st century.

My dilemma is a common one for those with historic cars. It stems from the fact that the phrase 'Historic Racing' is essentially an oxymoron. It's nice to think that people might just get out their old cars and drive them round in circles. But motorsport is and has always been about one thing: going faster next time than you did last time. Serious historic racers spend huge sums on their motors to achieve exactly that and, as a result, many historic cars are now virtually 'silhouette' machines that have been developed internally beyond all recognition.

With, it must be said, some exciting results. The St Mary's Trophy was a case in point. There was on-track equivalence between cars that wouldn't even have been on the same lap if competing back in their day but whose close rivalry, courtesy of some extravagant development, made for some very exciting racing.

You've just got to decide what you want to do with your car. I think I'm clear as far as the Jaguar is concerned: I'm going to allow the old dear out occasionally, but she's not allowed to go clubbing and she's definitely not allowed to wear skimpy tops. *End*

DEREK BELL DRIVES
JAGUAR MKI

Salvadori's old MkI has become a star attraction
at Goodwood, largely thanks to the exuberance of
driver Grant Williams. Derek Bell recalls his experience
as co-driver to the oversteering Welshman

PHOTOGRAPHY: JOHN COLLEY, STEVE HAVELOCK

THE 2003 GOODWOOD REVIVAL meeting was enormous fun. I joined the Welsh father
and son team, Anthony and Grant Williams, to share the drive with Grant in their outrageously
extrovert 1958 Jaguar MkI in the 20-lap, two-driver St Mary's Trophy race for production
saloons. Although their Jag is a 1950s car, it was accepted into this race because the Goodwood
organisers really wanted it to be there. And it is usually a front-runner.

Grant Williams has become a star attraction at the Revival meetings, racing this important
machine with real gusto. His car control is perfect and he relishes his time behind the wheel.
He really plays to the crowd, sliding the Jaguar through the corners at leary angles. Grant is
a superb driver, and I'm surprised he has not yet been offered a Touring Car drive, or
something of that level.

This MkI is a bit special. It was one of only three initially built as a Jaguar works car to
Group 3 specification. This meant that the factory could fit all the best bits from other models,
so it has an XK150 S head with three SU carbs, the brakes are from a MkIX and the doors,
bonnet and boot lid are constructed of lightweight aluminium. The rear hubs were wider,
from an XK150, to overcome the narrow rear track and its inherent handling limitations (this
Jaguar now runs a MkII rear end). Ivor Bueb, John Coombs and Briggs Cunningham each
took delivery of the first cars in 1958. This is the Coombs car, campaigned by himself and
raced by Roy Salvadori wearing the famous BUY 1 number plate.

Anthony Williams' father, 'Gordon F', was friendly with Lofty England and based close to
the Jaguar factory, so he had the chance to buy the car in 1962 and then contest it for a number →

of years. Then his son Anthony took over racing it before laying the MkI up until the Goodwood Revival was instigated in 1998. Anthony then prepared the car once again but found that his grandson, the young Grant Williams, was almost as quick as him first time out. Since then, Grant has been pedalling BUY 1 to good effect.

I have always had great affection for Jaguars. My father had the first E-type in East Sussex – and he was the first to crash an E-type there, too. It was the same car, and the smash occurred after an exuberant lunch. After that, he always drove Jag saloons. Years later I drove the 'Big Cat' for TWR (the XJ12C), which was a real handful, so my Jag background is half-reasonable. As you can imagine, I was really looking forward to racing this MkI in the St Mary's Trophy with Grant, with mechanical back-up and team management by Anthony.

We almost had a disaster during the Friday practice when a halfshaft broke. Anthony immediately set about stripping the rear end when a spectator, who had driven to the circuit in his Jaguar MkII, rushed into the pits and offered all the components from his car in the parking lot! Can you believe it? The man was so keen to help ensure BUY 1 was able to race he was prepared to offer his perfectly innocent car as a parts donor. But Anthony decided to pack all the bits and pieces into the rear of his van and roar off back to the workshop in Wales to fix the problem. After an all-nighter, the car was ready to go again the next morning. What a good effort.

During official practice on Saturday I took the Jaguar out only to find that it had hardly any brakes at all. Grant and Anthony did not seem in the slightest perturbed. 'Just pump the pedal a few times. The rear disc is a bit out of true

'A SPECTATOR RUSHED INTO THE PITS AND OFFERED THE COMPONENTS FROM HIS MKII IN THE PARKING LOT'

because of the halfshaft breaking, so it is pushing the pads back into the caliper. No real problem, though.'

I must say, I am not fond of racing cars without effective brakes, but I just had to get on with it. We qualified sixth and I got my lap time down to 1min 36sec. Grant's fastest was 1min 35sec so we were pretty close. My driving style is a little neater than Grant's. I would have been a second or so quicker if the brakes had worked, and Grant would have improved by about the same if he had stopped having such fun going sideways.

I started the race and got up to fourth place, having a great dice with Norman Grimshaw who was driving the Mini-Cooper S really well. We wanted to have a race with Leo Voyazides and Andy Bacon in the fast Ford Falcon. The Jaguar has a 3.8-litre engine (Anthony reckons it's putting out about 280bhp) but we were still giving away 100bhp and a lot of weight to the Falcon. Although the Jaguar is a racing car, it is very original and is fully trimmed. It's even road legal.

But the Williams' are a bit crazy and the Jaguar is set up for serious

oversteer. Once you get the hang of its 'pointy' nature, it is great fun. There is a lot of momentum and you do have to hurl the car at the corners, which requires a different approach to the much more sophisticated Porsches and things I have raced over the years.

Once the car is 'in', you steer on the throttle; a good thing as there is vast movement from one lock to the other. You have to make two bites at the tighter corners, and this means that if the car gets away from you your hands are in the wrong place on the wheel to catch it. I had a few hairy moments, but that's historic motor racing for you.

The Jaguar is good through the fast corners at Madgwick and Woodcote. I used third and top, with a quick downchange into second for the chicane. Fordwater can be tricky as the car goes light on the brow; just when you feel you should back off you must keep the power down. The Jaguar is terrific sliding through Lavant, where the line is not too vital but speed is all.

Anyway, after my stint, I came into the pits to hand over to Grant. I had undone the safety harness and was ready for a quick driver change. I have only ever climbed in and out of this car on two occasions, so I yanked the door handle towards me. I think this locked the door so Grant could not get in. Eventually we got it open, strapped him in and he shot out of the pits. He did his fabulous dance routine around the circuit and got the Jaguar up to second, just behind the Falcon. He closed a six-second gap down to about a second when the chequered flag dropped. That pit stop cost us the win, but there you go.

Driving a beautiful Jaguar that has been raced by Salvadori and three generations of lovely if slightly mad Welshmen was very special. It was a memorable occasion. *End*

Derek Bell
Five-times Le Mans and twice Daytona winner.

1958 JAGUAR MKI
ENGINE
3.8-litre dohc, straight-six, triple SU carburettors
POWER
(estimated)
280bhp @ 6000rpm
CHASSIS
Monocoque
SUSPENSION
Front: independent.
Rear: live axle with limited-slip diff

From far left
Rev counter is twisted around so that redline is at the top (an old racing trick); no need to rely on the original bonnet catch; is Derek grinning for the camera or because of the car?

xkExcess

Take a Le Mans winner and offer it in a roadgoing version.
Impossible? Not so. Jaguar did it with the XKSS in 1957

WORDS: PHILIP PORTER   /   PHOTOGRAPHY: JASON FURNARI

YOU COULD ARGUE it was the world's first supercar. It had prodigious performance, was rare and exotic, was utterly impractical in terms of luggage space and one was owned by Steve McQueen. Sounds like a pretty good definition of a 'supercar'!

The stunning D-type, for most of us the definitive 1950s sports racing car, had succeeded the C-type in 1954. The three-car factory team, led by Stirling Moss and Peter Walker, was unlucky not to seal a debut victory at Le Mans when Duncan Hamilton and Tony Rolt finished second by a mere 105 seconds after 24 gruelling hours of racing. The following year Hawthorn and Bueb took the first of the D-type's three Le Mans wins, but it was not one to celebrate as this was the year of the awful accident that cost over 80 lives.

In '56 two of the factory D-types crashed on the second lap, and Hawthorn's car was delayed by problems with its fuel injection. However, those gallant Scottish privateers from Ecurie Ecosse came to the rescue and took a memorable win with their lone D-type – a feat they repeated the following year when D-types finished first, second, third, fourth and sixth. There was no disputing the heritage.

In 1952 Jaguar had started building 'production' C-types, which were acquired by a number of the XK120 racers in the UK and America. Similarly, the factory laid down a small assembly line for 'production' D-types in 1955.

As the legendary Team Manager 'Lofty' England once told me: 'The reason for building 50 C-types and later 50 D-types, was that when entering a prototype at Le Mans, the manufacturers had to give a certificate that the car entered was the prototype of a car of which at least 50 examples would be built. I think we were the only company that in fact made 50!'

Ironically, Jaguar thought the D-type was not capable of winning Le Mans again in 1957, and so, in October 1956, announced its retirement from motor racing. The intention was to take a year out before returning with a team of E-types in 1958. Most unfortunately, life did not pan out like that. The ludicrously small team of engineers had to turn their efforts with some urgency to the aging range of real production models: the saloons and road-going sports cars. Furthermore,

'We got so much publicity from the fire that we didn't need to go motor racing – it was much cheaper to burn the works down!'

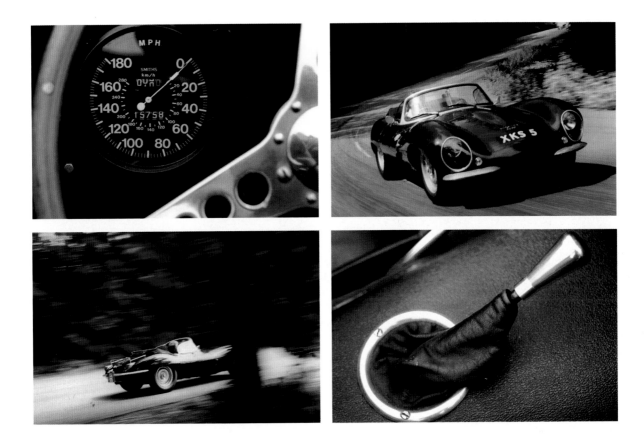

'When Jaguar announced its retirement from racing, some 42 production D-types had been supplied. But demand, believe it or not, had dried up, leaving 25 cars unsold'

a near-disastrous fire had broken out at the Browns Lane factory in February 1957. As 'Lofty' said: 'It was more important to keep the works going than go motor racing. In fact, we got so much publicity from the fire that we didn't need to go motor racing – it was much cheaper to burn the works down!'

When Jaguar made its announcement about retiring, some 42 production D-types had been supplied. But demand, believe it or not, had dried up, leaving 25 of the original batch of 67 unsold. Someone then had the brilliant idea of creating road cars out of the residue. I say 'someone' because several people subsequently claimed credit for the inspiration, and an air of mystery surrounds the real motives for conceiving what became known as the XKSS.

Duncan Hamilton, a wonderful, larger-than-life character, claimed he started the spark of an idea when he converted his ex-works car OKV 1, the 'D' he had shared at Le Mans with Rolt in '54, into a road car for Australian 'Jumbo' Goddard.

Another theory that has been peddled widely over many years is that the D-types were lying around going rusty and the XKSS was a desperate attempt to get rid of them. It is a small point, but aluminium does not rust!

When I wrote my book *Jaguar Sports Racing Cars*, Lofty gave me a great deal of help and debunked all these theories, saying: 'One of the important things in America, especially to Briggs Cunningham, was the Sports Car Club of America [SCCA], which ran production sports car races. The club should have

Above
Luggage rack is a nod towards road-going practicality. Everything else screams 'race car'.

accepted the D-type because it was used as a road car, but it didn't. So we decided to make the D-type acceptable to the SCCA, and had to build 50 examples of this revised car. We did use the remaining stock of D-types, but always planned to make more because we didn't have 50 lying around.'

Briggs Cunningham was, of course, the great American sportsman whose ambition had been to win Le Mans with one of his own cars. Having failed to do so he began racing Jaguars in his colours, and at the same time became the marque's New York dealer. So he had a vested interest in promoting Jaguar apart from the pure sport.

Another American, Bob Blake, played a major role in actually creating the prototype XKSS. Blake was a brilliant panel beater who had worked for Cunningham and claimed to have built every single Cunningham sports racer. When Briggs ceased building his own cars, Blake, who had a British wife, moved to England and joined the Experimental Department at Jaguar.

Lofty picked up the story again: 'Plans to convert to the XKSS were discussed by Sir William Lyons with Bill Heynes [Jaguar's engineering chief], and in turn with Phil Weaver [superintendent of the Competition Department], who got a D-type over to the competition shop. There, Bob Blake carried out the prototype work as instructed, but using some initiative. Sir William naturally went to the shop to see and approve the prototype work.'

The changes made to the D-types to create the XKSS largely →

'All 16 XKSS cars actually produced have their original D-type chassis number, too. Twelve went to the USA, two to Canada, one to Hong Kong and one remained in Britain'

consisted of additions. The most significant alterations to the bodywork – and none was of major structural importance – were the removal of the head fairing, the cutting out of the central division between the driver and passenger, and the provision of a door for the passenger on the left-hand side. A full-width, framed, wraparound windscreen was fitted, as were a pair of wipers. As the spare wheel lived in a compartment in the tail in what was the closest the D-type got to a boot, a luggage rack was mounted on the rear deck.

A rudimentary hood was provided, and Blake sketched his ideas for the top frame in an old exercise book. 'I made all the frames and bits and pieces,' he told me, 'including all the little wooden tools to make everything from. I made the front set of bumpers by cutting down the big old wide bumper, using the top radius and the bottom radius, cutting the flute out and welding the two pieces together. The back bumper went into production as a casting, quite thick but hollow in the back with bosses so that it could be bolted on – all made from my original.' These ideas led to the delicate bumper blades we would see on the E-type when it appeared four years later.

Tragically, the small production run of XKSS cars was cut short by the traumatic factory fire, which supposedly destroyed vital tooling. All 16 of the XKSS models actually produced have both their original D-type chassis number and an XKSS one as well. Twelve went to the USA, two to Canada, one to Hong Kong and

Above
The SS name is believed to stand for 'Super Sports', but this was never clarified at the time.

one remained in Britain. At least a couple of the cars had actually been completed as D-types before being converted to XKSS variants. This was so of XKSS 728, which was first displayed at the Barcelona Fair in 1956 as a 'D', and 769 which was on show at Appleyards, the Leeds Jaguar dealership. Stored by its long-term owner in the US for several decades, 728 emerged in 1998 in a wonderful time-warp state and today belongs to Gary Bartlett.

XKSS 757 (there was no apparent logic to the sequential numbering) went to Hong Kong, where it covered 1400 miles on the road and subsequently won the Macau GP on two occasions. The original owner of 707 was killed before he could take delivery, and the second owner died at Laguna Seca a few months later. Number 766 was sold to a Cuban living in New York, who then raced it extensively in his home country prior to the Castro revolution in '59. In the 1980s, dealer Colin Crabbe discovered this car and 725 in Cuba, and shipped them back to the UK.

XKSS 710 has been, in more recent years, converted first to a 'standard' D-type and then to a full Works long-nose specification, but all the original XKSS parts have been retained. Car 713 was owned by a succession of high-profile Californians, including rising movie star Steve McQueen. In 1967 he made a 'sale of convenience' to the Harrah Collection but, after a legal battle, managed to buy it back in 1978, keeping it until his death.

Of the Canadian cars, 716 was raced and hillclimbed with success and, many years later, converted into a D-type by

Lynx. Two D-types were also officially converted by the factory into XKSS models but not given XKSS numbers. XKD 533, which was originally raced as a 'D' in France, was returned to the manufacturer in 1958 for conversion and remained in France for some years. Today I believe it is owned by Ralph Lauren.

As to the other example, XKD 540, the factory chassis records mysteriously state 'redundant after experiment'. It was sold to Coombs of Guildford in Surrey for £2100 (the XKSS would be priced at £3878, so this sounded like a good deal.) Coombs later sold it to hillclimber Phil Scragg, who sent it back to the factory for conversion in the winter of '58/'59. That these two cars could be converted by the factory more than a year after the factory fire had supposedly destroyed vital jigs and tooling, thereby terminating XKSS production, rather seems to dispel that myth!

The example featured here started life as XKD 555. It was the first to be converted and was logically numbered XKSS 701,

the seven standing for the year. Its initial role was as the New York demonstrator, but 701 was also raced by the Vice President of Jaguar USA, one C. Gordon Benett who finished first at Mansfield, Louisiana. It was road-tested by *Road & Track* for the August issue, and staff concluded it was no dual-purpose car but did say it was a truly tremendous machine. Interestingly, they considered the ride was soft compared to the spine-jarring nature of Italian road-race machinery.

The XKSS continued to be raced in the States by its original owner Robert Stonedale, who later removed the screen, bumpers and boot rack, and added a roll-over bar. In September he finished fifth in a race at Oklahoma Airport with his left leg in plaster! The car then had a succession of subsequent owners, and in the early '60s suffered the period misfortune of having a Chevrolet V8 engine grafted in, which necessitated some altering of the frame. After an aborted attempt at restoration in →

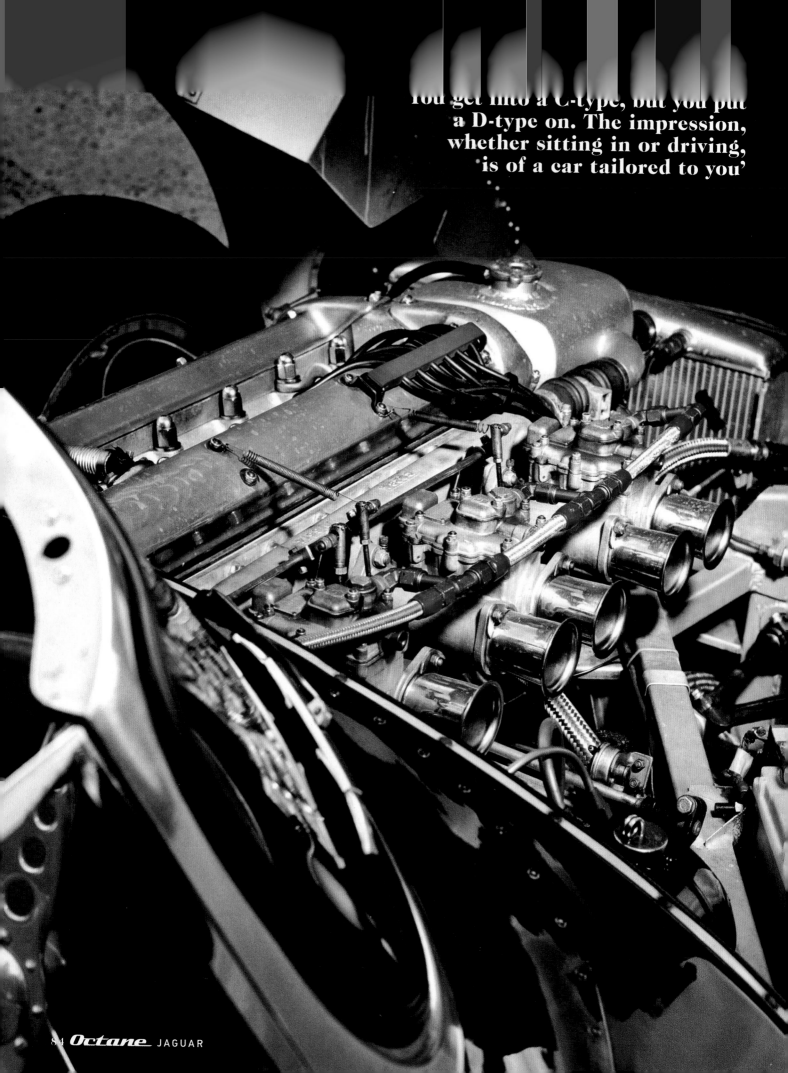

'You get into a C-type, but you put a D-type on. The impression, whether sitting in or driving, is of a car tailored to you'

1957 JAGUAR XKSS

ENGINE
3442cc, six-cylinder twin overhead cam XK engine with triple Weber 45 DC3 carburettors. Dry sump lubrication

POWER
250bhp @ 5750rpm
242lb ft @ 4000rpm

TRANSMISSION
Jaguar four-speed close-ratio all-synchro box

SUSPENSION
Front: Independent incorporating upper and lower wishbones with torsion bars.
Rear: transverse torsion bar, lower trailing arm and upper parallel trailing arms attached to live axle

BRAKES
Dunlop disc brakes all-round, triple pad front and twin pad rear

WEIGHT
1800lb (817kg)

PERFORMANCE
0-100mph: 13.6 secs.
Top speed: 149mph.
Standing quarter mile: 14.3 secs

VALUE
Around £750,000

Above
The XKSS folds itself around the driver. The full-width, wraparound screen makes it relatively civilised, too.

the 1970s, the car went to Lynx where, under the guidance of Chris Keith-Lucas, it was rebuilt for its Japanese owner as a D-type. Later the firm converted it back into full XKSS specification.

In early 2001 the car was acquired by Jaguar and TVR specialist Racing Green, which is based near Guildford. The vehicle was thoroughly overhauled mechanically for the Mille Miglia and shared on the event by Racing Green Chairman Graham Love and Mike Salmon, who raced D-types extensively in the 1960s. After a perfect, trouble-free run, Salmon commented that this was the best-driving D-type he had ever experienced.

Certainly an XKSS still feels a very quick car. The steering is delightfully precise and the whole machine feels very taut indeed. Thanks to the famous Jaguar torque, acceleration is vivid in any gear and, given the space and conditions, you could cruise at unprintably high speeds with complete confidence. The superb brakes add to that feeling, and I found the road-holding very predictable, allowing me to use the throttle to steer the rear end round the track we used for a very

exciting day's driving. Mechanically, the D-type and the XKSS are identical. The major difference you notice is the 'sophistication' of the full-width screen. The 'D' on the road is a pure, raw sports car, whereas the XKSS is a tad more civilised. It is said that C-types have recently become as sought-after (and thus as valuable) as D-types because they are more usable on the road. But the XKSS seems pretty happy pottering through suburbia, although is obviously at its most deliriously exciting on the open road.

The D-type was such a massive step forward from the C-type. I was forcefully reminded of this when, returning to Racing Green's extremely impressive premises, I climbed aboard a highly authentic C-type 'recreation' that it also markets. You get into a C-type, but you put a D-type on. The whole impression, whether sitting in or driving, is of a car tailored to you. Do I agree with *Road & Track* that it is not a dual-purpose car? Actually, I do not!

There may be virtually no space for the shopping, But it's the perfect, and maybe only, excuse to go shopping more often! **End**

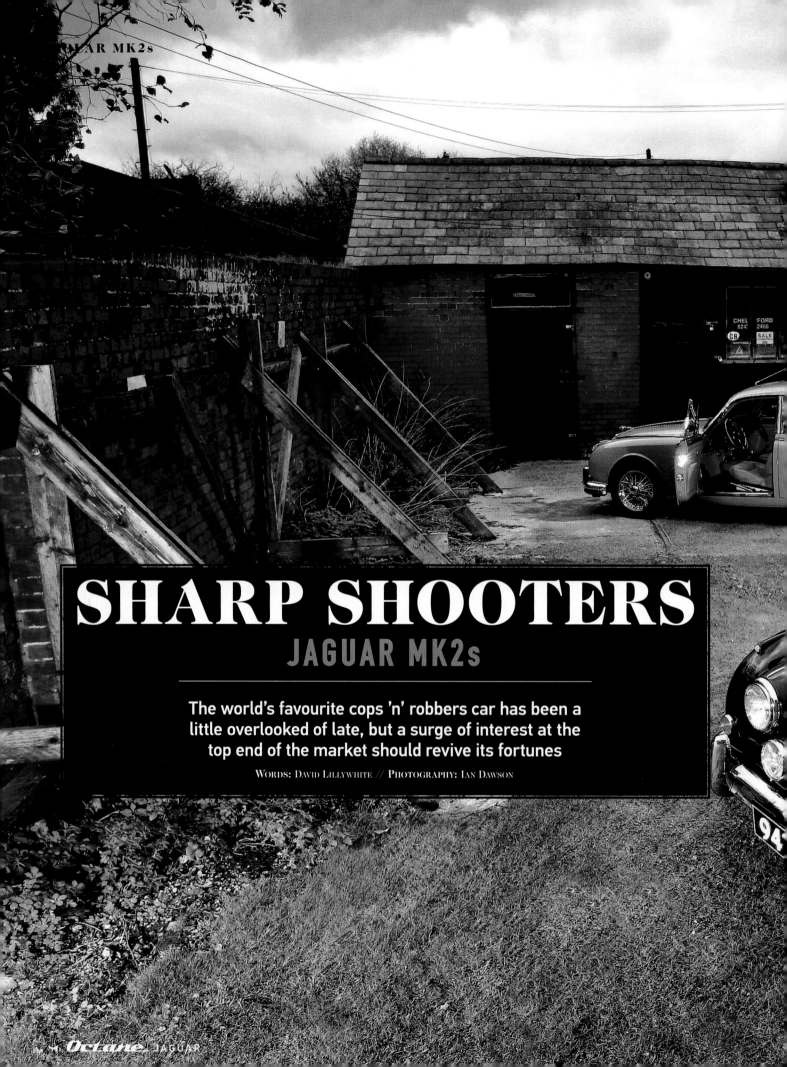

SHARP SHOOTERS

JAGUAR MK2s

The world's favourite cops 'n' robbers car has been a
little overlooked of late, but a surge of interest at the
top end of the market should revive its fortunes

WORDS: DAVID LILLYWHITE // PHOTOGRAPHY: IAN DAWSON

WE'RE BOMBING DOWN the bypass, tail squatting under the acceleration, speedo touching 100mph, XK engine growling, Moss gearbox whining, wipers just about sweeping away the drizzle. The rough, tough warehouses of industrial north-east London and Essex are behind us as we escape into the relative safety of the countryside.

Are we on a job, police on our tail? Or are we in fact wildcard undercover members of the Flying Squad, chasing down the bad guys?

Err, no; we're just a bunch of perfectly respectable middle-class 40-somethings who, ten minutes into a Mk2 drive, are already feeling the need to do the 'ton', arrive sideways outside a grimy lock-up, leave the engine running outside the local Barclays… You know the drill.

Ridiculous. But that's what Mk2s do to you.

There's been an air of menace about the Mk2 ever since it was launched back in October 1959. And it has somehow managed to hold onto that image right through its shabby time in banger territory during the 1970s, its gradual revival as a classic of ever-rising value through the 1980s, its steady days of the 1990s as a stalwart of the classic scene – and then its curious stagnation in recent years, left behind by the E-type and other classics.

Even now you'll find apparently sound Mk2s for sale for five or six thousand, and boy are they looking tempting. But most will be big trouble, and the smart money is on the very best cars, which are starting to attract a stronger following again. Yes, over the past couple of years the Mk2 has begun to make a comeback, and its slightly dumpy predecessor, the Mk1, and its less classy successor, the 240/340, are being dragged up with it.

Why? Think Michael Caine in *Get Carter*, Richard E Grant and Paul McGann in *Withnail and I*, assorted villains in *The Sweeney* (just don't mention *Inspector Morse*…). Think Goodwood: not just the Grant Williams/Derek Bell Mk1 slithering around the circuit to a standing ovation from the Revival crowd, but also the ever-growing desire for appropriate transport to the event itself, for which a Mk2 is absolutely perfect.

And think practicality, too – a perk of the increasing quantity and quality of spares and modification parts available, and the transformations so beautifully engineered by specialists such as Vicarage, Classic Motor Cars and JD Classics. Some even use modern Jaguar V8 engines.

So, over to Carl Moss of Essex-based classic Jaguar specialist JD Classics. 'It used to be that people bought XKs in →

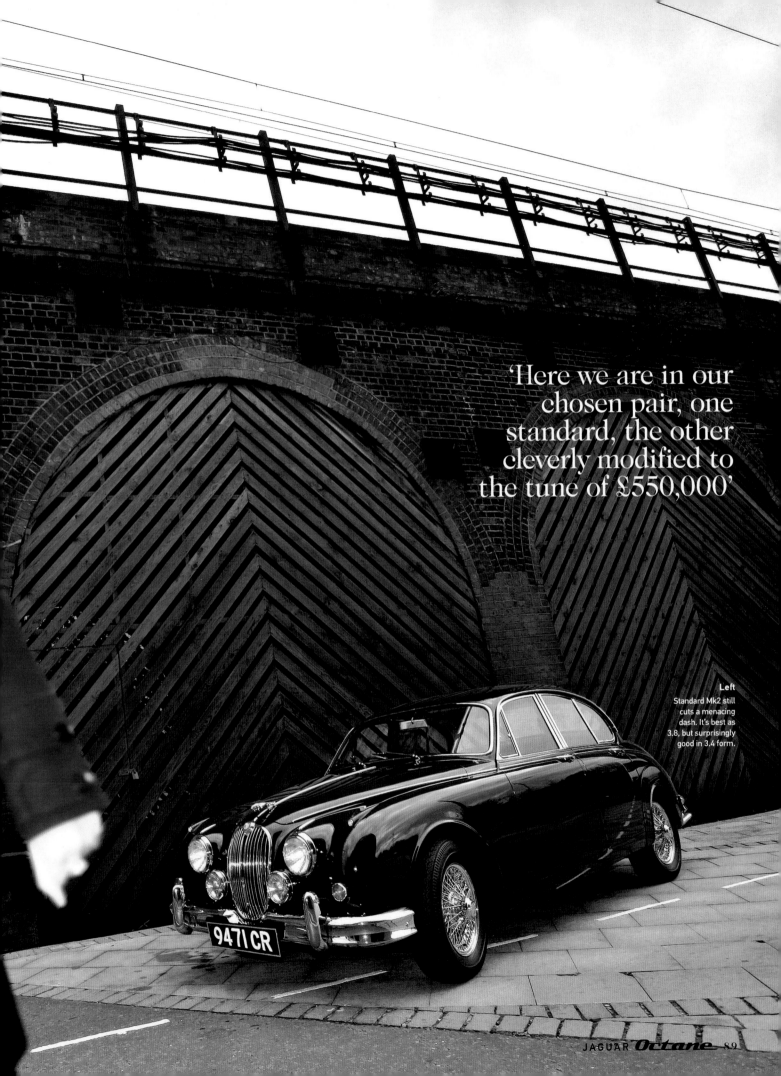

'Here we are in our chosen pair, one standard, the other cleverly modified to the tune of £550,000'

Left
Standard Mk2 still cuts a menacing dash. It's best as 3.8, but surprisingly good in 3.4 form.

9471 CR

the spring and summer, Mk2s in the autumn and winter . Not any more! We find that, at the top end, our customers have already bought an XK, liked it and found it to be reliable, and then they see their modern saloon and wonder why they're putting up with looking like everyone else and suffering terrible depreciation. So they buy the best Mk2 to use every day.'

Not surprisingly, then, there's a choice of Mk2s at JD (the place has to be seen to be believed). We could have chosen between the original red Coombs demonstrator (Mk2s modified by John Coombs, of Guildford, Surrey, are legendary), a wonderfully menacing Coombs-style black Mk2 sitting low on black wires, and a host of others, most carrying subtle upgrades.

But here we are in our chosen pair, one completely standard, the other as cleverly modified as you'll find any classic, to the tune of £550,000. Yes, that's a half a million – more on why later.

Both look fantastic in contrasting shades of Jaguar green – British Racing and Willow. The BRDC badge on the rear of the British Racing Green car looks exactly right, and I picture a race veteran hustling his much-loved machine between tracks,

crash helmet and overalls stashed neatly in the boot. He'd have no problems with the famously awkward Moss gearbox.

I, on the other hand, always suffer a few moments of struggle with standard Mk2s. The steering never fails to surprise me with its weight and low-geared imprecision, a world away from that of the E-type. And I invariably forget to take the gearchanges slowly enough – with a brief pause halfway – to avoid a crunch or, more likely, a flat refusal to shift (cars with the factory-option power steering and the new transmission fitted after September 1965 are much better).

This model, which is early and completely standard, will be no different. But sat in the wide leather seat, charmingly spindly steering wheel in hand and that lovely wooden dashboard with its Boy's Own row of switches up front, I'm feeling like I've returned to a long-lost friend. Why did I stay away so long?

Of all the Mk2s and derivatives, this is the most desirable: the 3.8 with manual overdrive gearbox that everyone hankers for. The first of the range, the Mk1, is good but not as good, with less power even in 3.4-litre form, bugger-all power as a 2.4, and

JD CLASSICS MK2 4.5

ENGINE
4460cc straight-six, DOHC, fuel injection
POWER
332bhp@6750rpm
TORQUE
330lb ft@4500rpm
TRANSMISSION
Five-speed manual, rear-wheel drive, LSD
SUSPENSION
Front: twin wishbones, coilovers, anti-roll bar.
Rear: independent, lower wishbones, coils, anti-roll bar
BRAKES
AP Racing ventilated discs all round
PERFORMANCE
Top speed 150mph
0-60mph 6.5sec

slightly suspect handling from the narrow rear track. Its smaller front and rear screens plus thick window pillars give the car a dumpy appearance compared with the Mk2, but do add period appeal.

The post-Mk2 models, the 240 and 340, deserve a better press (or, at least, the 340 does): the slender bumpers are lighter in weight and the much-criticised standard Ambla (plastic) upholstery lasts well and has usually been replaced by leather by now anyway. Again, the 2.4-litre 240 is painfully slow but the 340 is much better, with more power than a Mk2 3.4. And prices are significantly lower.

As for the Mk2s, while the 3.8 is the best option, and the 2.4 best avoided, the 3.4 is much better than it is given credit for, making up for its power and torque deficit with the smoothest engine of the bunch.

But for goodness' sake, let's get back to this lovely original BRG Mk2 and make the most of its 3.8 engine. These are quick cars, capable of 125mph and a 0-60mph time of 8.5 seconds, and it doesn't feel outclassed by moderns on the road. It feels rock solid, from the first satisfying clunk of the door through the strong, unflustered pull of the engine to the competence of the ride, despite the leaf-sprung rear axle.

It is let down by that steering, the brakes do need a shove, the gearshift does require care, but what a great car. Its pale green stablemate is in another league entirely, though, the ultimate example of the current trend towards well-engineered upgrades for Mk2s. It's built as the everyday car of Michael Gordon, founder of the American Bumble and Bumble hair salon and product empire, and it has taken around three years and £550,000 to develop.

Yes, you read that correctly – but don't let it put you off, because many of the upgrades featured are common to much more affordable Mk2s on the market. So, we'll start with the engine, a 4.2-litre XK unit from a Jaguar XJ6, bored-out to 4.5 litres and fitted with special forged pistons, a billet steel crankshaft, stage three camshafts and a gasflowed cylinder head. Crucially, it is running fuel injection – a JD Classics' conversion for XK engines – and a bespoke stainless steel exhaust, and it's cooled by an alloy radiator and electric fan.

Next up? Let's try the transmission, a modern five-speed, and again a staple JD conversion. The propshaft is carbon fibre and that leads us to the differential and consequently the rear suspension, which is no longer a live axle but a fully independent, alloy-wishboned affair, loosely based on the XK8's and now another JD Classics Mk2 conversion.

Back to the front, and the suspension is still based on the Mk2 front beam but is modified to take modern coilovers, adjustable for height and damping. The steering is assisted rack-and-pinion in place of the old steering box, once again a common (almost essential) conversion – but this one uses an electrically powered hydraulic pump that allows the amount of assistance to be adjusted from the dashboard. The brakes are gargantuan vented discs with equally massive AP Racing calipers, fed from custom-made billet alloy reservoirs. And →

'The beautiful pale green model is the ultimate example of the current trend towards well-engineered upgrades for Mk2s'

From below Standard model radiates luxury. Ultimate JD version boasts more than 330bhp, air-con, buffalo hide interior and umbrellas in A-pillars.

'It's shockingly fast, handling is massively improved, with better control over bumps, and it's wonderfully comfortable'

that's just the basics. Open the front doors and you'll find an umbrella neatly inserted into each A-post, specially made seats trimmed in a buffalo hide and resting on billet alloy plinths, sat-nav with a revolving screen (the reverse side is the original speaker grille), Becker Mexico sound system, a tyre pressure-monitoring system, radar detecting and blocking system (with sensors cleverly built into front and rear valances), parking detectors, heated screens front and rear, underdash and footwell lighting, puddle lights in the doors, a full air-con system with the controls neatly hidden, electric windows… Outside there are HID headlights, rear foglights concealed behind the reflectors, high-visibility brake lights built into the rear headrests, automatic rain-sensing wipers, unusually long louvres in the bonnet, with rain traps underneath. The list goes on. It's almost comical.

Yet the car is not tacky or inappropriate, and the way it drives is, well, sublime. With over 300bhp (and 330lb ft of torque), it's shockingly fast, the handling is hugely improved, with far better control over bumps, and it's wonderfully comfortable. I went to JD Classics expecting to find this car too over-the-top. I loved it.

But £550,000? That's mostly in development costs, yet if you own a Mk2 there are lessons to be learnt from this amazing machine. First off, thicker anti-roll bars and adjustable dampers improve the handling, four-pot brake calipers haul it up more efficiently, a decent-sized electric fan keeps it cool, and an alternator keeps it juiced. From there, rack-and-pinion power steering and a five- or six-speed box provide the finishing touches.

This is where the top end of the Mk2 market is going: owners looking for a stylish, trouble-free drive because they're not planning on getting their hands dirty. Sound machines start at £10,000 or so, but in this sector of the market there's big money being paid, to the tune of £80,000 to £180,000 for the best cars. Who'd have thought it? *End*

THANKS TO Michael Gordon and JD Classics, +44 (0)1621 879579, www.jdclassics.co.uk.

JAGUAR MK2 3.8

ENGINE 3781cc straight-six, DOHC, twin SU carburettors
POWER 220bhp@5500rpm
TORQUE 242lb ft@3000rpm
TRANSMISSION Four-speed manual with optional overdrive, or three-speed auto. Rear-wheel drive, LSD
SUSPENSION Front: twin wishbones, coils, telescopic dampers, anti-roll bar. Rear: longitudinal semi-elliptic leaf springs, live axle, radius arms, Panhard rod, telescopic dampers
BRAKES Dunlop discs all round
PERFORMANCE
Top speed 125mph
0-60mph 8.5sec

INFO

Mk1: Launched as 2.4 in 1955, with drum brakes and 112bhp. 210bhp 3.4 from '57, with drums initially, then all-round discs.

Mk2: 1959. Wider rear track, larger glass area, new interior and choice of 2.4, 3.4 or 3.8. Slightly heavier than Mk1.

240/340: 1967. With 2.4 and 3.4 engines, better cylinder heads, Ambla plastic interior (leather an option) and thinner bumpers.

Daimler 2.5 V8: 1962 version of Mk2 with excellent 2.5-litre Daimler V8, slightly different grille and revised interior.

BUYING

Rust is of course the enemy, and the complexity of Jaguar's first attempt at a unitary shell hampers restoration.

The join of sills, bulkhead and chassis members is really complex to repair. Front wings are pricey. Rear spring hanger condition is crucial.

Spares availability is generally excellent but Mk1 panels are scarce. Engines are strong yet expensive to rebuild, while transmissions, suspension and brakes are largely troublefree. Interiors cost a lot to restore.

E2A
Jaguar's lost opportunity

Jaguar's E2A was never the 'missing link' between D-type and E-type – but it was perhaps a missed opportunity. Tony Dron drives it and explains why this car could have been a Ferrari-beater at Le Mans

PHOTOGRAPHY: CHARLIE MAGEE // ARCHIVE PICTURES: LAT, JAGUAR HERITAGE, GODWIN-STUBBERT COLLECTION

PEOPLE CALL IT THE missing link between D-type and E-type, but this 50-year-old Jaguar prototype never went missing. This is the one and only E2A, a machine of huge significance. Former employee Roger Woodley and his wife Penny Griffiths saved it from routine scrapping in 1967 and, thanks to them, it was neither lost nor left to rot in some barn.

In 2008 it went for $4,957,000 at Bonhams' Quail Lodge sale, making E2A the most valuable Jaguar ever sold at auction. Its discerning owner now is Stefan Ziegler and the car is properly cared for by leading historic Jaguar expert, CKL Developments.

Back in 1960, the Jaguar public relations people worked hard to stress that E2A was not a works entry in the Le Mans 24 Hours. The marque had withdrawn officially from competition after 1956, claiming to rest on its laurels. Two days before Le Mans 1960, *The Autocar* published full details of the 'Jaguar New Competition

Car… Logical Development of D-type', including the words: 'The position is that Briggs Cunningham has persuaded Sir William Lyons to place at his disposal one of the several models on which the company has continued development during the past five years.'

That flowery, indigestible mouthful was subtly misleading. You can just hear that PR man: 'Now look, old boy, this isn't a works car, you know, and it would be frightfully helpful if you could make that clear.' Well, they all fell for it.

Far from being closed down in 1956, Jaguar's Competition Department remained secretly active, as Peter D Wilson revealed in his most readable 2008 book, *Cat Out of the Bag*. Peter joined the Competition Department in September 1961, recalling a clandestine operation which built prototypes and prepared 'competition Jaguars, all ostensibly raced by privateers, but invariably amongst them lurked works cars, attended by works mechanics…'

E2A was indeed a works racing car, a one-off competition prototype version of the new E-type, which was to stun the world in 1961. E2A's monocoque central section, extended to the rear, was of aluminium instead of steel. Following the trend in international sports car racing towards a 3-litre engine limit, E2A had an exquisitely built, fuel-injected, all-aluminium, DOHC straight-six of 2997cc. With a rev limit of 7000rpm, it produced 295bhp at 6800rpm.

When Briggs Cunningham, famous American sportsman, visited Jaguar before Christmas 1959, the mocked-up E2A was in Department 21, the innocuous name assigned to the Competition Department. Was it hurriedly prepared after Mr Cunningham's approach to Sir William regarding Le Mans 1960? It would, of course, be rude to imagine a carefully stage-managed set-up for anything so vulgar and un-English as a sale. Nevertheless, Mr Cunningham bought it. Well, he bought the project and agreed to fund its entry at Le Mans. He was not permitted to buy the car itself, which naturally remained the property of Jaguar, being a works prototype. Oops. With the deal →

sealed, E2A was built properly through January and February 1960, then tested extensively by Norman Dewis at MIRA. A condition of its use was that the legendary factory driver should oversee the car at all times. Some senior Jaguar people probably wanted Norman to drive in the 24 Hours itself. Quick and reliable, he was well up to that, but it was never on: Cunningham, understandably demanding an all-American driver line-up, had hired the famous veteran Walt Hansgen and Ed Crawford, a winner of minor US events.

At the Le Mans test weekend, E2A was fast, with talk of 190mph. At full revs the nominal top speed would have been about 179mph, but with the 'tyre growth' in those days a considerable increase in actual speed occurred. The tailfin, higher than a D-type's because of the windscreen demanded at Le Mans in 1960, was fitted between the test weekend and the race. Jaguar claimed it reduced turbulence, adding nearly 8mph to top speed.

E2A wasn't the quickest car at Le Mans, but it was probably fastest on the straight. The unfortunate Ed then destroyed the engine, probably by missing a gear. The Jaguar people pulled long faces, Cunningham dropped Crawford and, probably through Jaguar's Lofty England, approached Dan Gurney, a rising young American GP star. The softly spoken Californian F1 driver was, unexpectedly, available to drive at Le Mans.

Despite E2A's well-documented history, some corrections would not go amiss. I've also found the odd new anecdote. In the pits during the early part of Le Mans qualifying, Norman Dewis noticed that Dan Gurney looked pretty groggy. After what he had been through in the previous month, that's hardly surprising. On 22 May, Dan had won the Nürburgring 1000km, sharing a Camoradi-entered Maserati Birdcage with Stirling Moss. On 6 June he drove a privately entered BRM in the Dutch GP at Zandvoort, suffering total brake failure at 130mph and a spectacular accident at the Tarzan hairpin. Flying over the bank, the BRM demolished a barbed-wire fence and unfortunately killed a young spectator who was in a prohibited area.

Incredibly, Gurney emerged with only cuts, bruises and a supposedly sprained wrist, but there was a minor fracture. Nevertheless, Dan drove in the Belgian GP at the old Spa on 19 June, where his BRM's engine failed. That was the notorious meeting with four separate accidents in which Stirling Moss broke his back, Mike Taylor's racing career was ended, and Alan Stacey and Chris Bristow were killed.

A true professional, Gurney was at Le Mans for scrutineering two days after Spa. When I spoke with him recently, Dan preferred to discuss E2A: 'It seemed an excellent new car, breaking new ground on the aero side and in aesthetics, and I had the greatest regard for Jaguar's outstanding record of victories at Le Mans. I felt very positive about the whole deal, and was deadly serious, wanting to do a good job for a company that

I really respected.' Dan was impressed by the technical support that Jaguar put into that 1960 race. When I suggested that it was a works entry in all but name, but paid for with Briggs Cunningham's money, he agreed. Dan also got on well with Cunningham's technical man, Alfred Momo, and he very much appreciated sharing a car with the veteran American hero Walt Hansgen. Then 40, Hansgen was old-school, the strong, silent type who let his driving do the talking.

Norman's notes suggest that Walt was happy with E2A, but more recent statements by Dan reveal that, while Hansgen kept predictably quiet, Gurney complained of straight-line instability. The Jaguar people probably didn't enjoy Dan's criticism. It made him thoroughly unpopular, but he was right.

Bonhams' Quail Lodge auction catalogue included this quote from Dan: 'Through my constant questioning we finally found that they'd set up the car at the MIRA testing ground with a fair amount of toe-out on the rear wheels. If E2A leaned just a little, one way or the other, it was leaning on a wheel, which would direct the tail in a different direction. We got them to change it, and it became a normal, good-handling car.'

Dan cannot remember to whom his 'constant questioning' was directed, but his story rings true: it seems the rear suspension was dismantled shortly before the event for measurements to be taken. On reassembly, the geometry wasn't checked. The rear toe-out was indeed found and →

Below
Bonnet bulge was added to fit over 3.8-litre engine that was installed in July 1960, after Le Mans.

'At the Le Mans test weekend, E2A was fast, with talk of 190mph. Jaguar claimed the tailfin added nearly 8mph to top speed'

corrected at Le Mans during qualifying. With that done Dan set about serious qualifying, but he was hampered by rain.

He told me: 'I was trying really hard and, gritting my teeth, I'd managed to keep my foot flat down from Arnage to the old White House Corner. Next time round, coming up to White House, I ran into one of those curtains of rain you get at Le Mans. I was going really fast and could just see two balls of spray ahead, indicating two cars. They were going much slower than I was and, had they been in the way, I could not possibly have missed them. I shot past them, struggling on lock to lock, and made it through the corner okay. That got my attention, for sure.'

Maintaining a calm sense of control through such moments is the mark of the hardened ace. Had E2A proved reliable, Gurney and Hansgen could have won that Le Mans 24 Hours. Checking the results carefully, I found the little-known fact that Dan set the equal fastest race lap, matching early leader Masten Gregory's 4min 4.0sec in a Birdcage Maserati, which retired. As for E2A, a hairline crack in a high-pressure injection line led to lean running and engine failure. According to Norman's notes, E2A ran for just seven hours and six minutes.

How did Dan rate E2A against the Maserati he'd driven just before? 'It felt completely different, but Le Mans and the Nürburgring

Above
Scenes from E2A's abortive run in the 1960 Le Mans 24 Hours: it retired with engine failure.

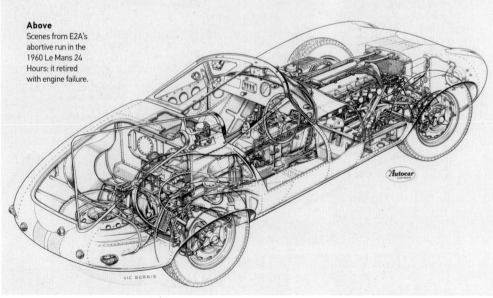

Above and left
E2A as it is today makes an interesting comparison with Vic Berris's cutaway for *The Autocar*, left.

Right
Just a few of the
fascinating detail
pictures taken by
CKL Developments
while fettling E2A.

are so different as circuits that I'd be guessing. Still, the Jaguar certainly had more top speed and it was much more comfortable. It felt more refined, more like a passenger car.'

Six years later, in 1966, brave Walt was fatally injured at Le Mans, qualifying a 7-litre Ford MkII and going all-out with slick tyres on a damp road. In 1967, of course, Dan Gurney and AJ Foyt won at Le Mans in a Ford MkIV.

In 1960, Briggs Cunningham made arrangements with Jaguar to extend the loan of E2A. Back in the factory, a 3.8-litre iron-block racing engine was fitted in place of the aluminium 3-litre. To accommodate the bulkier 3.8 a new bulge, in the now familiar E-type style, was pop-riveted to the original bonnet. As Norman recalls, the factory wanted to supply a fuel-injected 3.8 but Alfred Momo insisted on carburettors. With three twin-choke Webers, Peter D Wilson says this engine gave 294bhp at 5500rpm. After the bad experience in France, perhaps Momo didn't trust the new-fangled injection. The ugly big screen, meeting Le Mans rules, was replaced by a wrap-around Perspex job. E2A, still with its tailfin, was dispatched to the USA in July 1960.

Running on 15in wheels, in place of the 16in rims used at Le Mans, Hansgen put in some great drives, including one outright victory at a relatively minor Bridgehampton meeting at the end of August. On normal road-racing circuits, unlike Le Mans, E2A was no match for the much lighter, purpose-built sports-racing cars of →

the day. Bruce McLaren and Jack Brabham both raced it without success, and it was returned to Jaguar after the 1960 season.

The redundant E2A was left gathering dust until sometime in the summer of 1961, when instructions came down for it to be taken to Silverstone. David Hobbs, son of the Hobbs Mecha-matic gearbox inventor, was to test it on the Grand Prix circuit. Then 21, David had been an apprentice at Daimler when Jaguar took that company over. He had thus become a Jaguar apprentice, but in 1960 he had also started racing an XK140 with Hobbs transmission.

Driving to work, he frequently raced another Jag from Leamington Spa to Browns Lane. His rival, he discovered, was Lofty England, Jaguar's former racing manager but by then director of the Service Department. I tracked David down in his Milwaukee base: 'The only slight fly in the ointment,' he told me, 'was that I was supposed to be there an hour before Lofty, but I digress. He seemed to think I was quite good.'

Through 1961, his final year as a Jaguar student apprentice, David raced an Elite, winning 14 of his 18 races. Lofty was probably curious to know how young Hobbs would cope with E2A. The excuse for testing was a comparison between that machine and a standard production car, but it was surely the driver rather than the cars being tested at Silverstone on that occasion.

'I was not a good apprentice, spending all my time preparing (a loose term in my case) and racing cars,' admits David. 'I passed no exams at all and missed quite a few days of work, though I was blessed by the fact that Lofty was a fan. However, apprentice supervisor Mr Barker was not, and the day I left, in December just before my wedding, still sticks in my mind. He had me in his office, telling me that I was the worst apprentice he had ever had under his care and that if I never set

Above and right
Superbly patinated cockpit full of history – note 'Shot Firing' label from Maxaret brake testing days.

foot in the doorway at Jaguar ever again it would most certainly please him immensely.

'It was particularly pleasing when Lofty asked me to test E2A. I didn't know anything about it really, just that it was a sort of cross between a D- and an E-type. Imagine my pleasure as, dressed in my apprentice's brown overalls, I walked through the workshop and past Mr Barker's office, accompanied by Lofty himself, chief engineer Bill Heynes, Wally Hassan the engine man, and Mike MacDowel, who was responsible for all competition cars. Very satisfying!

'Anyway, they did send me to Silverstone, and in those days testing was done from the trackside at Abbey. Well, this was the quickest car I had driven to that point, and it felt a bit nervous. To cut a long story short I had an enormous long slide, half-spinning at Abbey, right in front of everyone, with the brakes hard on. I'm sure Mike Parkes, who could be a bit pompous, had also turned up. I have a memory of him saying "Silly boy" or something along those lines, and then we all went home. I had flat-spotted all four tyres and they hadn't brought any spares. I might have done about ten laps but it was worth it, just to see Barker's face.'

Next I rang Mike MacDowel, who told me: 'I warmed the car up first and it felt decidedly loose at the back. Hobbs went quicker and quicker until his huge spin, which ended literally at Lofty's feet!' Mike added that the car still had the tailfin and was still in Cunningham's colours.

David was criticised at the time for braking during his spin, wrecking the tyres, but locking up the wheels at the proper moment was correct to prevent an accident. Shortly afterwards, Stirling Moss himself defended David to the Jaguar hierarchy on that point.

In *Cat Out of the Bag* Peter D Wilson mentions this test, saying that David put up respectable times before his spin. But he goes on to relate that on the way back from Silverstone to Browns Lane, with Bob Penney driving, a rear hub broke and the wheel came away. Mike MacDowel had mentioned to me that Jaguar competition cars were always driven →

1960 JAGUAR E2A
(July 1960, 3.8 alterations in brackets)
ENGINE 2997cc straight-six, DOHC, triple Weber carburettors (3781cc) **POWER** 295bhp @ 6800rpm (294bhp @ 5500rpm)
TORQUE 236lb ft @ 6500rpm (n/a) **TRANSMISSION** Four-speed manual (from D-type), rear-wheel drive
SUSPENSION Front: independent by wishbones and torsion bars. Rear: independent by wishbones with two coil-over-dampers per side **BRAKES** Dunlop discs all round, no servo assistance **WEIGHT** 872kg (as weighed by CKL today: 919kg)
PERFORMANCE Claimed top speed at Le Mans c190mph

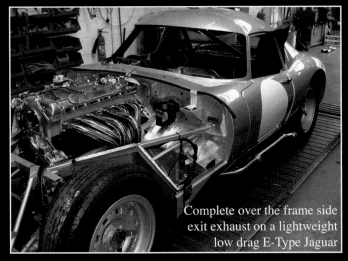

Below and right
Fast and light,
E2A handles well,
says Dron; engine
sports triple twin-
choke Webers.

'E2A was an advanced car which could have won at Le Mans, had it been thoroughly sorted and reliable'

on the road in those days. Maybe the hub was already failing when David was driving, causing that spooky feeling. As the innovative rear end used the driveshaft as a suspension arm, he was lucky it didn't let go at Silverstone. The point of this little story, as Peter says, is that racing improves the breed. Back in the chassis design office, where Peter was working at the time, Ray Kenney redesigned the hub to be stronger and simpler to service. The modification, which proved trouble-free, went into all subsequent Jaguar production independent rear suspension applications.

This failure was carefully hushed up and, even 26 years later, Andrew Whyte was told that E2A suffered a mere puncture with Bob Penney at the wheel. Whyte faithfully reported that yarn in his famous book on Jaguar competition cars.

In the second half of 1961, E2A was prepared as a test vehicle for the Dunlop Maxaret 'wheel slide protector' system, an early anti-lock device that was applied to the rear brakes only of E2A. For this, the Cunningham livery and the tailfin were removed and, when Peter D Wilson joined in September, E2A had a normal bootlid and had received a 'rather rough' respray in British Racing Green. The Maxaret tests in early 1962 proved inconclusive and the world had to wait for modern software before a genuinely practical ABS system could be devised.

E2A today still has a hole in its dash beside the words: SHOT FIRING 'PULL'. On this incredibly original car, that was for the chalk-firing gun that left measuring marks on the road during the Maxaret tests. The body was repainted in Cunningham colours many years ago and, probably, the long-lost tailfin should be recreated now. Roger Woodley and Penny Griffiths even saved the buck on which the original fin was made, so it wouldn't be hard to reproduce.

At Goodwood, one sunny spring day, I did some quick laps in E2A. It had been checked and serviced with meticulous care by Chris Keith-Lucas and Barry Burgess at CKL. Nothing was modified but this was no ordinary service – they checked the lot, right down to the rivets in the monocoque, which proved, surprisingly, to be perfect.

With close to 300bhp in an aluminium chassis, E2A felt predictably quicker and more responsive than a standard early E-type road car, which weighed about 300kg more. The old dampers were perhaps slightly worn in the middle of their travel, making it feel briefly vague when turning into the faster corners – perhaps CKL would have to change them. Once the car had been settled into a corner,

however, it felt superbly controllable and confidence-inspiring. Through Goodwood's tricky, top-gear Fordwater bend, a fast car like E2A was unlikely ever to be absolutely flat-out but, given a carefully chosen line, I was surprised at how fast it could go through there.

There was plainly nothing wrong with the geometry now and, although the grip on its old-fashioned tyres was relatively modest, the handling was excellent. You could encourage a little understeer or choose to hang the tail out at will if necessary. The 'quick change' D-type brakes worked well, too. The future for this gem from the Brit manufacturer's past was clearly one of preservation, but I thought it would be very tempting to race it in the Le Mans Classic, just for old times' sake.

Jaguar held all the aces in 1960, including a world-class ability in engineering and design to go with its glittering reputation on road and track. Despite that, and the new affluent society, by 1966 the firm was being swallowed up in mergers leading to the British Leyland nightmare. Was the marque too cautious, 'resting on its laurels' and pinching pennies when it should have been forging ahead? I think so. The factory fire of 1957 was a setback, but Jaguar should have recovered from that more quickly. In E2A, its engineers created a potential world-beater, and the company wasted it.

Later in the 1960s, it was the same story with the XJ13: the engineers produced a possible winner, the management dithered and the moment was gone. It's said that E2A's last official factory task was to distract attention while XJ13 was being tested at MIRA in 1967. Then Roger Woodley and his wife stepped in to rescue it.

E2A was an advanced car which could have won at Le Mans five decades ago, had it been thoroughly sorted and reliable, but it was all alone and crippled by a half-hearted company attitude. There should have been a proper works Jaguar team with half-a-dozen E2As, ready to face the hordes of Ferraris.

The once-charismatic Sir William Lyons, then nearly 60, had formed the view that Le Mans was the only worthwhile race, and he was reluctant to enter it unless Jaguar was guaranteed to win. Obviously, no such guarantee is possible. The spark had gone, but Sir William remained as MD until 1967. In 1960, with conditions perfect for confident investment, Jaguar behaved as if it could not afford to go racing. The reality was that Jaguar couldn't afford not to go racing. It could have been so different. **End**

THANKS TO Barry Burgess, Norman Dewis, Dan Gurney, David Hobbs, Peter Jones, Mike MacDowel, Peter D Wilson, Stefan Ziegler, and Chris Keith-Lucas of CKL Developments, www.ckldevelopments.co.uk.

50 YEARS YOUNG

In 1961, the very first E-type raced against time to reach the press launch in Geneva. Fifty years later, Peter Tomalin relived that epic 700-mile dash to find out if the iconic Jaguar could still deliver serious thrills

PHOTOGRAPHY: GUS GREGORY

Above and right
E-type settles to an easy
cruise on the autoroute,
shadowing the journey
taken in 1961 by Jaguar works
driver and PR man Bob Berry.

IR WILLIAM LYONS glanced at his watch again. Where the hell was Berry? It was the morning before the opening of the 1961 Geneva Motor Show, and the Jaguar boss had invited the cream of the world's motoring press to the Parc des Eaux Vives for an exclusive preview of the brand new Jag sports car.

Around 150 of them were now gathered in the park's famous restaurant, anticipation building deliciously as the clock ticked towards midday. The only thing missing was the car they'd all come to see. With just minutes to go before the appointed hour, Sir William was growing visibly agitated. Where the *hell* was Berry?

Bob Berry, sometime works driver and full-time member of the Jaguar PR team, had set out from Coventry the night before in the very first road-registered E-type, a gunmetal-grey coupé, 9600 HP. His mission: to deliver the car to Geneva some 700 miles away by 11am the following morning. He would have to drive solo, right through the night. And no autoroutes in those days, either. Plenty of fog, though, and snow in the mountains. It was, with hindsight, almost recklessly optimistic. 'I simply drove as if it was a

race,' he later admitted, 'going as fast as I dared – torn between being late and shunting the car. In retrospect I suppose 'foolhardy' is the best description of it. Youth often makes you do things you wouldn't normally have done…'

Fifty years later, photographer Gus Gregory and I are hammering towards Geneva in an E-type of our own, retracing Berry's epic drive – although we do at least have the option of using the motorways. We want to find out if this iconic Jaguar can still cut it as a driver's car in 2011. We also want to pay a small tribute to Bob – and to his test driver colleague Norman Dewis, who in a similar feat of speed and endurance piloted a second E-type out to Geneva two days later to satisfy the demand for demonstration drives.

We have given ourselves the best part of a day to get there, and while there's no irascible Sir William waiting to tear us off a strip if we're late, we're making good progress, travelling at very E-type speeds. I'd like to think it's what Bob and Norman would want. More than that, it just feels so good. Back in 1961, the E-type was simply the fastest thing on the road. Right now, on this French autoroute, as it eats up the miles at an indicated 95-100mph, straight-six blaring, the

years are just falling away.

We go back a long way, the E-type and me. Right to the very beginning, in fact. The model made its famous debut on Wednesday 15 March, 1961. Five days earlier, just after midday on Friday 10 March, at a maternity hospital not ten miles from Jaguar's Browns Lane factory, your humble correspondent made his own slightly less auspicious entry into the world. Yep, like the E-type, I'm celebrating my half-century. I know, and I don't look a day over 48…

All through my childhood the E-type was always there – in the Ladybird car books I'd pore over for hours on end; in dad's copies of *Motor Sport* when Denis Jenkinson drove across Europe in various (presumably loaned) E-types; in the shape of Dinky and Matchbox toys; in *The Italian Job*; and in rare sightings of actual E-types on the roads of rural Northamptonshire where I grew up. A mate of dad's, an engineer called Pete Slater,

'As it eats up the miles at an indicated 95-100mph, the years are just falling away'

who, incidentally, went to Korea in the early 1970s to help develop the first Hyundais, actually had a V12 E-type. This naturally conferred instant hero status in the eyes of Peter Tomalin, aged 13 and three-quarters.

I loved Aston Martins too – I coveted my cousin Simon's Corgi James Bond DB5 even after the baddy was ejected from the passenger seat and never found again – and Ferraris and Iso Grifos. But there was something about the E-type. Maybe it was the proximity to Browns Lane – dad worked there for a while, so Jaguar always felt like 'our team'. Maybe it was the legend of the first 150mph production car, maybe the Le Mans connections to the D-type. I think most of all, though, it was the shape.

Enzo Ferrari famously called it the most beautiful car in the world. The long, louvred

bonnet, the wire wheels with their eared spinners tucked up inside torpedo-shaped wings, that exquisite, tapering tail with its perfectly flush-fitting hatch… As a child it stirred up a strange, fluttery, yearning feeling in my stomach.

All these years later, I get that feeling again when Gus and I arrive at Eagle E-types in East Sussex and boss Henry Pearman leads us to the gorgeous silver-blue Series 1 coupé that he's generously agreed to lend us for this feature. It's a 1968 4.2-litre – not as 'pure' as the early 3.8s but generally considered the better car. It has the later, open headlights – the 3.8's faired-in lamps looked pretty but they were pretty hopeless – and the all-syncro four-speed gearbox in place of the ponderous Moss trans. This particular car also benefits from a few carefully chosen Eagle upgrades – electronic ignition, bigger, ventilated →

disc brakes, electric cooling fans, a modern alternator, and a longer fourth gear for those French autoroutes… In short, it retains the classic look and feel of an early E-type but combines them with a few sensible mods to help it cope with the 21st century (where do I sign up?). For the purposes of our trip, it's just perfect.

Gus and I load our bags into the surprisingly commodious luggage bay and drop into the cosy (but not too cosy) cockpit. Slide out the choke, twist the key in the centre of the dash, thumb the tiny Bakelite starter button and the big straight-six rumbles into life, responding to blips of throttle with a loud sniff from its three SU carburettors and a bark that resonates through twin big-bore stainless steel exhausts.

We ease out onto the damp Sussex lanes, gingerly at first, only too conscious of that long, vulnerable snout. The clutch is meaty but with a soft biting point, the gearshift slightly stiff yet positive, and the unassisted steering plain heavy at manoeuvring speeds – it lightens a little above jogging pace, but roundabouts and the like require inputs from the shoulders and a firm grip on the wood-rimmed wheel. The payoff is that at speed it is beautifully direct and perfectly weighted. The brake pedal has a nice, firm, high biting point, and you can swivel on the ball of your foot to blip the throttle on downchanges.

It's an hour and a half's drive from Eagle HQ to the Tunnel terminal in Folkestone, and we've slightly less than an hour and a half to get there for our 1.20pm crossing. And then we hit traffic. Buggeration! Eventually it ebbs away, and the final 25-mile stretch of M20 allows us to reel back lost minutes. What's immediately clear is that the E-type will have no trouble running with modern traffic. Peak power is an unimposing 265bhp, but the 4.2 is big on torque and the E weighs a modest (by modern standards) 1315kg.

Open the throttle at 70mph and the Jaguar surges forward with real urgency, exhaust pipes hollering. The brakes are strong, the ride excellent – fully independent suspension put the E-type years ahead of its early-'60s rivals, and this one's been fitted with modern Koni dampers, so it feels supple but nicely tied down. We arrive with only ten minutes to spare before loading. Just time for a cup of tea and a bacon roll.

A bag of apples and two pints of milk, snatched at a petrol station, was all Bob Berry had to sustain him. He left Coventry at 7pm on Tuesday 14 March to catch the midnight ferry from Dover – the last of the day. No M25 then, of course, and the North Circular was a nightmare, a series of bottlenecks. Incredibly, the fastest way was right through the centre of London, crawling out along the Old Kent Road. Thankfully the A20 to Dover was quieter. He made it to the ferry with 30 minutes to spare. Two hours later he gunned the E-type out of Calais – and straight into thick fog.

'It was very foggy as far as Reims,' he recalled. 'I →

'It responds with a loud sniff from its SU carbs and a bark through its big-bore stainless steel exhausts'

Above and left
4.2-litre version of the classic XK engine is big on torque (and sound effects); still cutting a dash in Geneva.

Right
Cockpit is cosy but perfectly habitable for long journeys. Toggle switches look dated yet add to car's character.

'Tunnels are a chance
to flatten the throttle,
exhaust note hardening
to a beautiful, savage snarl'

remember arriving in the centre of town in that huge square and really not being very certain where the hell I was. It was as bad as that. I wrong-slotted on two or three occasions, simply not being able to pick up the route in the fog.

'Just south of Reims the sun started to come up… the fog lifted quite rapidly and, not to put too fine a point on it, I just drove the car flat-out. I was so far behind schedule as not to be possible. On the long, straight roads it was running in the 120s, 130s, 140s – whatever speed I could get between the corners…'

No fog today, just chill, overcast skies, and our 4.2 settles to an easy 90mph lope at just under 3500rpm with the occasional foray into three figures. The days of 120mph-plus blasts across France are sadly long gone, even for E-types. At speed the loudest sound, above the hum of the engine and thrum of the tyres, is the rustling of the wind around the door-frames. It's one of the few things that betray the Jag's age.

Another shortcoming emerges as we approach Reims and drizzle begins to fall on the E-type's shallow windscreen – two out of the three wipers are barely on nodding terms with the glass. Fortunately the one directly in front of me is making a decent fist of things. I wriggle down a

little further into the plumply cushioned seat to get a better view out. Beads of rain form on the long bonnet, rolling back and flicking up off the rows of louvres. Just a few hundred more miles to go…

We find we can run for around 250 miles before refuelling, which works out at around 21mpg. Not bad for an old 'un. Away from each service station and péage booth, I pin the throttle through the gears; 0-60mph in about 7sec doesn't sound that quick today, but it's plenty quick enough to surprise other traffic. I half wish I was at the roadside, watching this impossibly pretty car howling off into the distance, tail squatting, wire wheels glinting…

It's late afternoon as we pick up the A26 towards Lyon. As darkness falls, the headlights cast generous pools of light on the tarmac, silhouetting the view over the bonnet, the priapic central bulge flanked by the rounded tops of the wings. Inside, the instruments glow, the heater pumps out warm air and we are snug as two bugs. Dijon next…

Bob Berry thought about approaching Geneva from the north, via Champagnole and the Col de la Faucille. It was a route he knew well but, figuring it might be closed by snow, he took the

safer but longer option, heading further south before turning east via Chalon-sur-Saone and Bellegarde. This was the main route into Switzerland – still a single-carriageway – and it was virtually nose-to-tail trucks all the way. It was also, he recalls, very steep and twisty, which made overtaking a nerve-shredding business. 'It was pretty tense stuff because time was really running out and it really looked impossible. I just kept forcing on and forcing on…'

Shadowing Berry's route, we've got it easy. Apart from the occasional shimmy as we pass through the bow-wave of the bigger trucks, the E-type tracks reassuringly straight and true. The rain's stopped now, and through the gloom we're aware of the outline of the approaching mountains as they begin to loom above us. Then comes the first tunnel and a chance to drop to 60mph, flatten the throttle and savour the exhaust note hardening and swelling to a beautiful, savage snarl. Towards Nantua, the road becomes truly epic, rising above the valley floor on giant stilts before plunging into the next tunnel. What a journey; what a car.

It's just after 10pm when we arrive at our modern chain-hotel on the outskirts of Geneva, still feeling remarkably chipper. After we have retrieved our bags from the luggage bay and

Above and below
Fifty years old and still fab (pity about Tomalin!); Sir William Lyons with his brilliant new sports car at the E-type's very first photo-call in March 1961.

locked the doors, it's simply impossible to resist a glance back – just as every E-type driver has always done. It looks tiny, delicate even, parked among the Renaults and Audis, but it's been simply magnificent today.

Berry, of course, charged on into the centre of Geneva. It was late morning by now and his first stop was the local Jaguar dealership, where the staff were waiting for him, ready to wash away more than 12 hours of accumulated road grime and give 9600 HP a quick polish ready for its appointment with the press. There was now just 20 minutes to go, but Bob knew that the Parc des Eaux Vives was only a short drive away. He could heave a relieved sigh. He'd done it.

'Good God, Berry, I thought you weren't going to get here.' Sir William was furious. But his anger soon melted away. The press reaction to Jaguar's new sports car was instant and unequivocal. They loved it, even more so when he told them the price – £2097 for the roadster, £2196 for the coupé, roughly half the cost of the Astons and Ferraris which were the only things that could catch it. In the photographs Lyons looks pleased as Punch, standing next to 9600 HP like the world's proudest father, and who could blame him?

The restaurant where the press assembled is →

'The E-type was created not by German engineers or Italian coachbuilders, but by stout English chaps with pipes and slide-rules'

E-TYPE JAGUAR 4.2

ENGINE
In-line six-cylinder, 4235cc
Max power 265bhp @ 5400rpm
Max torque 284lb ft @ 4000rpm
TRANSMISSION
Four-speed manual gearbox,
rear-wheel drive
KERBWEIGHT
1315kg
POWER TO WEIGHT
205bhp/ton
PERFORMANCE
Top speed 150mph
0-60mph 7.0sec

still there today. Next morning we mooch around the grounds, trying to work out where the car was parked – and then, in one of those moments that gives you goosebumps, we scan the tree-line, which suddenly looks very familiar. The trees have grown a bit, but there's no mistaking it from the old photos we've brought with us. We're standing on the very spot where Bob Berry roared to a halt 50 years ago.

Afterwards we search in vain for the local hillclimb where the car was demo'd, but that's fine because Gus has a better idea. To the north is Gex and the start of the run to the Col de la Faucille. This was Berry's favoured route, and indeed the one Norman Dewis took in the second E-type two days later, and it's not hard to see why. The road climbs and climbs through second-gear hairpins and third-gear ess-bends – the sort of road you dream of driving when you've got an E-type at your disposal.

The Eagle-fettled E is running on slightly wider rubber than the original, and it hangs on gamely, but the higher we climb and the more slippery the surface becomes, the more you can feel the initial understeer and the odd wiggle of the hips coming out of the hairpins. The steering is a touch too heavy and low-geared to make the Jag feel truly agile in the tighter turns, but when we hit the snow at the top of the Col it's impossible to resist giving it a bootful and riding out a little slide. This car just gets better and better. Yesterday it was a mile-eating GT. Today I'm throwing it around like

a sports car. From the top of the Col, we take the D991 down to Bellegarde, the tarmac flowing along the valley floor. It's the perfect E-type road, fast and sinuous, the sweeping corners requiring the gentlest rock of the shoulders before you pour out some of that ample torque, the chassis displaying its sublime poise. The perfect road to finish the perfect day.

But it's not quite the end of this story. There's the small matter of some 700 miles back to Blighty the following day – with a quick detour to take in the old road circuit at Reims – but once again the E-type just devours them.

Our journey finishes back in the Sussex lanes, just as dusk is falling. It's a very English scene – we even pass a village green with a Red Lion pub – and it's somehow fitting to end here. In 1961 the world's fastest and, many would say, most beautiful production car had been created not by German engineers or Italian coachbuilders, but by stout English chaps with pipes and slide-rules. The E-type was a world-beater, made in Coventry. That it can still be this great today – a consummate GT and a sports car, all rolled into one – is testament to their skill and artistry. And I'm not embarrassed to say it makes this particular Englishman very proud. Happy birthday indeed. *End*

THANKS TO Henry Pearman at Eagle E-types for the loan of the car, www.eaglegb.com. Thanks also to Philip Porter, current owner of 9600 HP, for allowing us to quote from his book *The Most Famous Car in the World*.

Above and left
Climbing the Col de la Faucille, just to the north of Geneva; pausing for breath at the summit; detour to Reims on the homeward journey.

THE TEN MOST IMPORTANT E-TYPES

Jaguar built more than 70,000 E-types during the car's 24-year career. Some are more special than others. These are the ones that really stand out

WORDS: PHILIP PORTER

THE LINDNER LOW DRAG LIGHTWEIGHT, 4868 WK

THIS CAR STARTED LIFE as a 'standard' Lightweight E-type, supplied to Jaguar's dynamic German importer and successful Mk2 racer Peter Lindner. He retained Peter Nöcker to drive the car, and they shared it for long-distance events. At the 1963 Nürburgring 1000km, Lindner famously led the field, including the works Ferraris of Scarfiotti and Surtees, for the first lap of the old 14-mile Nordschleife.

In 1964 the car's bodywork was modified: it became the only factory Low Drag Lightweight. In this guise it ran at the 'Ring, then Le Mans, for which it was fitted with the most powerful XK engine – 344bhp – that the factory produced. Lindner was tragically killed a few weeks later when the car rolled at Montlhéry.

Now, nearly five decades on, it's finally back on the road following a mammoth 7000-hour restoration by UK-based specialist Classic Motor Cars.

THE OPEN-TOP PRESS CAR, 77 RW

THE THIRD right-hand-drive roadster was the second car built by the production department and became the sister press car to the coupé 9600 HP. It was completed around mid-February '61 and was also lent to various publications prior to launch, including *The Times* and *The Motor*. The latter tested it in the UK and then took the car to Italy, where it achieved a mean maximum speed of 149.1mph. In its early days 77 RW was driven by Ritchie Ginther, Jack Brabham and Bruce McLaren.

Following the launch in Geneva, PR boss Bob Berry was kept busy demonstrating 9600 HP on a makeshift test circuit and, in fact, was so frantic that the factory received an urgent call requesting test driver Norman Dewis to bring along 77 RW to act as a second demonstrator. Like Berry, Dewis drove very rapidly to get to Geneva as soon as possible. And, as with the coupé, the roadster was sold to Coombs of Guildford in early 1962.

THE LUMSDEN/SARGENT LIGHTWEIGHT, 49 FXN

THE LUMSDEN/SARGENT Lightweight E started life as an 'ordinary' Lightweight, then had to be rebuilt with a new shell after Peter Lumsden had a massive shunt at the Nürburgring in 1963 (when he and Peter Sargent were lying fourth overall). The car was gradually developed independently of Jaguar (whose people did not approve) by two research engineers at Imperial College, London. Samir Klat and Harry Watson applied what was then cutting-edge technology and their considerable intelligence to most aspects of the car.

Constrained by the design of the XK engine and the regulations, they created their own 'low drag' shape and long nose, inspired by Costin's Vanwall. The result was a stunning-looking car which performed very creditably at the highest levels. ➜

THE CUNNINGHAM LE MANS FIXED-HEAD COUPE, 1337 VC

BACK IN EARLY 1962, Briggs Cunningham and his team began racing one of his three roadsters and took it to the Le Mans test weekend in April. For that year's race, Jaguar built him a very special coupé in the competition department. The bare shell gained an aluminium bonnet and Perspex side windows. Much of the ducting developed on the Coombs racer (see next page) was fitted and an engine was built up with a wide-angle head, dry-sump lubrication and triple DCO3 Webers. The unit produced 296bhp.

Roy Salvadori shared the car with Cunningham and they had a trouble-free run, which Roy described as: '…the best Le Mans I ever had. The car was just as good at the finish as at the start.' Their reward was fourth overall, third in the GT class – a remarkable result.

THE PROTOTYPE AND PRESS CAR, 9600 HP

THIS PROTOTYPE, BUILT in 1960, is the oldest-surviving E-type. The model was used for development work by Dewis in 1960 and early '61, including high-speed testing on the new M1 motorway. While still secret, it was lent to journalists so that their first published impressions could coincide with the car's unveiling. The magic figure was achieved by *The Autocar*, which set the 150mph legend.

In March 1961, Bob Berry made his famous dash to Geneva in it. Berry, who had raced D-types, drove flat-out to arrive in Geneva with just 20 minutes to spare before the car's launch. The E-type was then photographed with Sir William Lyons before becoming the press car for a year. Subsequent owners include film director John Paddy Carstairs and racing driver Jack Fairman. →

THE LOW DRAG COUPÉ, CUT 7

JAGUAR HAD ENVISAGED entering a team of E-types in GT racing in the early '60s but, due to some ridiculous decisions by GT racing's ruling body, the idea was dropped. However, aerodynamicist Malcolm Sayer had created his Low Drag Coupé design for just such use. In 1962 one example was built up and then sat around until Dick Protheroe managed to prise it out of Jaguar. He immediately took it to Reims for the sports car race supporting the French Grand Prix. He was beaten only by a Ferrari sports racer – and trounced all the 250GTOs.

Protheroe continued to race the E-type before selling it in early '65. The car went through a succession of hands and was raced by David Wansbrough (who famously put it in the lake at Oulton Park), Robbie Gordon, Martin Lilley (of TVR fame) and Brian Redman. It was hillclimbed and sprinted for several years by Mike Wright.

THE SOPWITH RACER, ECD 400

'LOFTY' ENGLAND, Jaguar's team manager of the 1950s and later the marque's MD, decided that 17 of the earliest cars should be allocated to owners for competition. The 'priority list' included Ecurie Ecosse, Peter Berry, Sir Gawaine Baillie, Peter Sargent, Robin Sturgess, George Wicken and Jack Lambert; Jack Fairman, Tommy Sopwith and John Coombs were at the top.

Sopwith, whose team raced under the Equipe Endeavour banner, had the fifth right-hand-drive roadster, and the Indigo Blue car was registered ECD 400. The Sopwith and Coombs cars were entered for the E-type's first race, at Oulton Park, in early April 1961. Graham Hill took a fine victory and began the E-type's long history of success on the racetracks of the world. In May, ECD 400 competed in the E-type's first international race when Mike Parkes drove brilliantly to finish second only to Mairesse's Ferrari.

THE COOMBS RACER, BUY 1/ 4 WPD

THIS CAR HAD several lives and became the most famous and active racer of the lot. Starting life as the sixth right-hand-drive roadster, it was supplied to Coombs and driven by Roy Salvadori in the model's first race, leading before brake trouble dropped Roy back to third. Registered BUY 1, it won at Crystal Palace.

For 1962, the car was re-registered 4 WPD and became a works racer in all but name. Graham Hill had joined Salvadori at Coombs. The model was modified further, and then rebuilt with a lighter-gauge steel bodyshell following a crash at Goodwood, yet it could not compete with the new Ferrari 250GTOs.

As a result, 4 WPD became the prototype Lightweight E and was rebuilt for the 1963 season with an aluminium monocoque and alloy-blocked engine. Driven by Hill, the car clocked up notable wins over the GTOs and was driven on three occasions in '64 by a young Jackie Stewart. In '65, 4 WPD took Brian Redman to several victories. ➔

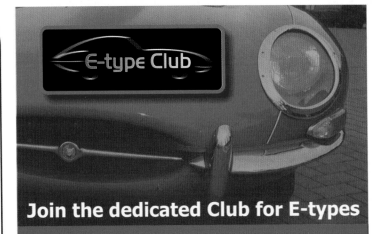

THE E1A PROTOTYPE

THE BEGINNING OF the E-type project, built in 1956 and designed to succeed the D-type at Le Mans where, following the dreadful accident in 1955, it was believed engine capacity would be limited. E1A was created with both racing and production in mind, and fitted initially with a 2.4-litre XK engine.

The body was slightly smaller than that of the eventual E-type, and it featured an early form of independent rear suspension. E1A – the A stood for aluminium – was developed by chief tester Norman Dewis and once sampled by Mike Hawthorn. Sadly, the car was later cut up, but large chunks survived and, eventually, a recreation was instigated.

THE EARLY RACER AND FILM STAR, 2 BBC/848 CRY

THIS MODEL HAD two distinct lives. First, registered as 2 BBC, it was raced extensively in 1961, being the most active competition example in the E-type's first season. During the week, the 12th right-hand-drive roadster was the demonstrator for Jaguar's long-standing Leicester-based distributor Sturgess. And at weekends Robin Sturgess took it racing. He was very successful with it, as well.

The car was sold at the end of the season and re-registered 848 CRY. Wearing this new numberplate, the red roadster appeared in the iconic film *The Italian Job*. It was driven by one of Michael Caine's henchmen, with Benny Hill as the passenger, and the E-type was attacked by the Mafia. Thankfully, it was not badly damaged.   *End*

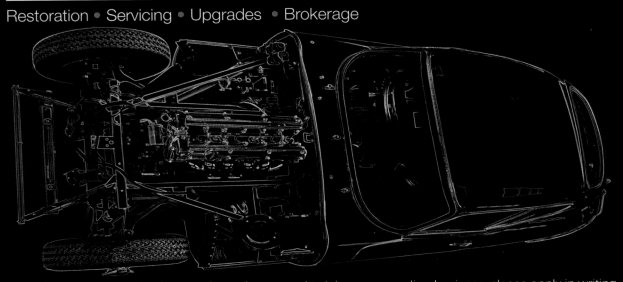

Science Class

Above
Le Mans veteran
Peter Sargent and
the special Low-Drag
E-type developed to
beat the factory cars.

The most aerodynamic E-type of the 1960s wasn't developed by Jaguar but by a small team of enthusiasts, using home-made test equipment – and the M1 motorway as a proving ground...

WORDS: PHILIP PORTER // PHOTOGRAPHY: SIMON STUART-MILLER

THIS E-TYPE started life as an 'ordinary' Lightweight, one of the 12 Competition E-types as they were known at the factory. In this form, as a roadster with a conventional vented hardtop, it was supplied in May 1963 to Peter Lumsden and Peter Sargent, who had finished fifth at Le Mans in Sargent's early E-type in '62.

For the 1963 event, they had a rather special Lister-Jaguar built up with a closed body designed by aerodynamicist Frank Costin. They took with them, as part of their crew for the April test weekend, Dr Samir (pronounced Sammy) Klat, because he could converse in technical French and it was thought this would prove useful at scrutineering. At that time, Klat was doing research into combustion at Imperial College and was captain of the university motor club. 'So I went along as interpreter, but I →

49 FXN

'I came over one hill to find it had been hailing on the other side, and a little voice said, "You are now going to leave the circuit." And I did'

Above and left
Modified E-type was clocked at 168mph in the wet down the Mulsanne straight, Le Mans, 1964. New roof section was based on a zero-lift wing.

could not just sit there and I asked if I could help,' says Klat. When he made several technical suggestions that were found to work, he quickly became a crucial member of the small team.

In May '63 the two Peters took their new Lightweight to the Nürburgring for the 1000km race. In spite of a field that included works Ferrari prototypes for Surtees, Mairesse and Parkes, and a pack of GTOs, it was the E-types of Peter Lindner and Peter Lumsden that led at the end of the first lap. Lumsden then heard a banging noise and thought it prudent to pit. Nothing wrong was found and he set off again with a vengeance.

'It was raining,' he recalls, 'but the car was going well, the rain was ceasing and I thought I was only about 20 seconds behind the chap who was third, so I kept the pressure up. I came over one hill to find it had been hailing on the other side, and a little voice said, "You are now going to leave the circuit". And I did.'

He rolled end-over-end at Flugplatz and demolished 150 yards of fencing. The car went back to the factory and was rebuilt with a new aluminium tub. Then Samir Klat and his colleague Professor Harry Watson started to develop it.

Working in a research environment, they viewed everything theoretically and then applied theory to practice. They soon realised the inherent constraints of the Jag engine. A comparatively narrow bore size meant a lack of space for big valves, so the engine, Klat comments, 'was always choked. And the shape of the combustion chamber was an absolute disaster.

'We then turned to the rest of the car. Having been involved with Frank Costin on the Le Mans Lister, I got to appreciate the importance of aerodynamics. So we decided to apply them to the Lightweight.

'The first thing we determined was that we had to reduce the drag. The most obvious thing was the top half. You could see on the normal one that you would have some turbulence, so we aimed for as near a laminar flow as possible... which meant the new roof section would be the shape of a wing, a zero-lift wing. The windscreen was fairly vertical, so we pushed the base of the screen right to the rear of the bonnet line and the angle was then quite different.'

Because they were running with quite a bit of blanking to the radiator, Samir decided they could reduce the opening in the bonnet and lengthen the nose. The result is distinctly reminiscent of Costin's Vanwall design.

Perversely, Jaguar did not appreciate their experimental work. Repeatedly Klat came up against the attitude that the factory had tried his suggestion and it did not work. Klat's own attitude was: 'Let's find out why it didn't work and see if we can make it happen.'

He says: 'After designing the hardtop, we ran along the M1 motorway with wool tufts [attached to the body]. Having painted on a grid, we put manometers all over the body and took readings.'

A manometer is a device whereby the air pressure pushes a column of water up or down and it allows you to measure the exact pressure at a certain point. The aim is to obtain gradual pressure changes with no turbulence. You then place your air exits at low-pressure points and your air inlets at high-pressure points.

'We also had a big rubber mallet and where the tufts weren't straight, we'd stop and bash away with the big mallet! We eventually got it so that the wool tufts were really smooth all the way.'

Klat and Watson also wanted to know if they were getting lift at the rear, and so rigged up Bowden cables between the suspension and the body, which were connected via an arrangement made of Meccano to a large board in the car. The cables carried two pins which the driver pushed to make holes in the board at different speeds. Measuring the distance →

'Klat persuaded Hill to circulate around Goodwood at racing speeds, while he, Klat, leant out of the passenger door and felt the suspension movement'

Above and right
Super-slippery
shape is still
beautiful and
elegant – just as a
racing car should be.

between the pin-holes proved, albeit crudely, that they had zero lift.

'Nobody believed us. We said we had measured it, and they said you couldn't measure a thing like that.'

The rear underside curvature of the body was changed, partly because the car was now longer and they had difficulty loading it up the ramps onto the transporter. Ironically, this modification actually improved the handling and generated downforce.

'We couldn't understand it and left it at that. Now, all these years later, we know we were getting a "ground effect".'

On one occasion Graham Hill, who was involved in gradually developing the factory-run Coombs Lightweight, tested the Lumsden/Sargent car. Klat had been concerned that, under heavy braking and acceleration, they were suffering from rear wheel steering due to suspension movement at the back. He persuaded Hill to circulate round Goodwood at racing speeds, while he, Klat, leant out of the passenger door and felt the suspension: 'Graham said, "You are mad, but if you're game, I am". I was wearing gloves, but when I got back they were torn to shreds.'

Nevertheless, Samir was able to feel a movement under braking, and so they

mounted the radius solidly with rose joints and hid them by attaching a pared-down section of the normal rubber mounting over the top!

At the Le Mans test weekend, the car was seventh fastest and beaten only by sports racing Ferraris and one Cobra. It was five seconds quicker than the fastest GTO and 15 seconds faster than the best Ford GT. *Autosport* commented that 'Sargent's light alloy E-type Jaguar was not exactly hanging about, haring down Mulsanne in the wet at 168mph'.

Meanwhile, they were getting zero assistance from Jaguar, with the notable exception of Malcolm Sayer. For example, Jaguar would not supply them with any hot camshafts, so they designed their own. At the same time, they were building a second engine with redesigned combustion ports, fabricated curved inlet manifolds, twin plugs, a 'home-made' 12-point distributor and asymmetric pistons. This motor produced 348bhp in comparison with the ultimate factory unit, which gave a claimed 344bhp.

The next major event was the 1964 1000km at the 'Ring. Peter Sargent recalls: 'We had a diaphragm clutch, and at the Nürburgring the bloody clutch centre suddenly fell out. As soon as we got back, Peter [Lumsden] rang the factory and

said they might like to know. "Oh," they said, "you haven't still got that in there, have you? We stopped using that some time ago because we found that the centre fell out".'

These were pioneering days for fuel-injection systems, and there was a cross-fertilisation between Klat and Jim Littlehales of Lucas that was to prove highly productive. Models fitted with the PI set-up were popping and banging in the mid-rev range.

'At the Nürburgring it was simply undriveable,' says Peter Sargent. 'You either had to have the throttle closed or flat open, and it was a bit difficult to get round some of the corners like that. Klat spent most of the night on it and finished up with a little blob of solder on a control. It made all the difference, and the next morning the car drove perfectly.'

In fact, in the paddock, Klat had modified the cams within the PI system with soft solder to change their profiles. By smelling the exhaust, he got the mixture right and cured the problem.

At Le Mans that year, Lumsden and Sargent were lying 14th after four hours and headed, in the GT class, by just two of the four Cobras and two of the four GTOs. The gallant Brit privateers gained another couple of places before having →

'The windscreen was fairly vertical,
so we pushed the base of the screen right
to the rear of the bonnet line and the
angle was then quite different'

Right
Fuel-injected engine
developed by Klat
and Watson gave
348bhp – slightly more
than Jaguar managed.

'Klat had modified the cams within the fuel-injection system with soft solder to change their profiles; by smelling the exhaust he got the mixture right'

JAGUAR LOW-DRAG E-TYPE

ENGINE
All-alloy 3781cc
six-cylinder twin-
overhead cam
XK engine with
Lucas mechanical
fuel injection
POWER
348bhp@6500rpm (est)
TORQUE
350 ft lb (est)
TRANSMISSION
Jaguar four-speed
close-ratio all-synchro
SUSPENSION
Front: Independent,
upper and lower
wishbones, torsion
bar springs.
Rear: Fully
independent, lower
transverse tubular
link, radius arms
and twin coil
springs per side
BRAKES
Dunlop discs. Jaguar
MkIX calipers. Special
Dunlop aluminium
piston blocks
PERFORMANCE
0-100mph 12 secs
Top speed 170mph
(depends on gearing)
Standing quarter mile
12.8 secs

to retire with a failed gearbox. This was 49 FXN's last international outing. Lumsden continued to race in the UK for another year, and then the model passed through a number of different hands before eventually ending up in the States. Some years ago it was bought by Sir Anthony Bamford, and then it was acquired by Lord Cowdray, joining the ex-Protheroe Low-Drag Coupé CUT 7, which, at the time of writing, he also owns.

Cowdray campaigns CUT 7 on serious European events, such as the Tour Auto, and intends to use the Lumsden/Sargent car for these and to race it at invitation events such as the Goodwood Revival. 'A

couple of the tours I do are back-to-back,' he explains, 'and if I have a bit of a problem with one then I've got a back-up car. I thought, why get something different? This is what I like.'

Cowdray has not been able to drive his new purchase in anger yet – but his co-driver Rupert Chevely has.

'It is different to CUT 7. In the wet CUT 7 probably would not be much slower but in the dry this model is much more rigid. It's a real racing car, whereas CUT 7 doesn't have that same feel.'

This very special machine benefited from the far-sighted approach of Peter Lumsden and Peter Sargent, and the

ground-breaking input of Samir Klat. He was one of the first of a new breed who brought a more scientific engineering attitude to motor racing, and 49 FXN was the beneficiary. Technically it is a very important machine, but that's not the only reason it's so special.

Peter Sargent sums it up. 'I think it's the most beautiful E-type anywhere,' he says simply. *End*

MANY THANKS TO Goodwood Motor Circuit, www.goodwood.co.uk. Thanks must also go to Lord Cowdray, Chris Keith-Lucas and Christopher Darwin – see www.gwtr.co.uk for details of his track days for older cars.

THE EXTRA E-TYPE

This V12 E-type is made from 100% genuine factory parts
– but Jaguar didn't put them together, an enthusiast did,
31 years after factory production ended

WORDS: NIGEL THORLEY // PHOTOGRAPHY: JOHN COLLEY

THE JAGUAR E-TYPE was the epitome of the British sports car, an icon of the 1960s that is still instantly recognisable today. It enjoyed a 13-year production run, during which 72,529 examples were sold – or could it now be 72,530?

Ray Parrott, a member of the Jaguar Enthusiasts' Club and a marque fanatic, knows all about E-types. He has five of them: a 3.8-litre Roadster, a Series 2 Fixed-head Coupé, a replica Lightweight and now two V12 Roadsters. An avid Jaguar devotee from an early age he's owned 25 models in 17 years, but he isn't completely obsessive – he now has a Sunbeam Tiger, a BMW 850 Alpina and a rally Aston DB6, to complement the everyday Jaguar XKR and XJ6.

A self-taught engineer, he has developed a significant number of skills in every aspect of vehicle restoration over the years. Now that he has set himself up with all the equipment and facilities needed to do most of the work on his cars, all his E-types get the 'Parrott touch' and have been adapted and improved for today's driving conditions. They are always kept in pristine condition and in regular use.

Ray's passion for what he terms 'the ultimate classic car' was further fuelled when he was contacted by Mike Wilkinson of M&C Wilkinson Jaguar Spares, a Yorkshire-based Jaguar parts business of which Ray was a regular customer. Through his many contacts, Mike had been able to acquire a cache of original E-type parts. They turned out to be highly significant.

Back in 1974, when the final E-type left the Browns Lane assembly line, all the remaining parts were sold off to one gentleman who kept them in storage with the hope of using them for his own needs. He had several lorry-loads of parts, all new and in their original packaging, which included significant items such as a complete Roadster bodyshell, an unused V12 engine and gearbox, a rear axle and all those little fixtures and fittings that go to make up a complete car. Eventually, due to age, the gentleman concerned sold the lot to Mike Wilkinson, who immediately thought of Ray because of his enthusiasm for all things E-type. What better person to benefit from some of these rare finds?

Discussions followed, and it became clear after viewing a hastily compiled list of all the parts that it just might be possible to create a new E-type from them. Ray and Mike made a detailed appraisal during Ray's numerous visits to Mike's premises in Yorkshire.

The amazing thing was that, although some parts were inevitably duplicated, there was sufficient of most things to actually build a complete Series 3 Roadster. In addition to the bodyshell, which had suffered only a few minor dents and surface rust, there were several made-up assemblies ready for installation, like the complete instrument panel with wiring, and the radiator with all its connections, electric fans and cowls. These had been assembled at Jaguar for despatch to the assembly line, and were ready to fit to a car.

Altogether, Mike and Ray estimated that there was 95% of what was required to complete the job, and that included a new set of original-spec Dunlop tyres! Among the numerous small packets of 'goodies' there was even a brand new RAC Running In →

Below
Series 3 E-type is one of the few roadsters that arguably looks better wearing its hardtop – especially when painted black.

'RAY PARROTT KNOWS ALL ABOUT E-TYPES: HE HAS FIVE OF THEM. HE'S OWNED 25 JAGUARS IN 17 YEARS – BUT HE ISN'T COMPLETELY OBSESSIVE'

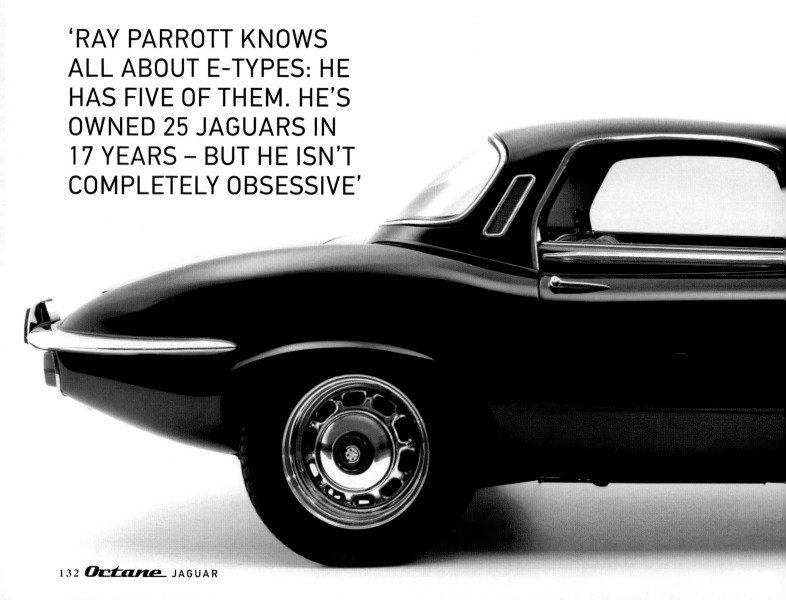

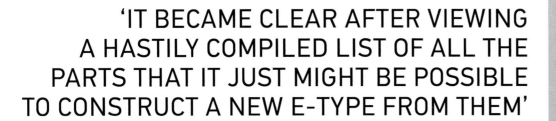

'IT BECAME CLEAR AFTER VIEWING
A HASTILY COMPILED LIST OF ALL THE
PARTS THAT IT JUST MIGHT BE POSSIBLE
TO CONSTRUCT A NEW E-TYPE FROM THEM'

THE PROJECT

Do-it-yourself E-type
Ray Parrott found that
he had 95% of the parts
he needed – and some he
didn't, such as 1974 tins of oil!

One man's workshop
Over the years, Ray has
built up an impressive
workshop to repair and
modify his classic Jaguars.

Back to black
E-type shell was painted
white when uncovered,
but was resprayed black to
match other 'last of line' V12s.

The test run
Ray's meticulous assembly
of all-original parts resulted
in an E-type that drives
literally like a new car.

'ITEMS LIKE THE BAINBRIDGE MILD-STEEL EXHAUST SYSTEM WERE ALL IN AS-NEW CONDITION'

sticker. A deal was struck and Ray, a haulier by profession, arranged for everything to be moved to his home in Essex for the project to commence. Mike agreed to supply back-up for any outstanding parts required, on the basis that they would be only original Jaguar parts and not reproduction items, so as to retain the authenticity of the finished car.

Ray's first priority was to get the bodyshell cleaned, the minor repair work carried out, and have the shell stripped and painted. This was the only work done by an outside contractor; Ray undertook all the other jobs himself.

Deciding on the colour that the body should be painted was very difficult. Ray is fond of red, but in the end he opted for black as this was the colour chosen for 49 out of the last 50 E-types. It turned out to be a wise move, because most of these black cars had a tan interior, and – while Ray again thought about using red – he found virtually a complete set of tan trim in his cache of parts.

With the bodywork underway, he started researching the minutiae of his project, realising that he had been given a unique opportunity to build a 'last E-type', provided he used only original parts. He meticulously worked through the factory Parts and Workshop Manuals, identifying every component he would need to build the car and cross-referencing them to other suppliers' information and to the packaging his purchased parts

---

**JAGUAR
E-TYPE S3**

ENGINE
5343cc all-alloy V12,
four Zenith 175CDSE
carburettors
POWER
276bhp @ 5850rpm
TORQUE
288lb ft @ 3600rpm
TRANSMISSION
Four-speed manual
SUSPENSION
Front: independent via
wishbones and torsion
bars, anti-roll bar,
telescopic dampers.
Rear: independent via
coils over dampers,
lower transverse links,
anti-roll bar
PERFORMANCE
0-60mph 6sec
Top speed 146mph

---

came in. His intimate knowledge of E-types and the fact that he already owned a Series 3 Roadster were extremely useful in understanding not only what was required but also how the different bits went together.

Ray also checked out the legal position with the DVLA. He was assured that, given the original content of the finished car, he could safely be granted a period registration number and chassis number.

As the parts identification continued, Ray never ceased to be amazed at what he had been lucky enough to find. For example, there were items that rarely survive long-term storage – such as a complete hood assembly, still boxed and with absolutely no damage or creasing to the clear plastic rear screen.

Other items, like the pre-formed fibreboard centre console surround and even the Bainbridge mild-steel exhaust system, were all in as-new condition. Most of the upholstery was present, and for those areas where he would need the trim finishing off – such as around the rear storage box – he even had a roll of new material!

Some of the exact material types used on the later E-types are no longer available, so Ray was lucky that he could either adapt 'spares' from his new parts or make up fresh trim using the raw material he had also acquired. Oh yes, it should also be pointed out that he has excellent trimming skills and his own industrial sewing machine – so none of this work presented any ➔

'NOT SURPRISINGLY, RAY WAS LOOKING FORWARD TO HIS FIRST DRIVE IN THIS "NEW" E-TYPE, AND HE WASN'T DISAPPOINTED. THERE WASN'T A RATTLE OR SQUEAK'

real problems to him. Over a period of eight months, Ray painstakingly worked night and day on the project, slowly assembling every component to exacting standards. The only large items he was missing were a windscreen and battery, which were easily sourced. Sensibly, he decided not to use the period tyres...

Any minor bracketry and trim pieces that he was short of were successfully sourced from spares suppliers and the Jaguar Enthusiasts' Club Spares Days held in March and October. Of course, there were no nuts, bolts, washers or rivets, so Ray scrupulously identified all the original fixtures and tracked them down, acquiring the entire stock from a business that was closing down locally.

One spin-off from the project was that it provided a rare opportunity to carry out direct comparisons between those original and still-packaged parts and the crop of reproduced items currently available for the E-type. Some incredible differences were revealed, which proved to Ray that there is still no substitute for using genuine parts. Everything, literally everything, went together like a knife going through soft

butter. Every screw hole matched up perfectly, every trim item fitted first time, and he found it a joy to put the car together. Ray has kept a detailed log of every part used or acquired and a photographic record of the work he carried out on this unique experiment. The icing on the cake was finding a brand-new factory hardtop for the car, again still wrapped up and in its original black paint.

Not surprisingly he was really looking forward to his first drive in this 'new' E-type, and he wasn't disappointed. There wasn't a rattle or squeak, and the Jag just felt right, even down to having the special smell that's peculiar to a car which is to all intents and purposes new.

The E-type has since been MoT tested and currently awaits registration. But what now? Ray has completed his challenge and has even built a new luxury garage on the side of his house to accommodate this and his other E-types. However, owning the finished car has turned into something of an anti-climax. The real joy for him was the detective work, the attention to detail and the actual construction. He is now undecided about keeping or selling the E-type – what would you do? *End*

THE ULTIMATE E-TYPE

Eagle takes the Jaguar E-type as a basis then makes it faster, handle better and – shock – look even sexier. This is what £600,000-worth of 21st century E-type feels like

WORDS: ROBERT COUCHER // PHOTOGRAPHY: GUS GREGORY/JAMIE LIPMAN

AS YOU CAN IMAGINE, the classic car world went mad for the E-type in 2011. Every event celebrated the model's 50th anniversary, and values continued to strengthen after decades of languishing behind those of Italian, German and other British marques. Yet Henry Pearman and Paul Brace had already spent years developing the now famous Eagle E-types into some of the most beautiful and dynamically capable sports cars you can buy.

Back in 2009, *Octane* drove an Eagle E-type and compared it with a beautiful Aston Martin DB4. While both were absolutely the best examples of their respective marques, the Eagle impressed with its engineering, dynamics and serious speed. Pearman's ethos is to improve an E-type, not by stuffing a modern V8 into it, but by taking the original and upping the level of engineering of its componentry in a manner that Jaguar might have done had it developed the car itself.

The E-type has tremendous raw ingredients. Engineering hours cost, though, so a full-house Eagle model will set you back some £250,000 depending on final specification. But in effect you have a brand-new sports car with 2011 standards of performance.

Having got used to the quarter-of-a-million-pound Eagle E-type, you'd better brace yourself for the rarefied Jaguar Lightweight Eagle Speedster you see here. Only the second constructed, with a very limited number of further Speedsters planned, this example costs around £600,000. The first, Speedster No 1, was specially commissioned for an American enthusiast who wanted something even more special →

Left
Experiencing the Eagle
Lightweight is like a game
of spot the difference: it's been
fundamentally altered yet, in
isolation, the changes are subtle.

than a bespoke Eagle. So Development Engineer Brace set about designing the Speedster as a one-off. However, the car generated such interest, Eagle built this second example in Lightweight form.

The firm is interested in maintaining Jaguar history and heritage, and as such stresses that Eagle cars are 'proper' E-types, even if the transformation is dramatic. In 1963 Jag produced 12 Lightweight E-types, all constructed in aluminium and featuring an engine with a lightweight aluminium block, fuel injection and a five-speed gearbox. Those great old racing machines inspired the new Lightweight Speedster, which also has an aluminium body and differential casing as well as an ally 4.7-litre block. The result is an impressively low kerbweight of just 1008kg. With the big-bore E-type straight-six pumping out an easy 310bhp at a lowly 4800rpm and a torque figure of 340lb ft at only 3600rpm, the Lightweight promises shattering performance of at least the level of one of the dozen originals.

Altering one of the most beautiful automotive designs – one that is on permanent display at New York's Museum of Modern Art – is a tough call, but Brace's Lightweight looks extremely striking. Any criticism of the original E-type's design usually centres on its narrow track, especially when it's shod with thin wire wheels and skinny original tyres. This can also make the car look like it is teetering on its toes. And 'delicate' is a word often used to describe the beautiful classic.

Brace's Speedster has addressed these qualms, and the Eagle has a much more aggressive, almost dangerous countenance. It's more bad boy than pretty boy, and this has been achieved by employing the old hot-rod trick of chopping and raking the small windscreen with shaped, wind-blown side glass and hidden A-posts. This gives the Speedster sleekness and lowers the stance of the car.

The more pumped-up appearance is further enhanced by cleverly deepening the sills, which necessitates a lower floorpan. Muscle is added by increasing the track and fitting specially made wire wheels that fill the curvaceously flared arches. The exaggerated rear haunches give the impression of coiled urge, and the upswept tail shouts power, with the twin tailpipes 'frenched' tightly under the narrowed numberplate recess.

The result is a stunning-looking beast that is low and muscular, promising serious speed. But what really elevates the Lightweight Speedster is all the thoughtful detailing. This Jaguar is seamless, smooth and pure, and this is set off by the luscious paintwork, which at first appears to be black but, as the sunshine strikes its haunches, turns out to be metalflake claret. The sparkling aluminium wire wheels have three-eared spinners with the word Speedster etched into them, as does the hand-turned steering wheel boss.

The sculpted cockpit, with its authentic dotted aluminium facia and 'waterfall' rear decking that drops in from the rear, mirrors the smooth exterior lines and enhances the flow of the Speedster. Beautifully shaped seats covered in soft red leather finish off the interior.

Opening the aluminium bonnet reveals the heart of the E-type – that magnificent six-cylinder engine, with its polished cam covers, rows of head bolts, individual throttle-body fuel injection and airbox shaped out of carbon fibre. And it is the mechanical engineering that makes an Eagle special. Since 1982, Pearman and his dedicated team have concentrated on perfecting these Jaguars, with impressive results.

The shaped bucket seat is cosseting and, although unique to the Speedster, the interior is still that of an E-type. The Nardi steering wheel is a matter of taste and feels good, though I would prefer the original E-type wheel. It's one of the best.

Turn the ignition key, then dab the starter button, and the big 4.7-litre six fires. Its note is deep and more industrial than the normally quiet E's, alluding to the extra capacity and grunt. The clutch is hydraulically light and the Eagle-engineered five-speed gearbox slips into first with ease. Almost all of the prodigious torque is available from as little as 1800rpm, so the Speedster moves off the mark effortlessly and is quiet and demure down the country lanes. The free-flowing exhaust maintains →

'The result is a stunning-
looking beast; low, muscular
and promising serious speed'

a deep yet restrained note, a bit like an opera singer chatting quietly. Mellifluous but constrained.

The Speedster feels tight and taut, but the suspension soaks up the rutted country lanes with well-damped responses. Yes, it is firmer than a stock E-type, but that's what you expect – and would surely hope for – with 310bhp under your right foot. A feeling of unstressed lightness pervades and the steering is similarly easy, even though the front tyres are 225/50x16s (with larger 245/55x16s at the rear). The large tyres are modern Pirelli P6000s and they impart a degree of wide-rubber softness to the otherwise crisp steering response, while the vented disc brakes with four-pot calipers shed speed with disdain and inspire great confidence. Soon you're loafing along the lanes at an easy 80mph, with just 2500rpm showing on the tachometer.

By today's standards an E-type is a small and narrow car, and even this muscular Speedster feels diminutive enough to punt along narrow roads. Naturally the adjustable Eagle suspension, set here for comfortable road use, keeps the car razor-sharp.

The roads open up and so does the chance to unleash some power. It isn't strictly necessary to change down a gear, but do so just to enjoy the gearshift action and suddenly the bad boy arrives. The revcounter needle has been lazily dawdling below 3000rpm until now, yet get it above that and it heads for the redline in a blur. At the same instant the quiet exhaust note changes to a full-bore roar, and the Speedster becomes not so much a Jaguar but a charging lion. The way it gathers speed is shocking and is in no way in keeping with a classic car of the 1960s. You have to grab an up-change and the relentless shove continues, the rev needle goes straight back to the redline and you go for the next cog almost immediately. Unbelievable!

Once you've savoured the savagery of the Speedster's raw power, it's time to settle down and enjoy its flowing handling. Incredibly, it combines the E-type's deftness and lightness of touch with huge grip and precision. Those fat tyres bite and really work as the supple suspension allows insane rates of undramatic cornering speeds. This Speedster is one of those rare sports cars: you don't have to work it along, it simply flows as the dynamics are so capable of turning undulating tarmac into a perfect palette for all that power. The Eagle Lightweight Speedster is a pure Jaguar E-type. Only more so. *End*

FOR MORE INFORMATION see www.jaguarspeedster.com.

JAGUAR LIGHTWEIGHT E-TYPE SPEEDSTER BY EAGLE

ENGINE 4.7-litre straight-six, DOHC, fuel injection
POWER 310bhp@4800rpm **TORQUE** 340lb ft@3600rpm
TRANSMISSION Five-speed manual, rear-wheel drive
STEERING Rack and pinion
SUSPENSION Front: double wishbones, torsion bars, telescopic dampers, anti-roll bar. Rear: trailing arms, lower transverse links, fixed-length driveshafts, twinned coil springs and telescopic dampers, anti-roll bar
BRAKES Vented discs with four-piston AP calipers **WEIGHT** 1008kg
PERFORMANCE Top speed 160mph (est). 0-60mph 4.8sec (est)

RACER'S DOZEN

Jaguar's XJ13 prototype has barely been driven
since the 1960s. *Octane*'s John Simister followed
its recommissioning – and has now driven it
further than any other journalist in history

PHOTOGRAPHY: MATTHEW HOWELL, IAN DAWSON

Left
Jaguar's Heritage cars are now the only vehicles being worked on at Browns Lane

'The heritage volunteers are the only people who remember how the XJ13 went together originally. There's no shop manual for this car'

JAGUAR'S BROWNS LANE plant is practically deserted. People, plant and machinery are gone to the much newer, higher-tech Castle Bromwich factory, leaving a litter-strewn shell as if the former occupants had fled at zero notice before the headwind of an invading army. But there are a few pockets of survivors around the edges: the administration offices and the Heritage Centre are the obvious ones, while over at the far corner the past is still the present.

Gary Jones used to work in Jaguar's emissions laboratory, but the building had a much more exciting past as the marque's competition department. 'See where the wall has been bricked up?' he's saying. 'That's where the exhausts used to come out. You can imagine the noise.'

Inside the run-down building of cheap red brick, you can see how the space was once divided into sections. Each one was an engine test cell, and just a few paces away all kinds of competition cars would be built. Gary can almost see the ghosts, and one of them looks like the Jaguar XJ13.

Experimental Jaguar 13, built in 1966 and first

run in 1967, was meant to be the sports-racer to take on GT40s and Ferrari P4s. The mid-engined, V12-powered, 502bhp XJ13 would take up the racing-green baton where the D-type left off a decade earlier, and bring glory back to Britain. That never happened, not least because the FIA changed the prototype rules for 1968 and the XJ13's engine was considerably bigger than the new 3-litre limit. All that effort, all that hope and expense, for nothing – except that it did result in one of the most beautiful racing cars ever built.

Maybe that unlucky number was the reason. Maybe an XJ14 would have won Le Mans and history would have been different. Who can tell?

THE PAST IS still the present. Next door to the Marie Celeste-like emissions lab is where Jaguar's Heritage cars live and are maintained when they're not on display.

Gary has just helped to dismantle that most mysterious and valuable of all the old Jags, the one I am going to help resurrect. The XJ13 is being dismembered that it may live again, and the old guard is back. They're Heritage volunteers now,

and they are the only people who remember exactly how the XJ13 went together originally. There's no workshop manual for this one-off car. It's all in their heads.

But why do it now? The history of the XJ13 is the stuff of Jaguar legend, and ill fortune has been the recurrent theme. After the car's racing plans were kyboshed, it went into hiding until the production version of Jaguar's V12, of which the XJ13's unit was the precursor, was about to be launched in the E-type and XJ12 saloon. So, in 1971 the XJ13 was dusted off and taken to MIRA, the Motor Industry Research Association's banked test track near Hinckley, Leicestershire, for some filming.

Veteran test driver Norman Dewis was doing the driving, and near the end of the day he went for a final rapid run on the banking. The authorised version has it that the right-hand rear wheel collapsed, instantly pitching the Jaguar down the banking and into the infield, where it dug in, flipped end-over-end twice, rolled twice and finally stopped the right way up, a quick-thinking, miraculously undamaged and fortunately compact Dewis cowering under the dash. Strangely, though, there are photographs showing the wrecked XJ sitting with all four wheels seemingly intact. What really happened has gone fuzzy in the mist of history…

In 1973, the XJ13 was comprehensively rebuilt with nearly every panel re-made and replaced. It made occasional public appearances, and at one event its engine was terminally over-revved. The other surviving motor was pressed into service but one of its pistons had been welded, which inhibited maximum-effort use. And so the XJ13 →

'My task today is to help with the final reassembly. The engine and gearbox have been reunited with the tub, and my jobs include getting the gear linkage to work properly'

'I peel off from its backing a brand-new stick-on Jaguar badge, confirm the centre line, then attach adhesive to metal. The XJ13 is finished'

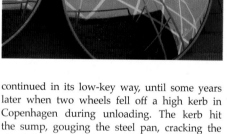

Above and left
XJ13 is wheeled into daylight for the first time since its rebuild, prior to ritual badge fixing.

continued in its low-key way, until some years later when two wheels fell off a high kerb in Copenhagen during unloading. The kerb hit the sump, gouging the steel pan, cracking the aluminium casting above it and breaking a stud. That was that, then. No more running, and the XJ13 was relegated to static display only.

'WE'VE BEEN waiting to get our hands on it for the last two years,' says Richard Mason, chief Heritage spannerman. I'm at Browns Lane, it's the end of March, and before me is half an XJ13. It terminates shortly after the cockpit, and the rear suspension, ZF transmission and subframe are sitting as a unit some distance away. The missing structural element is the engine, vital to the rear end's integrity and now over at Jaguar's Whitley design and engineering centre.

While the dismembered XJ13 looks tidy and pleasingly patinated, the paint is dull and scuffed and there's a general air of tiredness. The big task

for the recommissioning is to bring the engine back to race-ready health, even though the XJ is hardly likely to be raced. It just needs to live at speed once again, to recall those heady days when David Hobbs and the XJ13 set a new UK circuit lap record of 161.6mph at the tricky MIRA track with its three flipped-up banked corners. The second-biggest task is to repair and refinish the body.

Otherwise it's just a thorough clean and check of everything else. Just. Oh, and some new tyres would be good. And it all has to be ready for a parade at Le Mans in June.

Three weeks later, Richard and I meet again to catch up on progress. We're off to Chesman Engineering in Coventry, where the XJ13's heads have been lightly skimmed and the ports cleaned up. Starting and stopping the engine over the years, without giving it time to warm up, has caused corrosion from condensation and the head gaskets have been weeping. Chesman will also machine some new camshaft bearings. The heads

are quite unlike later production V12 units, most obviously because they have twin instead of single camshafts and the inlet ports sit between the cams, as they do on a Lamborghini V12. There are still two valves per cylinder but the combustion chamber is hemispherical in typical race-engine (and XK-engine) fashion.

Next stop Whitley and the engine development department, where the heads are delivered to the eagerly waiting Graham Hughes and Paul Harris. The rest of the motor is laid out on benches, apart from the block which is mounted on a stand next to the other XJ13 engine. That one, long presumed vanished but eventually found, has a chunk missing from a head and a very battered cam lobe, the result of that over-revving. It will donate its steel 'sump' – actually merely a bottom cover plate because this is a dry-sump engine – to the rebuilt engine, and the Whitley boys will weld and re-machine the aluminium casting above it that had the crack and the broken stud. →

'Feel that V12 sing as it hasn't sung in years; try to imagine what it would have been like to race the XJ13 at Le Mans, had rules not killed the dream'

JAGUAR XJ13

ENGINE
4994cc all-alloy V12, quad-ohc, two valves per cylinder, Lucas fuel injection, dry sump
POWER
502bhp@7600rpm
TORQUE
386lb ft@6300rpm
TRANSMISSION
ZF five-speed manual transaxle, four-wheel drive
SUSPENSION
Front: double wishbones, coil springs, anti-roll bar. Rear: double wishbones using driveshaft as upper lateral link, coil springs, anti-roll bar
BRAKES
Ventilated discs front and rear
WEIGHT
1125kg (2478lb)
PERFORMANCE
175mph on gearing as tested

Right and facing page
Simister sets off on a cautious tour of the Browns Lane access roads, before a proper high-speed run at MIRA.

Both engines' builds were recorded when new on detailed data sheets. Which unit was used during Hobbs' 1967 record run and Dewis's crash isn't known, but the motor being rebuilt now is definitely the better basis for a resurrected XJ13. Its con-rods are beautifully polished, for example, and everything seems machined a little more lovingly.

Time now to look more deeply at what makes this Claude Baily-designed engine what it is. Jaguar made seven prototype four-cam V12s (this one is number seven), one of which was used in a MkX test mule, but just the two XJ13 motors used gear drive for the camshafts – four straight-cut gears per bank, the first in each geartrain driven by chain from the crankshaft, mesh adjusted by moving an eccentric idler shaft. Also gear-driven is the scavenge pump in the sump; it and the pressure pump have a massive six gallons of oil to move between them.

The block is similar to those of later production V12s apart from its smaller bore (87mm instead of 90mm). The stroke is the same short 70mm, resulting in a 4994cc capacity. Lucas mechanical injection squirts fuel straight into the intake trumpets, outboard of the throttle butterflies in typical racing practice. The distributor uses Lucas Opus electronic ignition and has the biggest cap I've ever seen.

Surprisingly, the aluminium castings exposed to the outside air have been painted in aluminium paint. It looks garish, but I'm told it quickly tones down once the engine gets hot – and that's how the unit was finished originally. As for gaskets, potentially a problem in a near-unique motor, Federal Mogul (which nowadays owns the Payen gasket name) has offered to make new major gaskets using the original dies that have miraculously been found. Paul and Graham will cut out the minor gaskets themselves.

Now, it's off to the Coventry Boring and Metalling Company with all 12 pistons. This fantastically useful machine shop already has the crankshaft, whose crankpins have been machined by 20 thou' to take new big-end bearings. CBMC will machine the ring grooves in the pistons to take new, wider rings. And good news: X-ray analysis has shown that the repaired piston is perfectly fit for maximum-effort use and it won't be necessary to make a new one. (The pistons in the other engine are of a different 'grade' and so are fractionally different in size.)

MEANWHILE, the front half of the XJ13 and its rear body panels are at XK Engineering, a short distance north-east of Coventry. Prime mover Graham Hall once worked on Jaguar's E-type lines and subsequently branched out into XK and E-type restoration. Nowadays the bread and butter comes from building Range Rover Autobiography special editions, but Graham is thrilled to have the XJ13 in his emporium.

'We're painting it in two-pack because it's durable and keeps its gloss,' he's saying. 'We've matched the colour with a spectrometer.' The panels aren't all stripped to bare metal – it's difficult going round all the rivets and there's the danger of stripper residue damaging the paint in later years – but sound paint is flatted back and re-primed. 'Yes, even around all those louvres…'

The last part to get its coats of dark green is the main rear body section, in the spray booth as we talk. The other parts, newly resplendent in their dark gloss, look fantastic.

IT'S EARLY JUNE and all the pieces are back at Browns Lane. The engine has gone together perfectly, with valves re-lapped and everything else found to be in excellent condition. AP Racing has rebuilt the twin-plate Borg & Beck clutch, the gearbox has been cleaned and flushed out and its oil pump – actually a standard SU electric fuel pump – has been brought back to life.

What else? Brake and clutch hydraulics stripped and cleaned, all seals re-usable. All rubber bushes found serviceable, all joints greased as needed. All oil and water pipes – they run through the cockpit – removed and flushed through, then refitted with new hoses. Sill end plates removed to inspect the fuel tanks – just the right-hand one is used now. Injector pump and alternator drive belts replaced. Pump flushed and bled, alternator and starter checked and cleaned. Wiring checked all over. A thorough recommissioning, in other words. My

task today is to help with the final reassembly. The engine and rear suspension have been reunited with the tub, and my jobs are to bleed the clutch, to get the gear linkage to work properly, to fit the covers over the differential and the exhaust manifolds and to wire in a rev-limiter. Then in with a new pair of batteries, wired in parallel for the normal 12 volts but ample amps.

And now, easy does it, it's on with that fragile, curvaceous and unwieldy rear body section. Mind the new paint, engage the pegs, lock the side sections to the sills with wire rods like the shaft in a piano lid's hinge. The side louvre panels go on next – they guard the engine's air supply – and we're done. Except for one thing. I peel off from its backing a brand new stick-on Jaguar badge for the nose, confirm the centre line, move the badge back and forth until we achieve aesthetic consensus, then attach adhesive to metal. The XJ13 is finished.

WHEN I WAS LOOKING to buy my house, I saw in a bedroom a grey-painted scale model of a familiar shape; it was the XJ13 wind-tunnel model, because the owners of the house were related to aerodynamicist Malcolm Sayer. I never thought then that I would drive the real thing, but that's what is about to happen…

Richard Mason has warmed it up, checked that everything is working as it should. Now it's my turn to trundle the XJ13 up and down the Browns Lane access roads. Just it and me, now, in real time, past made present once again.

I climb over the bare aluminium sill, pull the featherweight door shut, settle into the minimalist bucket seat behind a woodrim steering wheel and

one of two Abbey Panels plaques (the company both built the body and rebuilt it in 1973). The cabin has been left as it was, four decades-worth of patinated functionality, and it's cosy in here. Pretty hot, in fact: a pair of oil pipes runs above two water pipes right next to what passes for a passenger seat, and they're radiating a lot of surplus heat energy.

Ignition on, by toggle switch. Fuel pump on, ditto, accompanied by a loud whirr. Push the ignition switch further down against a spring, hear the constant-note churning of a hefty starter against 12 hefty compressions, and 502bhp of impatient V12 erupts into busy, gear-whirring, cam-chattering life. The exhausts are loud and sound angry, but the V12 is ticking over as if plucked straight from a production car.

I've heard past stories of a heavy clutch and a cantankerous gearshift, but the clutch rebuild has fixed everything. It must have been a clutch-drag problem before, because now the tiny, right-hand lever finds gears easily as long as you don't move it out of sequence. And you nearly always have to →

'The cabin has been left as it was, four decades-worth of patinated functionality, and it's cosy in here. Pretty hot, in fact'

Above left
V12 is one of seven prototype four-cam engines and one of only two built to XJ13 spec, with gear-driven cams.

Above
Malcolm Sayer's aerodynamic shape is still gorgeous, 40 years on.

select second before you can have first; it's a deliberate lock-out system.

Good grief, this is a torquey engine. It's still tight and we shouldn't venture beyond 4000rpm, but the smallest throttle-squirt hurls the XJ13 forward. The Experimental Jaguar lives again.

IT DIDN'T MAKE the Le Mans 24 Hours parade. The Heritage people ran out of time. But the XJ13 did make the Le Mans Classic three weeks later, after a 67-mile shakedown run at MIRA which uncovered one easily cured oil leak and a balance problem with the new Dunlop front tyres. At Le Mans it ran faultlessly and fast; four decades late, yes, but who's complaining?

And now we're at MIRA again, for a proper drive in an unfettered space. Now run-in –although Richard asks that I don't go over 5500rpm (peak power arrives at 7600) – the XJ13 is fully and finally the racing car reincarnated. The new paintwork even has smoke-marks around the exhaust pipes.

First, some gentle runs on the banking where disaster struck in 1971. It doesn't like small throttle openings, hunting and fretting impatiently, but

'The XJ13's eagerness is infectious. The hard-edged bellow is intoxicating as I pass 5000rpm with the accelerator pressed down as hard as I dare'

further pressure unleashes huge energy and I back off immediately.

But after Richard has taken me for a rapid blast around the banked track, breaking his self-imposed rev limit because the engine is running so well and sending the most fabulous sound waves searing across Warwickshire, I get another go. This time it's on the Dunlop handling circuit in the infield, and there's a distinct impression that it's all right for me to exercise the XJ a little.

Can this be real? I'm in this unique racing car, for which Jaguar was once offered £7.5m and which has just had an expensive restoration so it can be used and enjoyed in the future. If I do

something daft, there won't be a future. But the XJ13's eagerness is infectious. Its breadth of torque is breathtaking, the hard-edged bellow from intake trumpets and four lots of three-into-one exhausts is intoxicating as I pass 5000rpm with the accelerator pressed as hard as I dare.

Snick-up, blip-snick-down, aim for a corner, feel the light nose bite on those surprisingly squidgy Dunlops (they run at under 20psi), feel the instant turn-in and tail-loading typical of a mid-engined car designed for handling-literate drivers. I just know that a burst of power now would bring on a delicious drift, but there's too much at stake here and many eyes are watching.

So back on the straight, feel that V12 sing as it hasn't sung for years, try to imagine what it would have been like to race the XJ13 at Le Mans had rules not killed the dream. What would it have looked like in race trim? Would it have sprouted spoilers and scoops, sullying the shape so it could stay on the road at 200mph? We'll never know. But I've just driven it further, faster and for longer than any other motoring writer in history. And gentlemen, it's been a privilege. *End*

THE MEN WHO MADE HISTORY

Sir William Lyons surrounded himself with creative, engineering and business geniuses. Here we profile just a few of the key men who turned a small coachbuilding operation into a global luxury and sports car brand

WORDS: PAUL SKILLETER

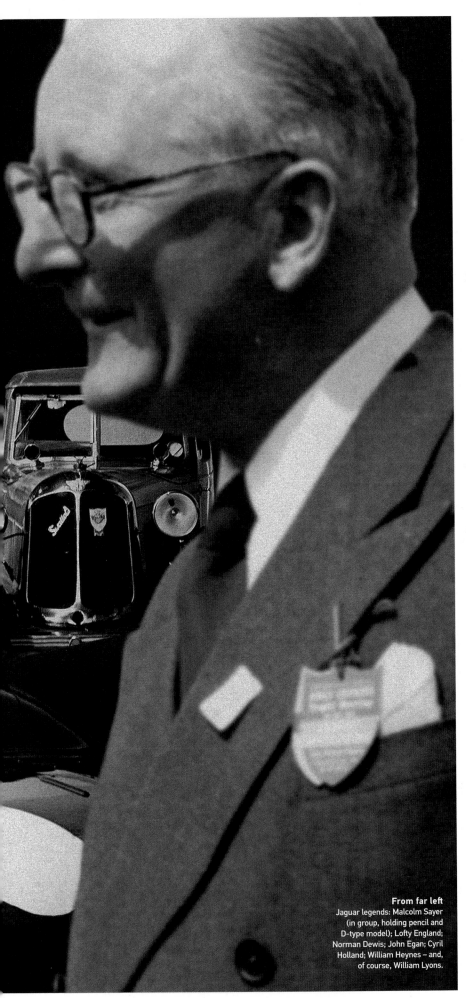

SIR WILLIAM LYONS

BEHIND EVERY GREAT CAR there are great people, and over the past eight decades Jaguar has been particularly fortunate in the quality of those who have worked for it. Sir William Lyons, of course, founded the whole enterprise, so it's only right to start with him. He was born 109 years ago; his father was an Irish musician who settled in Blackpool, his mother the daughter of a wealthy mill owner (who so strongly disapproved of the union that he 'cut her off without a penny'…). After a false start as a motor car salesman – he was sacked – the young Bill was languishing in his father's music shop when the Walmsley family from Stockport moved into his road.

William Walmsley's gleaming aluminium sidecar changed Bill Lyons' life; in 1922 the two men formed a partnership to produce it commercially, which led to the Swallow-bodied cars and, in Coventry in 1931, a distinct marque – the SS. Then, in 1935, Lyons created the Jaguar, spearheaded by a 'pocket Bentley' 2½-litre saloon but priced at a third of the real thing. The company's progress was rapid after that, and led to the sensational XK-powered cars of the 1950s and '60s.

Jaguars were popular because they (usually) went like the clappers, looked fantastic and were affordable. Lyons secured this combination of virtues by recruiting some brilliant engineers, who complemented his own natural talent for styling. Vitally, he also possessed a shrewd grasp of economics, growing the business just enough to obtain economies of scale, but without losing exclusivity.

As a person, Lyons was a man of two halves: the 'Jaguar' Lyons was formal almost to the point of being dour, and his penchant for stringent economy became legendary. Some translated the latter as meanness, but his abhorrence of waste and inefficiency was actually ahead of its time, and the practical outcome was that Jaguar achieved much on minimal resources.

Not that William was without humour, as his PR man Bob Berry recounts: 'He was amused by situations… He used to laugh with his eyes – they were a very steely blue, and unwavering. If he was annoyed with you he'd bore holes through you. If he was going to relax, you would see it in his eyes… he had a sort of twinkle if he was amused by something.'

Lyons was knighted in 1956, but he and wife Greta remained without affectation. Among his family and small but close circle of friends (very few of whom had motor industry connections), Bill was a different person, relaxed and informal. He was often extremely generous to his employees on his Wappenbury estate and farm, even to the extent of building a bungalow for one of them.

He rarely allowed even his closest colleagues into this private world, but I once glimpsed both sides of Lyons – while conducting a photoshoot of the new XJ12 at Wappenbury Hall in 1972. Sir William and Lady Lyons were part of it, and initially Lyons issued peremptory instructions to PR man 'Whyte' (Andrew Whyte; Lyons almost never used forenames) and the shoot was stalling. But then Greta had the idea of bringing out the Yorkshire terriers; immediately the austere, blue-suited Sir William dissolved into Bill Lyons, the smiling family man and dog-lover, everyone relaxed, and the shoot ended in success...

Perhaps Sir William's business acumen let him down badly only once, when he merged Jaguar with the British Motor Corporation in 1966. Too trusting, only later did he discover that BMC was steeply in decline – which led to the merger with Leyland and the BL debacle. He died in 1985, but was happy to have seen Jaguar thrive once more as an independent company under John Egan.

From far left
Jaguar legends: Malcolm Sayer (in group, holding pencil and D-type model); Lofty England; Norman Dewis; John Egan; Cyril Holland; William Heynes – and, of course, William Lyons.

JAGUAR HEROES

CYRIL HOLLAND

In 1926, Lyons felt the need to progress from sidecars to coachbuilding but, as he later wrote: 'Coachbuilding was an art about which I knew nothing.' An advertisement in the Midlands papers produced master bodymaker Cyril Holland; his CV 'sounded too good to be true', but it wasn't. 'What delighted and impressed me the most,' recorded Lyons, 'was his ability to work with nothing more than a rough sketch of what he had to do.'

For nearly 20 years Holland acted as Lyons' 'interpreter', turning his styling concepts into practical realities. Had he not joined Swallow at the critical time, it is quite possible that the little company might never have made the transition from back-street sidecar maker to prestige car manufacturer. When, shortly after the war, Cyril decided to leave (partly because Jaguar was adopting mass-produced all-steel bodies, so leaving little scope for his skills), William Lyons was genuinely sorry.

WILLIAM MUNGER HEYNES CBE

The mark of a good leader is their ability to choose the right people. When in 1935, after a series of searching interviews, Bill Lyons hired a quiet young man from Humber to become his first chief engineer, he certainly placed the engineering future of his company in good hands. Heynes took the 'cad's car' SS and made it into a gentleman's conveyance in the form of the Jaguar. He must also be given the major credit for choosing an advanced but complex twin-overhead-camshaft design for Jaguar's first all-new power unit after the war. The move was risky (had the new engine failed in service it would probably have ruined the marque), but sound design and execution ensured its success. The XK motor went on to power all Jaguars until the advent of the new V12 engine in 1971, and the majority of them right up until 1986.

Yet Heynes was really a chassis man, and it is equally to his credit that Jaguars have always handled well. It was also Heynes the motor sport enthusiast who took up the challenge of Le Mans and – at a time when Britain was a nobody in motor-racing terms – won it. The C-type, victorious in 1951 and 1953, led to the D-type which won the 24 Hours in 1955, 1956 and 1957. Heynes wanted to return with a mid-engined car in the 1960s but, although Sir William benevolently allowed him to play, what became the XJ13 never raced. Meanwhile, however, models such as the Mk2, E-type and finally the XJ6 were all evolved under Bill Heynes' aegis before he retired in 1969. It was an amazing and unique engineering legacy on which the success of today's company is founded.

FRANK RAYMOND WILTON ENGLAND

A literally towering figure in Jaguar history, 'Lofty' England arrived as the company's service manager in 1946. The ex-Daimler apprentice and racing mechanic (he had worked for Sir Henry Birkin, Dick Seaman and Prince Bira) quickly became a key player in the business. Lyons had a particular regard for England and placed great trust in him; Frank took an ever-greater responsibility in the running of Jaguar, and ultimately succeeded Sir William as head of the company.

Although the position occupied only a small percentage of his time at Jaguar, Lofty is best remembered for his role as team manager during the marque's Le Mans years of the 1950s. A shrewd race tactician, he also possessed a steady nerve – as was shown by his resolve at the time of the 1955 Le Mans disaster which involved Mike Hawthorn's works D-type. Lofty became joint managing director in 1968, and after Sir William's eventual retirement in 1972 guided Jaguar through some very tough times within BL until the arrival of the dynamic young Geoffrey Robinson in 1973. England retired the following year.

'As a person, Lyons was a man of two halves: the "Jaguar" man was formal to the point of being dour, but among his friends he was a different person, relaxed and often extremely generous'

MALCOLM SAYER

Sir William is rightly hailed as a supreme designer, but it was the gentle-giant Malcolm Sayer from Bristol Aircraft who produced some of Jaguar's best-known shapes. Brought in to pen the original 1951 C-type, Sayer went on to use the basic contours of his sports-racing D-type design to evolve the E-type – one of the few cars on permanent exhibition in the New York Museum of Modern Art.

It might be supposed that Lyons could have been jealous of Sayer's talents but there is no evidence of this, perhaps because of the clear demarcation line: Lyons styled the saloons, Sayer the sports cars. The former, made in far higher numbers, brought in the cash, but it was the sports machines that established Jaguar in America and created the 'beautiful, fast cars' image that still sells the marque's models today.

SIR JOHN EGAN

To some, the outcome of John Egan's tenure of Jaguar was failure: it was on his watch that in November 1989 the firm succumbed to Ford's blandishments, and the following year once more became a small part in a major group. But justifying his inclusion here is the fact that, in 1980, with Jaguar in real danger of being closed down, Egan stepped in and initiated a remarkable revival process. This culminated in the company's privatisation in 1984 and a glorious five years of freedom, during which he raised morale and tackled many of Jaguar's quality problems.

Long-term, a specialist manufacturer making only 50,000 cars a year was never going to survive. But Sir John made the best of what was there, and gave Jaguar back a lot of self respect. *End*

Left
The young Lyons' first love was motorbikes; his Harley-Davidson Daytona Special was a cherished possession.

CLASSIC MOTOR CARS
LIMITED

RESTORING JAGUAR'S HERITAGE

This fabulous XK120 was a 1952 Jaguar's works press car. It underwent a complete CMC restoration before its successful competition debut in the 2010 Mille Miglia.

A John Coombs prepared Mark 2, is a very rare and special car. This one has just been delivered to our client after a full restoration and Classic & Sports Car will be featuring it soon.

This beautiful and unique car recently completed its 4 year restoration and on its international debut at Villa D' Este it was awarded a Medaglia D'Onore. A wonderful example of the special skills at work at CMC.

THE WORLD'S PREMIER JAGUAR RESTORATION COMPANY

SALES | RESTORATION | UPGRADES

Classic Motor Cars, Bridgnorth, England.
Tel: +44 (0) 1746 765804 Email: mail@classic-motor-cars.co.uk
www.classic-motor-cars.co.uk

The JUDGEMENT of PARIS

Jaguar's new XJ saloon sees the company deliberately moving away from its past and looking to a fresh future. So can you make any kind of meaningful comparison with the 1960s original? *Octane* drove both cars in Paris to find out

WORDS: MARK DIXON // PHOTOGRAPHY: TOM SALT

PHP 42G

AUNCHING ITS NEW XJ saloon in Paris was a bold move by Jaguar. The XJ is a big car, and Paris is an unforgiving city. Whether negotiating the ceaseless whirlpool of traffic that encircles the Arc de Triomphe or threading through the maze of narrow side-streets that link the broad boulevards, you take your life in your hands wherever you go. And don't even mention Parisian parking techniques.

But the new XJ itself represents a bold move, so maybe Paris was an appropriate choice of venue. In recent years Jaguar has started to drag itself away from the 20th century – and, more specifically, the 1960s – and to embrace the 21st. First came the XK coupé and then the XF, each of which marked a progressive loosening of the heritage bonds that have tied Jaguar to the past rather than the future. The new XJ sees Jaguar almost liberated from those shackles. As a classic car person, you may not see that as a positive step, but you might feel rather differently if your job depended on selling the damn things.

All credit, then, to Jaguar for allowing *Octane* to drive and photograph the new machine back-to-back with its 1960s predecessor. Not every car company would have the confidence to do that. In fact, Jaguar design chief Ian Callum is a big fan of the original XJ6, and there are a couple of nods to its lines in the shape of the new car. Pretty subtle nods, it has to be said, but that's as it should be.

It seems right to renew acquaintance with the older car first, and it would be impossible to find a more appropriate example: PHP 42G was Jaguar founder Sir William Lyons' personal transport for the first two years of its life. Finished in Sable – a dark brown colour that's now back in fashion and suits the XJ6's understated lines – it's covered fewer than 70,000 miles since new and is part of Jaguar Heritage's collection.

Heading into Paris from Jaguar's launch base in Versailles, you're immediately reminded of just how modern the XJ6 must have seemed in 1968. It was, in fact, a revelation. *Motor* magazine's road test the following year said that the XJ6 'comes closer to perfection than any other car we have tested, regardless of price'. *Autocar* reported that 'the handling was, if anything, better than that of the E-type, and certainly unmatched by anything in the saloon car class'. *Car* named it 1969 Car of the Year.

High praise, indeed, and yet in some ways the XJ6 is actually better now than it was then. Over the past four decades, cars have become generally bigger: safety considerations have fattened them up in every dimension. Windscreen pillars are thick and obstructive. Doors are built like castle walls to resist side impacts. The XJ6 was a very strong model for its time, but it also has a remarkable feeling of delicacy. To use the old cliché, it's a big car that shrinks around you.

You notice that the moment you slip into its leather-faced, armchair-like seats, and grasp the thin-rimmed steering wheel in one hand and the equally delicate T-bar gear selector with the other. Actually, you don't grasp them: you hold them precisely with the tips of your fingers. To drive an XJ6, at least in town, you naturally adopt the posture of someone taking tea with the vicar, except that hard black plastic and chromed steel have

Above
New chases old
into Paris centre:
2010 car is wider
and longer than 1968
model, but weighs
about the same.

replaced the porcelain china. That lightness of touch is apparent everywhere. The 'screen pillars and door frames are slender strips that hardly interrupt the panorama of glass surrounding you. Despite the car's considerable bulk and the confidence conveyed by its fat, doughnut-like tyres, it has beautifully understated detailing of a kind you rarely see nowadays, from its pencil-thin door handles to the tiny, lancet-like rear lights, seemingly inspired by the pointed arches found in cathedrals of the Early English period.

And all that has an effect on you, the driver. Comfortably seated in the XJ6's cosy interior, you feel relaxed and at peace with the outside world. It's a world you feel secure in because you have superb all-round vision through that large glass area, while the twin peaks of the headlamps are reassurance that, yes, you will miss the beaten-up Mégane that's hurtling towards you between unbroken lines of parked cars. Under your foot are maybe 200 horses of smooth six-cylinder power (Jaguar claimed 245bhp for the 4.2, but that was wildly optimistic) and they're harnessed to a Borg Warner automatic transmission that gives smooth if not seamless changes. When that suicidal teenage scooter rider – the original Crazy Frog – cuts across your path, you'll keep your cool because you know you have four-wheel Girling disc brakes awaiting a stab from your right foot.

More than anything, however, it's the XJ6's sublime ride that still impresses after all these years. Jaguar went to enormous trouble with the XJ's suspension, using a mixture of synthetic and rubber mounts to insulate the shell from vibration and incorporating anti-dive geometry to maintain →

'Heading into Paris from Jaguar's launch base in Versailles, you're immediately reminded of just how modern the XJ6 must have seemed in 1968'

stability under braking. The result was a car that cushions its occupants from the rumble-thump of Paris cobbled streets while cornering relatively flatly and gripping strongly. What's more, Jaguar achieved this miracle with Dunlop radial tyres while the likes of Rolls-Royce were still relying on crossplies to maintain ride comfort.

Press the accelerator and the XK engine responds with a muted growl, pushing this big car forward with respectable urge. The antique Borg Warner slush-box blunts the power delivery, extending the manual car's 0-60 time of 8.7sec to 10.4, but that's still far from embarrassing. And while you can punt the XJ6 along remarkably quickly if you have a mind to, why bother? Far better to sit back and bask in the appreciative looks of other motorists. Even the French have the good grace to admire this icon of perfidious Albion.

Flaws? It has a few, but then again, too few to mention. Well, almost. The infamous row of rocker switches across the dashboard looks impressive but is horrible to use at night if you're not totally familiar with the car – or if you drive it only occasionally. And the twist-action, umbrella-handle handbrake under the dash is an unmitigated pain. Taller drivers must lean forward to release it, and half the time you're not sure you've completely pushed it free of its ratchet, leading to obsessive-compulsive checking while on the move.

But these are mere quibbles. The XJ6 is a wonderful, fabulous car. Jaguars were always built down to a price, so they say, but there's little sense of it in this womb of wood and leather. Although it's a perfect grand tourer, whistling along at high speeds and low engine rpm with relatively little wind noise, it's arguably an even better city model. Here the feather-light Adwest Varamatic power steering, so light you can literally operate it with finger and thumb, feels most at home, and the age of the Borg Warner auto 'box is mitigated by lazy, low-rev upshifts. What's most incredible of all is that you could buy an identical car today – less the William Lyons connection, of course – for just a few thousand pounds. A Series One XJ6 is the classic bargain of the moment.

Jaguar's new XJ will set you back rather more, of course. At launch, the 'base' 3-litre V6 diesel version, which actually has a level of luxury →

1968 JAGUAR
XJ6 4.2

ENGINE
4235cc straight-six,
cast-iron block with
alloy head, DOHC, two
SU HD8 carburettors
POWER
245bhp
(claimed)@5500rpm
TORQUE
283lb ft@3750rpm
TRANSMISSION
Three-speed Borg
Warner Type 8
automatic
(four-speed manual/
overdrive optional),
rear-wheel drive
SUSPENSION
Front: independent
by coil and wishbone,
telescopic dampers,
anti-roll bar.
Rear: independent by
paired coil/damper
units with lower
links and driveshafts
serving as upper links,
radius arms
BRAKES
Girling discs all round
WEIGHT
c1600kg (kerbweight
minus fuel)
PERFORMANCE
Top speed 120mph
0-60mph 10.4sec

'Although the XJ6 is a perfect grand tourer, it's arguably an even better city car, where the feather-light Adwest power steering feels most at home'

Above and right
Original XJ is one of
the most beautiful
saloons ever made.
Comfortable interior
and powerful engine
add to its charms.

unimaginable just a few years ago, costs £53,775 and is expected to account for 85% of sales in fuel-price-crippled Britain. The car we drove in Paris was the next model up, the 380bhp petrol V8, which starts at £64,355; top of the range is the twin-supercharged 5-litre SuperSports, with 503bhp. That will cost you £87,455. (Some markets, but not the UK, also get a 464bhp 'blown' XJ.) Long-wheelbase versions of any model add 125mm of extra rear legroom and about three grand to the price.

First things first. What about the styling? It's a talking point, that's for sure. There's nothing retro about New XJ. The front grille is an obvious XJ6 reference, and the roofline was supposedly inspired by the '60s car's, but you'd be hard pressed to tell unless someone pointed it out. The thick D-pillars have been disguised with black inserts, which is an old trick (remember the black-painted sills of 1970s Rover P6s?) but one that works. Trust us, you don't notice them when you see the car in the metal.

New XJ looks sleek, it looks fast and it looks impressive. It doesn't look like a traditional Jaguar, which as we've already explained is rather the point. But it's a handsome machine and one whose styling will easily hold its own among exalted German company, while remaining distinctly different. Again, just as a Jaguar should be.

The rear lights are intriguing. Sloping vertically inwards, to an imaginative mind their slatted lenses could be suggestive of a cat's extended claws. A deliberate reference, or just an attractive myth in the making? Other notable features include a long glass sunroof (though divided by a central stiffener) which increases headroom; it lifts out and slides back when opened.

New XJ's most attractive aspect, however, is the bit you see most of: the interior. It's beautifully finished and the 'piano black' specification of our test car is the one to go for, contrasting with some lightly-applied chrome accents. The high-mounted circular air vents are reminiscent of a Ferrari 599's, but the quality of the detailing is far superior to the Italian car's: these days the Brits actually do this sort of thing much better. (Talking of Italian exotica, we spotted another XJ press car that →

2010 JAGUAR XJ 5.0

ENGINE
5000cc all-alloy V8, fuel injection, normally aspirated, variable inlet manifold and switchable camshaft profile

POWER
380bhp@6500rpm

TORQUE
380lb ft@3500rpm

TRANSMISSION
Six-speed automatic with paddleshift for manual control, Winter/ Comfort/Sport modes, rear-wheel drive

SUSPENSION
Front: independent by coils and unequal length wishbones, active variable dampers. Rear: independent, multilink with air springs, active variable dampers

BRAKES
Ventilated discs all round, electronic braking and stability controls

WEIGHT
1605kg (kerbweight minus fuel)

PERFORMANCE
Top speed (limited) 155mph 0-60mph 5.4sec

'New XJ looks sleek, fast and impressive. It doesn't look like a traditional Jaguar, which is rather the point. But it's handsome and different'

Above and right
New XJ marks new design direction for Jaguar. Interior beats rivals' for style and finish; V8 engine sounds gorgeous

had a very appealing tan leather interior and '30s Bugatti-like flat-dish alloy wheels. With some careful perusing of the options list you could commission a Continental-style Jaguar that would play the Quattroporte at its own game.)

Still in the front seats, techno-geeks will enjoy the 'Dual-View' central touchscreen, which allows driver and front-seat passenger to simultaneously see full-screen images of completely separate displays – sat-nav and a DVD film, for example – because they're viewing them from different angles. And technology is also on display, literally, for the instruments, which are analogue-style 'virtual' dials and needles. You have to wonder whether Jaguar could add some alternative programmes that would allow you to choose your own typefaces and detailing – surely the logical next step in owner customisation, and one that would make a surprising difference to the driving experience.

Ah yes, the driving experience. Two words: bloody good. Our car is 'only' the 380bhp version, but it's plenty quick enough for all but the most psychotic. Most of the time you can bumble along in Comfort mode; turn the rotating gear selector to Sport, press the Dynamic vehicle setting button (at which the virtual dials take on an appropriately red tinge) and you can feel the big Jag tense itself for action. Even the seatbelts tighten slightly.

In this guise, New XJ has crushing acceleration – 5.4 seconds from rest to 60mph and an electronically limited 155mph top speed. That's Ferrari Daytona performance, in our world. Pleasingly, it's accompanied by a subtle but noticeable V8 throb, which emphasises how Jaguar intends New XJ to be as much a driver's car as an executive limo. Opt for the Supersport version and the 0-60mph time comes down to 4.7 seconds, which is all of a tenth of a second behind a DB9... Jaguar hasn't quoted any in-gear acceleration times but it's a pretty safe bet that even a Parisian taxi driver won't make that gap ahead of you.

Sheer speed is all very well, of course, but it means little if it's accompanied by F1 levels of suspension compliance. Inevitably, New XJ will be shod with either 19 or 20in alloy wheels (18in for some markets – India, perhaps?) but the engineers have managed to keep the ride, at least, recognisably Jaguar. Continually variable dampers and similar electronic trickery provide a smooth-ish passage at all times; only at low speeds and the worst of surfaces (those Parisian cobbles again) are you aware of its firmness.

Yet that underlying hint of purpose is in keeping with Jaguar's new focus, and it's backed up by steering that is pleasingly sharp and →

Below
Even in the heart of the French capital, both Jaguars drew appreciative comments from passers-by.

'With some careful perusing of the options list, you could create a Continental-style Jaguar that would play the Maserati Quattroporte at its own game'

precise. But we've saved the biggest revelation until last. Because it's mostly made from aluminium and magnesium alloys, New XJ weighs almost exactly the same as the 1968 original, despite being longer, wider, plusher, faster and, yes, safer. That is quite remarkable. After decades of motor industry institutional obesity, Jaguar is taking a lead in fighting the flab.

That's what makes New XJ just as significant now as the XJ6 was all those years earlier. Weight reduction may not be as sexy as lots of horsepower or trick suspension, but its importance to creating a true driver's car is something that enthusiasts have been harping on about for years. Gordon Murray will be delighted, and so are we. *End*

'New XJ's rear lights are intriguing. To an imaginative mind, their slatted lenses could be suggestive of a cat's extended claws. A deliberate reference, or just an attractive myth in the making?'

Right
C'était un rendezvous… No Ferrari this time, but XJs old and new at the Basilica of Sacré Coeur, Montmartre.

XJ220

THE SUPERCAR THAT CAME IN FROM THE COLD

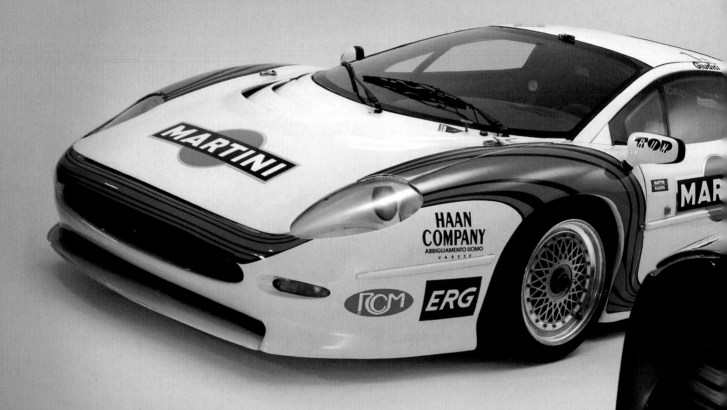

There's still a stigma attached to Jaguar's 200mph supercar, but is that fair? **John Simister**, who was in on the XJ220 from the early days, finds that clever mods and a solid market are transforming its fortunes

PHOTOGRAPHY: JOHN COLLEY

PEOPLE CAN BE VERY CRUEL towards fallen idols. There is glee to be gained from hubris, even when the pre-fall status was not gained by self-aggrandisement.

Hurrah! we all cheered, when Jaguar revealed its XJ220 supercar. Wow! we all exclaimed, as deposits were placed and late-'80s fortunes were poised to be made as the putative fastest car in the world became the must-have investment. Ha! we cried, knowingly, when the car-greed bubble burst just as the production XJ220 was ready to go its first customers. Naughty Jaguar. Of course the buyers would want their deposits back: the XJ220 they were to receive wasn't what they ordered at all.

What they were fobbed-off with, as they saw it, was short of six cylinders, two driven wheels and eight inches of wheelbase. Never mind that it was more powerful than the car they thought they had bought, that it still had the pedigree of a →

'WITH A FRACTION OF THE
BUDGET AND RESOURCES
AVAILABLE TO PORSCHE
AND FERRARI, BRITAIN HAD
PRODUCED THE SUPERCAR
TO TOP ALL SUPERCARS'

Group C-derived engine, that with its shortened chassis it actually looked better. Jaguar, in the eyes of a public always baying for the blood of a self-destructing British motor industry, had fouled up again.

Had it? Decades on from the production XJ220's début, with dust and values settled, air cleared and reality biting, the truth seems a little different. Forget the hype, forget the howling, look at the car. It's a marvel, and the fact that it exists at all is similarly marvellous. It is imperfect, too, but today there are ways of remedying most of the imperfections, as today's guru of all things 220, Don Law, will shortly reveal. Yes, Jaguar's sensationally curvy XJ220 has finally come in from the cold.

IT WAS 1988, in the spring. I was sitting next to Jaguar's then chief engineer, Jim Randle, at dinner in Juan-les-Pins. The marque was launching the XJS convertible, but I knew of something much more interesting than the XJS. I worked at *Motor* magazine at the time, and I'd got wind of something called the Saturday Club.

Motor's photographer had been recording the Club's activities on film but was sworn to secrecy. Other in-office references had been similarly guarded, but this much I knew: something big and supercar-shaped was going to appear at the 1988 British Motor Show. Jim Randle, however, would not be pressed. 'Wait and see,' was all he would say.

'FORGET THE HYPE, FORGET THE HOWLING, LOOK AT THE CAR. IT'S A MARVEL, AND THE FACT THAT IT EXISTS AT ALL IS MARVELLOUS'

THE SATURDAY CLUB was an unpaid, voluntary agglomeration of Jaguar petrolheads: engineers so infused with the desire to see the firm compete with Ferrari's F40 and Porsche's 959 that they would willingly sacrifice their weekends to make it happen. The motor industry supplier base in England's Midlands was behind the Club, too, notably Park Sheet Metal (which made low-volume Jaguar panels) for the aluminium structure and outer skin, and FF Developments for the four-wheel-drive transmission. Everyone wanted beleaguered Jag, then in its second, brief period of independence between BL divorce and Ford acquisition, to show what it could do.

As presented by Jim Randle and his team at Birmingham's NEC in October 1988, the XJ220's Keith Helfet-designed body clothed a 6.2-litre, four-cam, 48-valve version of Jaguar's V12 engine. Related to the unit used in the successful Group C racing Jaguars – the team won Le Mans in 1988, remember – it was calmed down for road use but was still reckoned to make over 500bhp, more than any other car of the time.

Yet the machine it powered was enormous: over seven feet wide and not far off 17 feet long. Even so, great promises were made, with more than 200mph on offer and a computed 0-60mph time of 3.5 seconds. The world loved the XJ220. With a fraction of the budget and engineering resources available to Porsche and Ferrari, Britain had produced the supercar to top all supercars.

And the world's rich just had to have one. Not necessarily to drive, though. This was the time of madness for high-end car values, of people buying motors (even blown-over, filler-filled E-types) for inflated sums and keeping them as investments

ready to sell for even more inflated sums. Cars were the new gold standard. And about 1500 deposits at £50,000 apiece rolled in, even though Jim Randle had initially thought in more modest terms of a few hundred XJ220s, not thousands.

THAT PROTOTYPE never ran. And even if did run, it wouldn't run far because there's no space behind the cabin for a decent-size fuel tank. It sits, majestic but static, in the Jaguar Daimler Heritage Trust's museum. A K-registered production 220, also in silver, shares Heritage space with the prototype, and despite the difference in length it's as faithful a visual progression from concept to real car as any I've ever seen.

So, what happened to the V12 and four-wheel-drive idea? With orders taken, Jaguar and Tom Walkinshaw, architect of Jaguar's then-current racing success under the TWR banner, together formed Jaguarsport based in Bloxham, Oxfordshire. That's where the XJ220 would be made, but not before the TWR brains had worked out how to turn concept into reality.

The structure would be made from aluminium honeycomb, like those of the Group C cars. The engine's length and the fuel-tank problem made the prototype's packaging unworkable, even though there have been other mid-engined supercars with longitudinal V12s; they tend to have tanks in the side sills, not possible in the XJ220 if it was to retain those signature side scoops. And the weight would have been huge, and the brakes wouldn't have coped, and the expense of four-wheel drive would have been prohibitive, and there was no time to develop it properly, and so on.

Interestingly, XJ220 chief development engineer Alistair McQueen, on a recent visit to Don Law Racing, spotted a V6 →

Above
XJ220 isn't as dramatic as, say, the F40 or McLaren F1, but it will probably prove more timeless.

and a V12 alongside each other and, unprompted, commented on the significant size difference: 'Is it any wonder that we went for the V6!'

The Jaguar Group C and IMSA race cars had moved from a giant V12 to a 3.5-litre, twin-turbo V6 to reduce weight and size, and the engine had worked pretty well. The V6 was derived from that used in the Metro 6R4 rally car, and Walkinshaw had bought the rights to its design. For the XJ220 it got another redesign, so all-embracing to suit it for a roadgoing role that hardly any parts were left in common. For example, the oil pump was moved from within the vee to the front of the crankshaft, so it could be got at without dismantling the entire induction system (less of a problem on the race engine because they were forever being dismantled anyway).

Two Garrett T3 turbos force-fed the induction to help create the epic 542bhp at 7200rpm; a large, transverse silencer absorbed some of the exhaust noise and precluded a rear boot (cue one of Don Law's upgrades). The camshaft drives involved straight-cut gears at the bottom, cambelts at the top. And – a legacy from the block's origins as effectively three-quarters of a Cosworth DFV – the cylinder banks were still at 90 degrees to each other, great for free breathing but death to refinement.

A V6 should have a 60-degree vee angle to be properly

Below
Cabin is well-fitted with neat extra dials in the driver's door; V6 engine was derived from the 6R4 rally car.

smooth with even firing intervals, or else the crankpins of opposite cylinders should be offset by the amount by which the vee-angle departs from the 60-degree ideal. Not in the XJ220, though; the three crank throws were paired, with no offset (it weakens the crankshaft), and set 120 degrees apart from each other. This was not going to be a smooth engine; goodbye to one of a V12's main attractions.

Shoreham-based consultancy Ricardo, one of Britain's great engineering success stories, designed and built the five-speed transaxle. The all-round double-wishbone suspension remained from the prototype, complete with aerofoil-section rear lower arms because they were in the airstream of the underside's downforce-creating ducts. The brakes were a bit small because the wheels were similarly so, as part of the design (cue another Law enhancement, although TWR itself spotted the problem early on). The XJ220 was ready to roll in 1991, yours for £415,544. That the McLaren F1 was poised to spoil the Jaguar's fastest-car claim was just unfortunate, but then the F1 did cost half as much again.

TROUBLE. JAGUAR had managed to slim down the order bank to a manageable 350, hoping in the process to have weeded out the speculators, but even some of these 'enthusiasts'

'BUT IS THE XJ220 ACTUALLY ANY GOOD AS
A SUPERCAR? AT SPEED, YES. AROUND CORNERS,
GUARDEDLY YES, AS LONG AS YOU'RE
CIRCUMSPECT IN THE WET. THE ACID TEST
IS HOW IT COPES WITH TRAFFIC JAMS...'

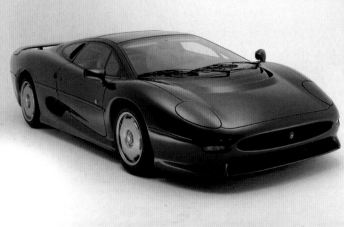

'WAKE THOSE TURBOS AND BY GOD IT'S QUICK... WELCOME TO THE REAL WORLD, XJ220'

decided they wanted their deposits back when they saw what had happened to the XJ220. (And to the value, post-crash, of their early-'90s investment portfolio. Cue bleeding hearts.)

Ford, new owner of Jaguar, didn't want bad publicity and was also keen to keep the XJ220 out of the US, where there would be no service back-up for what would be a high-maintenance car. So a tricky situation was about to develop, even though Tom Walkinshaw had already told the deposit-placers that the XJ220 wouldn't have worked in its original form. For the would-be buyers, though, including some high-profile names in the entertainment world, the specification change seemed an excellent excuse to pull out of the deal and not worry about the fact that £415,544 was not, after all, going to double itself in a matter of months.

It went to court, and the court saw through the crocodile tears. Jaguar was within its rights to change the specifications, and any defaulter should pay the marque £100,000 on top of the deposit to get out of the deal.

It was a decent result for Jaguar; some people did pay not to own the XJ220, leaving 150 cars unsold and in storage, some ended up paying the full price to become owners. And some, coming fresh to the party having not paid a deposit, gained a

Above
This Martini-liveried car was built to Group N specification – much less radical than the XJ220Cs that were raced at Le Mans, for example.

bargain by buying the rejected XJ220s for around £200,000 each. What a steal…

Jaguar didn't make as much money as it had hoped after ending production at 288 vehicles, especially as some of those unsold cars remained so until the late-1990s, but neither was the XJ220 a disaster. The final ten examples did end up in the US despite the firm's wishes, having been sold to a New York dealer by an Essex Jaguar agent, but by then Jaguarsport was history and the parent company was losing interest fast.

ENTER DON LAW. The Staffordshire race-prep and Jaguar expert, whose son Justin is a rapid driver of historic Jaguar race cars, has become the XJ220's stepfather. Among other things, he has built on the modifications that created the XJ220S, a TWR-developed machine of which only five examples were ever actually built. They were painted and trimmed by XK Engineering, in these pages for their repaint of Jaguar's XJ13, but were never completed to the intended mechanical spec.

TWR created them from 220s used in the Fast Masters Championship, run in the US – that forbidden market – in 1993. The veteran racers crashed the Jaguars frequently, so they needed rebuilds anyway. Various mods were specified to add an extra 100bhp and 19mph to the already adequate →

'WHEN CUSTOMERS STARTED
ASKING FOR MODIFICATIONS
– BRAKES, DRIVING POSITION,
THE WAY THE DOORS OPENED
– JAGUAR COULDN'T DO THAT.
SO IT SAID "GO TO DON"'

Above
Road car and Group N
racer are very similar
in specification, both carrying
aluminium panels on a
honeycomb aluminium structure.

211mph top speed. The idea was to convert the cars as they were sold but none went to retail, and the conversion never went further than bodywork changes. The aluminium panels were, doors excepted, replaced by carbonfibre. A giant rear wing precluded an opening bootlid, so the entire tail section was fixed (the Le Mans examples had removable nose and tail sections, though). Three-piece BBS wheels were fitted to aid brake cooling.

The XJ220S is a mad car – Law looks after the original, bright yellow TWR demonstrator – but it does address some of the standard model's failings. Most serious of those is the braking: 'John Nielsen [who raced the Group C Jaguars] did a lap of the Nürburgring Nordschleife in a production car and the tyres and brakes were wrecked,' says Don, although he goes on to explain that it was in the name of setting a lap record (sub-7.5 minutes).

Don Law Racing is a temple to all things XJ220. There's a dark green left-hooker with some of the upgrades, a silver car with its engine out, another silver one that's an XJ220S. In a neighbouring workshop are motors undergoing rebuilds, in another a phalanx of XJ220s including a couple of race cars built from two of the ten pre-production machines. Number seven has carbonfibre panels and was once raced in the Italian GT championship, as did number nine which still wears its Martini colours.

'We look after seven of the pre-production cars,' says Don, proudly. 'The first two were nothing like a 220 and had scissor

doors. The third was the first one to look like a 220.' And what's this? It's a Ford Transit.

Don explains. 'We went to TWR to buy the last engine and some spares. "Is there anything else?" we asked. "Only the secondhand engine in a van," they said. I thought they meant an engine on a pallet that happened to be in the back of a van, but it's a complete XJ220 under the Transit shell.

'It was an XJ220 mule. They were going to scrap it when TWR was liquidated but I rescued it. It looks just like a twin-wheel Transit apart from the XJ220 wheels, and it's road registered.'

The Transit XJ220 once did 179mph around the Millbrook test track's bowl in Bedfordshire, and it made an appearance at the Festival of Speed in the livery of Goodwood's usual Transit fleet.

A CARMAKER is supposed to keep a parts and service back-up alive for its cars for at least ten years after production ends. For Jaguar, with all its big-company systems, doing this for the XJ220 was going to be a headache. The XJ220 had already, in 1993, had a Le Mans outing; five years later Don Law ran that Martini-liveried race car in the AMOC Intermarque championship, driven with great success by Win Percy. Helped by this experience, he found himself looking after ever more road machines.

'Jaguar had a ramp for the XJ220,' Don says, 'but it wanted to pass responsibility on. It couldn't do this officially until the ten years was up, but when customers started asking for modifications – brakes, driving position, the way the doors opened – Jaguar couldn't do that. So it said, "Go to Don."'

It's a strange position. Don Law Racing isn't an official marque agent so Jaguar can't officially recommend Don's operation. But his company can supply parts that Jag cannot, including enough body panels to satisfy XJ220 ownership for years to come, and it carries out not just upgrades but running modifications, learned over years of XJ220 maintenance, to ensure reliability.

Currently there are about 100 cars on Don's books, including models from mainland Europe and beyond which are sent to him for work. The two-year service (£4456 plus VAT) is vital. It includes replacing the twin-plate clutch, which copes badly with low-speed manoeuvring and has been known to fly apart if suddenly abused on a little-used car. Don had to get a gearbox casing re-cast to fix the aftermath of one such episode.

The service's other crucial component is replacing the cambelts and checking the valve timing, which will usually have moved thanks to strange vibratory forces between the pulleys and the camshafts, locked together only by being a taper fit. Don does a mod to prevent this, without which valve-to-piston contact is a permanent worry. This means removing the engine, but that's easy because it sits on a subframe which drops out underneath.

Then there is the big one every six years, which involves replacing the fuel tank for £3500 plus VAT (running an XJ220 was never going to be cheap even if, in relative terms, the £130,000 you'll now pay for a good, regularly used one is surprising value). This is foam-filled, and contains a collector pot plus two lift pumps →

'AND THE UPGRADES? BETTER BRAKE SERVOS, BETTER DISCS AND PADS, MODIFIED CALIPERS, AN ALTERNATIVE MASTER CYLINDER AND A DUCTING SYSTEM. THEN THERE ARE CHANGES TO THE DRIVING SEAT AND TO THE DOOR HINGES'

Top, left and right
XJ220C racer
used carbonfibre
body panels; 1988
prototype now at
Browns Lane museum.

Above
Race car interior carries original digital display; tweaked V6 produces around 620bhp.

and internal filters, the whole assembly fed into the XJ220's structure via holes. Old tanks can leak into the honeycomb structure, damaging the epoxy, so replacement is important.

Oh, and should you come across an XJ220 which has done nothing more than delivery mileage and has lain dormant ever since, don't get too excited. It will need £20,000-worth of recommissioning before you can use it, including all the hydraulics, all the valve springs, many of the gaskets and the full belts/clutch/tank treatment. Tyres, too.

And the upgrades? Better brake servos (there are two of them), better discs and pads (technology has moved on since 1991, and the brakes were under-specified then), modified calipers, an alternative master cylinder and a ducting system. Going for the fully ducted XJ220S type of system is expensive, though, and you'd have to lose those lovely 17in front, 18in rear wheels. Then there are changes to the driving seat so tall motorists can get their legs in and not have their eyes staring at the header rail, and to the hinges so the doors can open wider (access as standard is highly awkward).

That's the practical stuff. Don Law can also reproduce the planned 220S niceties, with changes to the engine management, the valves and the pistons, plus the straight-through exhaust system which adds power and drowns out the engine's bag-of-bolts clatter at low speed (it's derived from a race motor, remember). Don offers recalibrated dampers and new springs to sharpen the handling and cure the pitching, too, and even a mod to enable a suitcase to be stashed in the boot.

FINE. BUT IN THE end, is the XJ220 actually any good as a supercar? At speed, yes. Around corners, guardedly yes, as long as you're circumspect in the wet. The acid test of usability, though, is how it copes with traffic jams and traffic calming, rigours to try any supercar's patience.

I drove the JDHT's example from the Houses of Parliament to Buckingham Palace as part of the Queen's 80th Birthday celebrations, crawling sometimes at just 10mph behind a police escort. Slightly acrid clutch aside, it was as good as gold, with a surprisingly docile engine for all its gnashing and uneven 90-degree thrum. Earlier that day, though, the Embankment was near-deserted and, well, I just had to, didn't I? Wake those turbos and by God, it's quick…

Welcome to the real world, XJ220. **End**

THANKS TO Don Law, +44 (0)1782 413875, www.donlawracing.com.

JAGUAR XJ220

ENGINE
3498cc, 90-degree V6, aluminium block and heads, four overhead cams driven by gears and belts, four valves per cylinder, two turbochargers
POWER
542bhp@7200rpm
TORQUE
475lb ft@4500rpm
TRANSMISSION
Five-speed manual, viscous limited-slip differential, rear-wheel drive
SUSPENSION
Front and rear: double wishbones, coil springs, anti-roll bar, telescopic dampers
BRAKES
AP Racing ventilated and cross-drilled discs all round, two servos
PERFORMANCE
Top speed 211mph
0-60mph 3.6sec
VALUE
£100,000-150,000

TO JAGUAR ENTHUSIASTS, the words 'Browns Lane' and 'MIRA' are shorthand for two icons that are inextricably linked with the post-war history of the marque. From this combination, three great sports cars emerged – the XK120, the E-type and, more recently, the XK8. At time of writing, after 50 years of producing the most famous Jaguars, Browns Lane is about to cease car production but MIRA, where every Jag has been tested, continues to play a valuable role.

The history of the Motor Industry Research Association (MIRA) goes back to 1946, and Jaguar moved to Browns Lane over a period straddling 1951/'52. Previously the marque had a rather more modest factory at Swallow Road in the Holbrook district of Coventry in the Midlands, to which it had moved when it made the brave but crucial trek south from Blackpool, Lancashire, where everything had begun, in 1928.

Until the MIRA facility in Warwickshire became available, testing had been a much more haphazard business, mainly involving the use of local roads and the odd Continental foray – the XK120's first test outside factory grounds was a run up the nearby Keresley Road. The rapidly developing facilities at MIRA allowed Jaguar to raise its game considerably, and the two would work in parallel to create the exciting →

TESTING
TIMES

As Jaguar production came to an end in Coventry, *Octane*
took three generations on a nostalgic trip from
Browns Lane to the MIRA test facility

WORDS: PHILIP PORTER   PHOTOGRAPHY: MATTHEW HOWELL // ARCHIVE PHOTOS: MIRA

'Norman Dewis, Jaguar's chief tester from 1952 until 1976, was one of a number of engineers who decided what facilities were needed at MIRA'

Above and right
Norman Dewis in front of XJ13, another car he tested at MIRA; Browns Lane workers reminisce about E-type.

sports cars, the volume small saloons, the prestigious large saloons and even the C- and D-type racers. All could be labelled: 'Developed at MIRA, built at Browns Lane.'

Jaguar is most famous for its sports cars. The sales of saloon cars were, of course, considerably greater and crucial to the prosperity and evolution of the company, but it was these sports cars that added the excitement, the zest, to the whole range and to the Jaguar name. Today we would call it 'the halo effect', and it is precisely what the marque lacks at present.

The three generations of sports cars represented on our pilgrimage from Browns Lane to MIRA are very different indeed. If you were searching for just one word to quickly sum up the differences, it would probably be 'weight': as Jaguar's sports cars evolved, they successively felt lighter and lighter to drive.

As is well-known, the XK120 happened almost by accident. Hastily created to stir up some publicity and steal a few headlines, and as a means of trying out the seriously exciting new twin-overhead-cam engine on long-suffering enthusiast customers, it just blew everybody's socks off. Demand was overwhelming. Jaguar had a problem because it was already outgrowing its

factory and, when the engine was launched in the Mark VII saloon, the pressure on space was to be intense.

The XK120 was without a doubt the pre-eminent sports car of its day and, while it now feels quite a heavy machine, it still has highly respectable performance. It is a model that demands driver involvement if it is to driven quickly, and, to owners, that's what gives it character. The steering is a little heavy and lacking in feel. The brakes, unless uprated, are pretty feeble and the gearbox is slow. These judgements, however, are being made more than 50 years after the car burst upon the dour pre-war motoring scene. At the time, the XK120 was a revelation.

What makes this model so good today? Probably most outstanding is its reliability,

coupled with excellent performance; and, of course, the classic good looks that captivated people so in the 1950s and still do in this more cynical age. The 120 is an old sports car that can be used. It can potter down to the shops or be driven thousands of miles on rallies. That brilliant engine is still the heart of a landmark sports car.

The same is true of that star of the '60s, the sensational E-type. Again, the model set new standards when launched in 1961. Again, one can, in hindsight, criticise the brakes and the gearbox on the original examples, but they did not take the shine off the exceptional package that was clothed, once again, in a body of pure, unadulterated, sexy beauty.

The difference is that over a decade Jaguar's standards had jumped and the steering was now superb, the ride and roadholding positively sophisticated and the performance leagues ahead of anything but a few ludicrously expensive esoterics. For that reason, the E-type also makes a very practical classic car because, like its forebear, the 'E' can be used for tootling or for rapid long-distance motoring in style.

Climbing out of a 120 and into an E-type you would think there was more than a decade between them. Their characters are ➔

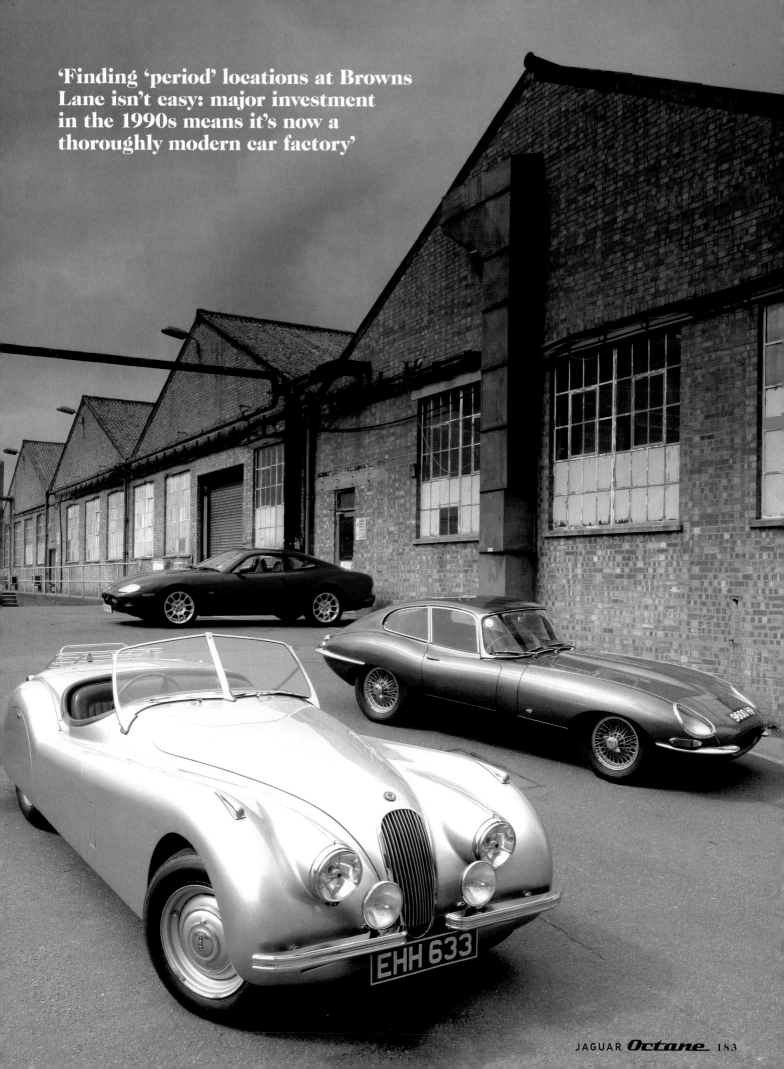

'Finding 'period' locations at Browns Lane isn't easy: major investment in the 1990s means it's now a thoroughly modern car factory'

'Before the war all Coventry's roads were made of cobble stones, and after the Blitz they were shipped to MIRA and used for the Belgian pavé'

Left and facing page
Crash-testing an E-type; historic raised banking is still in daily use.

Above and right
Building the banking used for the action shots in this feature; MIRA opening was, appropriately, by a Jaguar MkVII saloon.

totally different, which is how it should be. Both have their own flavour. The E-type feels much more modern, much lighter, with livelier performance, precise steering, greater roadholding powers and just more sophistication all round.

Both XK120 and E-type were at the pinnacle of sports design in their respective eras, but what about the more modern XK8? We are jumping two generations here, so it's not surprising that the XK8 is a very different animal. It is not pure sports car; it is a grand tourer. For a start, it has automatic transmission, it is almost silent, it is supremely comfortable and it is very quick indeed. The convertible version even has a power-operated hood.

Times have moved on. Customers' requirements and aspirations are very different from what they were 50 years ago, and the 21st century XKs have done a fine job for Jaguar. They are also undoubtedly classics of the future. As their predecessors did in their time, they will no doubt plummet in value when their replacement is launched, and will endure a period in the doldrums before better examples start to be sought and revered. Perhaps now is the time to start hunting out exceptional XK8s and XKRs.

Of the cars we drove on our sentimental journey from Browns Lane to MIRA, the

XK120 was bought by David Nursey more than 30 years ago. It was a bargain at £600, as it was actually worth nearer £800 at the time… David is often Clerk of the Course at Shelsley Walsh, and the car always looks stunning, parked in an old hay barn right by the start-line at meetings.

The E-type was bought by me in 1977. It is the oldest in existence and was used for publicity, including the infamous 150mph road test in *Autocar*, and a mad dash to Geneva for the press launch. In 2000 the car, which had become pretty sad and been off the road for 25 years, was transformed by an amazingly dedicated conservation restoration by Classic Motor Cars of Bridgnorth. The model was handbuilt in 1960 and originally had a blueprinted engine to achieve the magic 150mph top speed: a level of performance that has been faithfully recreated, so it feels pretty lively on the road. It still retains that wonderful E-type combination of relative sophistication and superb balance.

The 1997 XK8 was provided by Coventry-based Jaguar specialist Chris Forbes of CF Motors. To say the XK8 is light years ahead of the classic sports cars is to be unfair to the older models. When the XK8s and XKRs were launched, they put Jaguar back at the top of its niche: a niche holding relatively few competitors, of which

the Mercedes SL was the most obvious. Early XK8s are now relatively affordable but, as Chris explains, you have to be very careful about what you're buying.

Find a good one and they are very rewarding models, offering terrific value for money. Like most things in life, the more you pay, the better the car. Generally you should get the youngest example you can afford, because earlier examples suffered from engine problems with the piston bores, though a number have had replacement motors or major rectification work. Parts are expensive, but a good specialist – such as Chris – will know which aftermarket spares made for the higher-quantity saloons can be used on the XKs. There are not many of them, mind you.

Browns Lane was the obvious place for our three classics to rendezvous, although finding a location that looked 'period' to suit the older cars isn't as easy as it was a few years ago. Major investment in the 1990s and a corporate update since the Ford takeover means that Browns Lane today is a thoroughly modern car factory, right down to the obligatory heritage centre that any prestige marque worth its salt now boasts.

But the Browns Lane story started when the XK120 was in its infancy, and company founder William Lyons had to go through

some pretty tortuous negotiations to move his business up another gear. After WW2 had ended, Britain needed to rebuild its economy and earn crucial foreign currency. The emphasis was totally on export business, and sheet steel was allocated to companies on the basis that they would export virtually all their production. Jaguar led that overseas charge and set a brilliant example with its success, particularly in America.

The Mark V and XK120 models were launched in 1948. Perhaps helped by some reflected glory from the sporty 120, the more practical Mark V enjoyed full order books, and the completely new Mark VII saloon was also being developed.

This healthy situation meant increased production and that translated into a need for an expanded facility – not easy at Swallow Road. On one side the site was bordered by the Dunlop factory, on the other by open fields. Lyons applied for planning permission to expand the site by 50% and was turned down.

It seems that the authorities, which were still exerting a wartime level of control over trade and industry, wanted Dunlop to expand on its existing site and Jaguar to sell the firm its own factory. So Lyons began a rather tortuous dialogue with various officials at the Ministry of Supply about acquiring a wartime 'shadow' factory that had been occupied

> **'The XK120 and E-type were at the pinnacle of sports design in their eras, but the XK8 is not a pure sports car; it is a grand tourer'**

by Daimler during hostilities. It was situated at Browns Lane, on the outskirts of Coventry in an area called Allesley.

Over the next months Lyons would show himself to be a shrewd and tough negotiator. Initially, the Ministry wanted an annual rent of £75,000. Lyons was not impressed and looked at other sites in Scotland, Wales and Northern Ireland. But the export effort desperately needed Jaguar and, by shrewd bargaining and some brinkmanship, Lyons finally agreed a rent of £30,000 per annum for the first five years and the sale of his current factory to Dunlop for £450,000.

So Lyons had a deal that brought two massive benefits to his marque. He now had a one million square foot factory (nearly twice the size of Foleshill and one of the largest in Coventry) and some useful capital to invest in new models, such as the forthcoming small saloon range. A few →

'The facilities at MIRA allowed Jaguar to raise its game considerably, and the two worked in parallel to create the sports cars, saloons and even the racers'

Above
Long bonnets are still a feature, but Jaguar's sports cars have become much more sybaritic to meet the expectations of today's buyers.

years later, long after the move to Browns Lane, he re-opened negotiations with the Ministry of Supply and finally bought the site outright for £1.25m in early 1959.

At about the time that Jaguar was moving shop from Swallow Road to Browns Lane, a wartime airfield at Lindley, near Nuneaton, Warkwickshire, was being transformed into the MIRA research and testing facility. In the early 1950s it had already been used unofficially for testing for a while, as the perennially young Norman Dewis – Jaguar's chief tester from 1952 until 1976, who was then with Lea Francis – explains. 'We used to go up Higham Lane and there was a big steel gate which we could open sufficiently to get a car through. We would then use the old runways for basic test work. It was just a disused aerodrome with grass growing on it.

'The MIRA was then based at Brentford in London, but it decided it wanted to build up its facilities and become more connected with the motor industry in the Midlands. It chose Lindley as being a good central point, and "Ossie" Dolby was put in charge of the track. He made his office up

in the old control tower.' Dewis was one of a group of test engineers who formed a committee to decide what facilities were ideally needed for vehicle development.

'One of the first things created was the Belgian pavé, for testing for structural weaknesses. Dolby went to Belgium and measured the size of the cobbles and the depth of the gaps between them. The pavé was then constructed exactly as it was in Belgium! Before the war, all Coventry's roads were made of cobble stones, and after the Blitz the city didn't know what to do with them, so they were shipped to Lindley and used for the Belgian pavé.'

One of the other major facilities was the triangular high-speed track with seriously banked corners. Lyons played a hand in this important development. He was a member of the National Advisory Council (NAC), and the minutes of a meeting held in October 1951 report that: 'Mr Lyons urged that since the need for the high-speed track was generally accepted, the sooner it came into operation the better.' When completed, this high-speed circuit was to be used by most of the manufacturers, day in, day out. Towards the end of 1960,

one of the cars Dewis was driving most days to develop the E-type was 9600 HP. The XK8 was also extensively tested at MIRA and I recall, when I was writing a book about the model, being taken by one of the testers over some unbelievably vicious curbs that would be mounted at 40mph – rough treatment, but all in the interests of preparing vehicles for whatever a customer might throw at them.

Today MIRA is continuing the work it pioneered back in the early 1950s, when the 'export or die' dictum meant that British cars had to be capable of dealing with the worst kinds of roads found in the world's remotest areas.

And Browns Lane will remain Jaguar's spiritual home, even though production of cars is being moved to Birmingham. They can take the cars out of Coventry, but they will never take Coventry out of the cars. At least, that's what Jaguar enthusiasts hope.

THANKS TO David Nursey for the use of the XK120 and Chris Forbes for the XK8; Ken McConomy at Jaguar; and Neil Bradley and Richard Adams at MIRA.

Jaguar wins the world's two toughest races: Daytona and Le Mans.

A DAY LIKE NO OTHER

Some thought the glory days of Peter
Whitehead's 1951 win for Jaguar, and the four
victories that followed, would never be repeated.
But in 1988 the marque proved them wrong...

WORDS: DAVID LILLYWHITE

WERE YOU THERE IN 1988 when Jaguar returned to the Le Mans winners' podium, 31 years after the company's last win there? If you were, then there's no need to describe the ecstatic reaction of the crowd, the waving of the flags, the general air of relief that a British team really could deliver at La Sarthe once more.

Le Mans has always been popular with the British, but by the mid-1980s attendance was falling and major manufacturers seemed to have lost interest. Porsche had been left to dominate but, in the background, Jaguar had been building up to the event for several years in a bid to increase its worldwide credibility. Curiously, it had all started in America when Bob Tullius, of Group 44 Racing, decided to build his fifth competition Jaguar. This new Group 44 car, to be named the XJR-5, would be a far cry from XJRs one to four – an E-type, followed by three XJ-S racers, all with V12 engines.

Group 44's XJR-5 also used a V12, but was a pure race car, rather than being based on a road machine. Although on the heavy side, two XJR-5s competed at Le Mans in 1984 and 1985. In 1984 both retired at around the 14-hour point. Yet in 1985, although one XJR-5 retired after nine hours, the other survived to finish 13th. Suddenly the motoring press and the British public began to take more interest in Le Mans again.

Group 44's efforts had been supported by Jaguar Cars

Above
Group 44's Bob Tullius.

Top left
The Group 44 team
(here with an XJR-7
in 1987) was always
immaculate in white.

Top right
1990 Le Mans-winning
XJR-12 was evolved
from the '88 Jaguars.

North America. But in the UK, Jaguar Cars engaged Tom Walkinshaw's TWR to oversee its Group C racing efforts. TWR had achieved great success with Rover, Ford, Mazda and BMW, before getting involved with Jaguar in 1982 (with a successful adaptation of the XJ-S for the European Touring Car Championship).

There was immediate rivalry between the two Jaguar-supported siblings; to make matters worse, Walkinshaw commandeered the XJR moniker for TWR's new carbon-fibre monocoque, V12-powered racer, named the XJR-6. In 1985, just a few months after Group 44's 13th place at Le Mans, TWR entered the XJR-6 into its first race. It wore Silk Cut purple and white livery in place of traditional British Racing Green.

The TWR XJR-6's first full season, 1986, was a success on the whole, yet not at Le Mans. Three cars were entered: one ran out of fuel, one retired with a broken driveshaft and the last was damaged when a tyre blew. Porsche won the race once again.

Bob Tullius was still fighting, too. TWR might have used his XJR tag, but it didn't mean that Group 44 couldn't use it too. Jumping in ahead of TWR, Tullius named his next car the XJR-7, and raced it 28 times between 1985 and 1988, although never at Le Mans. However, it wasn't long before he lost Jaguar's backing.

Group 44 had planned an XJR-8 (it was built and has

'THE LEADING XJR-9 REGULARLY SWAPPED THE LEAD WITH THE THREE
FACTORY PORSCHES – THE LEAD WAS NEVER MORE THAN A LAP'

appeared occasionally since). Instead, Walkinshaw's next car was named the XJR-8, an evolution of the XJR-6. Three were taken to Le Mans by TWR, which prompted *Autocar* to preview the event with the headline 'Jaguar's three-car team looks set to triumph at Le Mans on Sunday'.

So it was that the 1987 Le Mans crowd was swelled by thousands of British, many visiting the circuit for the first time. It looked like the race would be a straight battle between the Silk Cut XJR-6 Jaguars and the Rothmans Porsche 962Cs, but thanks to gearbox breakage, an accident caused by a blown tyre and valve spring failure, all three Jaguars retired. Porsche won again.

In 1988 the Jaguar/TWR returned, backed by a massive British crowd. Mercedes was entered for the race yet withdrew just before the start after a 220mph tyre blow-out on the Mulsanne straight in practice left the team feeling less than confident in its equipment.

Porsche was looking for its eighth win but TWR was not going to make things easy for its German competitor. It took five cars, all XJR-9s (updated versions of the XJR-8), which travelled in two articulated transporters, accompanied by three truckloads of spares, 14 drivers, 75 full-time staff, 21 volunteers, with a plane on hand to fly in spares from TWR's Oxfordshire base.

There were a further 80 staff for catering, another plane to ferry around VIP guests and a dedicated Dunlop tyre

Above
Tom Walkinshaw of TWR took over where Group 44 had been forced to leave off.

Top
Le Mans 1988 and three XJR-9s take Le Mans by storm, finishing first, fourth and 16th.

engineer with 2500 tyres! When the 1988 race began, the cars set off at unusually high speeds, eventually breaking speed and distance records for Le Mans. The leading XJR-9 regularly swapped the lead with the three factory Porsches, in a race so close that the lead was never more than a lap. By the end of the race, all 3313 miles of it, the XJR-9 of Jan Lammers, Johnny Dumfries and Andy Wallace won by just two minutes and 36 seconds, with Porsche second and third and another XJR-9 in fourth. The last of the three surviving XJR-9s was 16th overall.

The crowd went mad. This was the first Jaguar Le Mans victory since Ron Flockhart and Ivor Bueb's famous 1957 victory in a D-type. On a worldwide scale, the good feeling and publicity which were generated by the win confirmed to other manufacturers that the Le Mans 24 Hours was still a race worth working for.

What happened next? Well, for 1989 the XJR-9s reappeared at Le Mans, but managed only a fourth and an eighth position. For short-circuit racing, Jaguar switched to new cars, powered by turbocharged V6s (starting with the XJR-10) but the V12 was developed into the XJR-12, specifically for endurance racing.

The policy paid off, and the XJR-12 took first and second places at the 1990 Le Mans, and second and third in 1991. Jag returned only once more to La Sarthe, this time competing in the GT class (and winning) with three XJ220Cs. **End**

BIG CAT DIARY

Could there be a tougher first test for the 542bhp Jaguar XKR-S
than to chase the Mille Miglia for three days and 1000 hard-
driven miles? **Henry Catchpole** finds out how it fares

PICTURES DAVID SHEPHERD, SAM RILEY, HENRY CATCHPOLE & JAGUAR

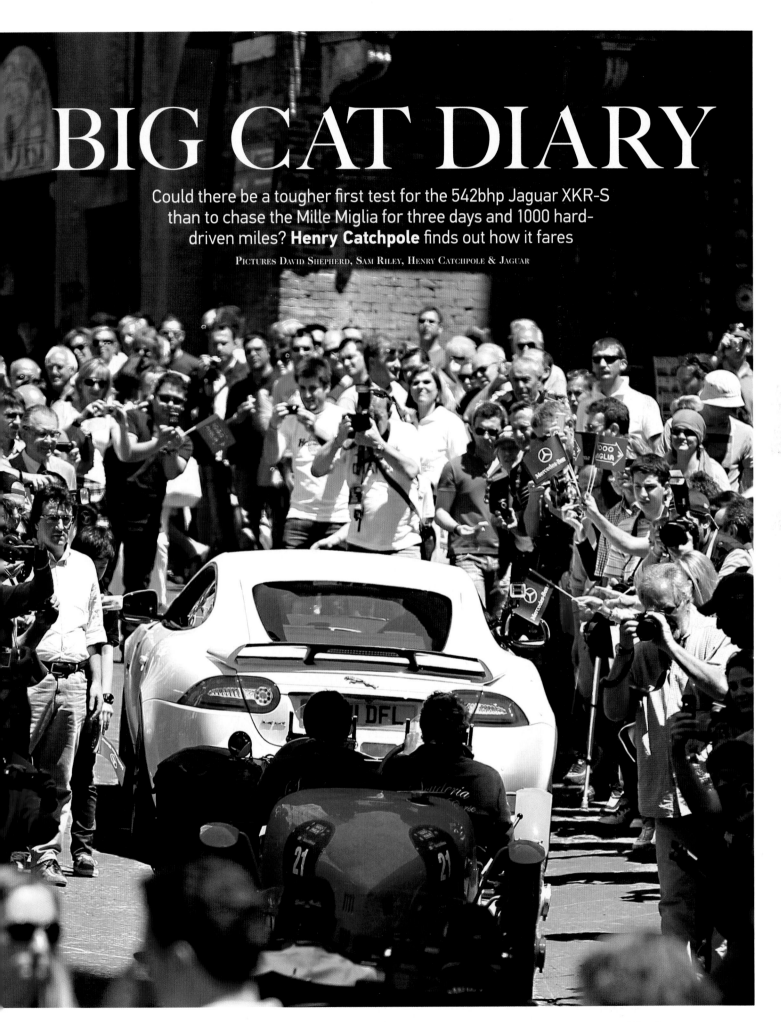

THREE ABREAST. About £3m-worth of classic cars has just gone through a red traffic light side by side by side, and then tried to jostle and out-brake each other into a single carriageway. What is more, holding my breath, I followed them through… Welcome to the three days of utter insanity that is the Mille Miglia.

The famous thousand-mile race round Italy ran for the first time in 1927 and ended in 1957 after Alfonso de Portago's fateful 150mph puncture and crash into a crowd. Twenty years later the modern event rose from the ashes, no longer a race but instead a regularity rally for cars that could have competed in the original. It still follows a route from Brescia through Verona, down over the mountains of L'Aquila to Rome and then back up through Tuscany and across the plains of the Emilia Romagna to Brescia again. Our aim for the next three days is to follow said route and the cars competing in the 2011 Mille Miglia. And to do so we'll be using a brand new Jaguar XKR-S, which is nice.

When I saw the first photos I wasn't sure about the big wing and gilled snout of the R-S, but sitting in the sun in a scruffy hotel car park on the outskirts of Brescia, it looks absolutely ace. Even parked next to a C-type. This is a relief, because if you are about to try to mix it with over 300 of the most glorious cars ever produced then you want something that looks a bit special. I also have a sneaking suspicion that we'll need to do a certain amount of blagging over the next few days and it's easier to outflank people in high-vis if they're drooling.

It's Thursday morning and we're about to go and watch the ceremonial sealing of the cars (where a metal cord with a lead seal bearing the Mille Miglia logo is attached to each competing vehicle) in the Piazza della Loggia in the centre of Brescia. Our passport round the Mille Miglia is a big green circular 'press' sticker on the bonnet of the Jaguar. We're hoping that this will open doors and let us get close to the action, but as I have no previous experience of the MM it's all a bit unknown. Nearing the centre of the city, the

sticker seems to be doing the trick though, as blue-shirted policemen wave us past barriers and up cordoned streets. Eventually we enter a corridor of spectators and join a long queue of aero screens, chrome bumpers, cycle wings and body shapes penned with single-minded artistry. I look in the mirror and see Mika Häkkinen pull up behind in an ex-works Fangio Mercedes 300 SLR. Surreal – and it won't be the last we will see of him…

Many spectators – both British and Italian – clock what is actually the first right-hand-drive XKR-S fresh off the production line. 'How much…?' always gets an impressed coo when I reply 542bhp, or 501lb ft, or £97,000.

Eventually we find the limits of our sticker and get siphoned off into a side-street before the piazza, so I suggest to colleague, co-driver and film-maker Sam Riley that we go and have a look at the start/finish ramp, which is a few streets away on the wide and imposing Viale Venezia. Naturally the huge stage is behind barriers and there is security everywhere. However, I am not a complete beginner at this sort of caper, and a speculative left turn sneaks us and the Jag behind the railings and onto the ramp for a few seconds before I have to deal with heavy-set security using only a puzzled look and my best Valentino Rossi accent to say, 'errr, Inglese?'

The first cars don't set off until the evening, and the crews all gather in the grounds of an old convent until the allotted hour. It's here that the breathtaking quality of the cars taking part becomes clear. Häkkinen's here again, a mechanic →

'If you're mixing it with over 300 of the most glorious cars ever produced, you want something that looks a bit special'

'It feels crazy haring through a city at over twice the normal speed limit. It's like *Gran Turismo* brought to life'

revving the SLR's 3-litre in-line eight-cylinder to warm it up. Standing near the Silver Arrow as the mechanic stabs the throttle at metronomic second intervals, my ears throb and I can feel every hot gust from the side-exit exhausts. My particular favourite is a Ferrari 500 Mondial in French racing blue that seems to have remained cosmetically untouched since it finished its last race in the '50s. Not only is it a beautiful shape, but it also possesses a patina that oozes history – like a dimple in a smile, I even love the dent in the back.

After a while, we drive up towards the centre of Brescia again and manage to join the crowds lining the sides of the road not far from the start. Our plan is to just drive onto the route behind a police convoy and then try to hang on in the hope that they don't object. We wait and watch in the XKR-S, then when a couple of Jags come hurtling past with a police motorbike, we give chase.

They're already heading round the next corner as we pull out, but we manage to keep the flashing blue light in view and the corridor of cheering people makes it fairly obvious where to go. It feels crazy and initially slightly uncomfortable haring through a city at over twice the normal speed limit. It's like *Gran Turismo* brought to life. As we near a junction, we've just managed to reel in and tag onto the tail of the fast-moving convoy, so policemen and flag-waving officials rush us through whilst holding up the evening traffic.

Roundabouts litter the way east out of Brescia, but following the bobbing rump of an XK120 we only touch the brakes or change down just enough to jink right-left-right on the straightest line possible through each one. And still there are crowds of people; I had expected them near the start, but as the race heads into the countryside and the gathering gloaming, they are still there, the elderly sitting in chairs outside bars, mothers clutching babies outside houses, teenagers standing on traffic islands, all cheering and inciting you to go faster.

The R-S is already proving a hit, both with me and those watching. I've been driving with the windows down not only because the evening air is warm but because I want to feel the atmosphere of the cheering spectators as much as possible. Select Dynamic Mode so a little chequered flag appears on the dash and the sound from the exhausts is truly epic, which delights all those we pass. Turn the traction and stability controls off, and with 501lb ft of torque and quick steering it's as easy as you like to hold a slide out of the dusty roundabouts too, again to the smiling whoops and cheers of the onlooking Italians (and me!).

A bit like in cycling, you don't want to drop the slipstream of the car in front. If you haven't got Castrol R fumes constantly flooding up your nostrils then you're probably not close enough. Convoys of sometimes a dozen cars seem to be charging across the countryside in a manner that isn't what I'd imagined from a historic regularity rally. Even without any police escorts in attendance the pace remains astoundingly, lawlessly high, and as night falls the insanity just seems to increase.

There are not just the historics but also support and event cars and occasionally enthusiastic locals all tearing around too. Plus, of course, 'ordinary' traffic. I've never driven an emergency vehicle that's got its 'blues and twos' on, but I imagine my concentration levels wouldn't be any higher if I did. I'm constantly scanning the way ahead, watching, positioning, judging gaps, accelerating hard yet expecting to have to →

Clockwise from far left
1955 Ferrari 500 Mondial is Catchpole's fave; gorgeous Mercedes 300 SL; Italian-registered Jag XK120; D-type in parc fermé; freaky funfair at end of first night's driving; Aston DB3 with police escort.

'Front-end grip is tremendous, so you can turn in hard and then just light up the rear tyres'

brake. All this in darkness with a mixture of lights in red, green, white, blue and very occasionally orange, ranging in brightness from candle-dim to xenon-blinding, both flashing and constantly on. And still there are people waving and cheering at every junction and through every village.

Ah, yes, villages and towns. The pace simply does not drop as you dash between houses. Most of the time there are police and officials stopping traffic and creating clear passages through lights and junctions, but not always. The roads we're using as we charge towards Verona and then Bologna are not big either, and for hour after hour there is no chance to relax. The only occasional pause comes when the historics are siphoned off towards a town-centre checkpoint and we get diverted around the outskirts to wait on the other side. Out here, waiting at the side of the road, there's a camaraderie of its own amongst the supporting vehicles as people listen for the approach of a particular blaring competition exhaust. Then they run for their car and it all starts again.

We eventually reach parc fermé in a Bolognese multi-storey at about 3am. We've been driving for six hours, and Riley and I have still got to find our hotel, 20 miles out of town (via the world's most annoying motorway diversion and a frustratingly incorrect postcode). Just before I

flop onto the bed and fall into instantaneous sleep, I consider the fact that on their record run in 1955, Stirling Moss and Denis Jenkinson would already be past Rome…

Just three hours later the Jaguar's supercharged 5-litre V8 fires into life, the deep cacophony reverberating around the hotel's underground car park. Minutes after that we're back out in the mêlée, this time mixing it with some of the oldest pre-war cars at the head of the cavalcade.

Daylight doesn't diminish the drama, it just means you can see the lunacy more clearly. Long southbound straights (where Moss et al would have been hitting over 170mph and the R-S could potentially reach 186mph) are clogged with Friday-morning traffic. But this doesn't seem to bother the competitors. There are priceless Alfa Romeos and Maseratis being driven like they are motorbikes, overtaking down some mythical middle lane at incredible speeds towards oncoming traffic. Solid lines mean nothing. Only when something too wide, like an artic, appears and spells imminent doom do they haul on their ancient drum brakes at the last minute and force a gap in the traffic back on their side of the road.

Cars queuing for a red traffic light? Simply overtake the lot and cut in at the front before negotiating the crossroads like you're colour-blind. What's even scarier is that I'm not just an

observer in all this, but following them. Sometimes I'm safely in their wake as they scythe a path through the turmoil, but sometimes I'm forging my own way through non-existent gaps. By mid-morning, I feel like I know the width of an XKR-S to the nearest half-millimetre.

After climbing up to the precariously perched hill-top principality of San Marino, we head down onto smaller, quieter roads that twist through the trees. The road surface we are tackling is far from pristine, the tarmac frequently contorted and writhing like it's in pain. This must be a car-wrecking event for the historics and it's a stern test for the XKR-S. Fortunately, despite 28% stiffer spring rates, the R-S's ride remains everything you would hope for in a Jaguar, smothering the vicious bumps and leaving our spines immensely glad they're not travelling 1000 miles in a GT3.

Mid-afternoon we pop out onto a section of dual carriageway… which promptly grinds to a halt. While sitting there, glad of the brief respite but wondering if we're ever likely to reach Rome, the barely silenced gnashing and wailing of an Allard J2 rips past my open driver's window, causing me to jump. Silly me. Why sit in traffic when there's a perfectly good hard shoulder to hammer down? Eventually even that clogs up, so everyone gets out and has a wander around →

Clockwise from above right
Hard-shoulder shortcut past queuing traffic on a dual carriageway eventually becomes a jam, too; spectators line much of route, cheering cars on; Allard charges down wrong side of the road – a normal state of affairs on the Mille Miglia; XKR-S's supercharged 5-litre V8 has 542bhp, so there's lots of fun to be had in hairpins; snow can still be seen from highest roads.

JAGUAR XKR-S

ENGINE
V8, 5000cc, supercharged
CO2
292g/km
POWER
542bhp@6500rpm
TORQUE
501lb ft@2500-5500rpm
TRANSMISSION
Six-speed automatic gearbox, rear-wheel drive, eDiff, traction and stability-control systems
SUSPENSION
Front: Double wishbones, coil springs, adaptive dampers, anti-roll bar.
Rear: Double wishbones, coil springs, adaptive dampers, anti-roll bar
BRAKES
Ventilated discs, 380mm front, 376mm rear, ABS
WHEELS
9x20in front, 10.5x20in rear, aluminium alloy
TYRES
255/35 R20 front, 295/35 R20 rear, Pirelli P Zeros
WEIGHT
(kerb) 1753kg
Power-to-weight 314bhp/ton
PERFORMANCE
0-60mph: 4.2sec (claimed)
Top speed: 186mph (claimed)

Clockwise from above
XKR-S heads into Siena alongside classics – and parts crowds just as successfully. Catchpole enjoys a hard-earned, extra-large beer after three days' hard driving in Jag. XK120 Fixed-Head Coupé gets its moment on finishing ramp.

'The XKR-S really couldn't have been a better companion for our 1000-mile blast around Italy'

Below
Chasing the pompieri on
the final leg to Brescia.

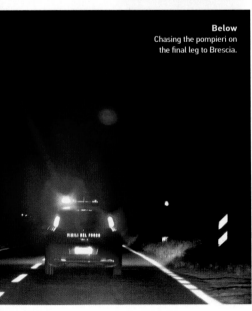

until things start easing and we head for the hills once more.

The jam has spaced everyone out a little and we get a wonderfully clear run down a fast valley road before climbing up through broad hairpins. The R-S's chassis is exactly the same as the one that sits underneath the limited-edition XKR 75, but now you've got even more power to exploit it – another 19bhp, so 39bhp up on the standard XKR.

The steering is undeniably light, but it is phenomenally accurate (whether picking an apex or squeezing through traffic…) and the chassis is beautifully balanced. There is still a softer edge to it than you might expect from a car with an R-S badge on its rump, but only when you're really pushing does it lose a little ultimate bite. However, it is huge fun through the switchbacks. There's tremendous grip from the front end, so you can turn in hard and then just light up the rear tyres. The eDiff will lock initially before opening again to stabilise the slide in a wonderfully benign manner as you continue painting black lines all the way through the corner.

There's still some snow at the top of the Micigliano pass and we pause to take some photos as the sinking sun turns the sky orange. We hear a car approaching, hard charging, no revs being spared. Then we see it, that shock of very blond Finnish hair hunkered down behind the low screen as it comes howling up and over the crest, flat chat. A timeless machine, a timeless road, a timeless scene. It's like a spine-tingling snapshot from 1955.

Sometime around 10.30pm we descend into the heart of Rome and the usual buzzing throng of multitudinous scooters. It's a mark of the craziness of a day chasing the Mille Miglia that the manic Roman traffic feels relatively tame. A litre of beer (in one glass!) and a pizza make up the first proper meal in over 24 hours, and it tastes just wonderful. All that lies ahead is the return leg to Brescia…

Five hours later I fall blearily out of bed, having slept through my alarm half an hour previously. I feel like I need a Red Bull to get me going, like an alcoholic needs a whisky to start the day. We tag onto the now familiar police convoy rushing through traffic lights on the way out of Rome in the early morning mist, before stopping to fill up alongside an Aston Martin DB3 at an Esso garage.

As the race makes a diversion to Vallelunga, we press on past cypress-lined driveways to Tuscan villas and the ever-present crowds, and head for Siena. We're in front of the entire race – sorry, regularity rally – by the time we get there, and as we're early we manage to sneak past the flustered official who is meant to be diverting any car younger than 54 years old around the city walls. Once in, we slowly edge down the quiet and oh-so-narrow renaissance streets and find somewhere to park up and wait for the volume to increase.

Colleague Harry Metcalfe eventually passes us in his Bruschetta, and then the field proper begins arriving. We get back into the Jag and ease out into the stream of cars between two blue pre-war Bugattis. As you do. Just around the corner we emerge, blinking from the confines of the

shady street, into the brightness of the enormous, sky-ceilinged Piazza del Campo, where the Palio horse races are held. It's mayhem. People are four or five deep either side of the car, taking photos and standing in the way. You feel like a Group B driver in slow-motion, parting the sea of spectators as you drive through. An official looks at us scathingly, but there's nothing he can do and the crowd clearly loves the sound of what must be one of the loudest Jaguars ever to roll out of the factory. Half a mile the other side of the piazza we park up outside a small church, and while Sam does some filming I wander off in search of a celebratory gelato for each of us.

The afternoon sees us being chased across sun-drenched Tuscan hills by an original Gullwing Mercedes and then us pursuing a Porsche 550 Spyder down into Florence. As an art history graduate it is one of the most bizarre experiences of my life to cross the Arno River with the medieval Ponte Vecchio bridge on our right and then drive through the Piazza della Signoria. Bowing to the crowd's hollered wish and lighting up the tyres on the cobbles whilst Michelangelo's David looks down through the windscreen will stay with me forever.

From Florence we head up over the Futa and Raticosa passes, following a hard-charging C-type. Its driver is clearly making up time and it's just as well the XKR-S is such a monstrously effective overtaking tool, able to surge past lines of cars in the shortest of straights, treating the overtaken to crackles and explosive reports on the overrun when you lift off the throttle sharply to dive back into a gap.

Bologna, Modena, Maranello, Fiorano and Parma all slip by as night falls once more. Eventually, with the final few hours to Brescia ahead, we settle in behind an incredibly loud 328 BMW and the flashing blue lights of the pompieri (firefighters) who do the route each year. I'm incredibly weary, but the crowds are still out in force in the last few towns and it seems churlish not to get the XKR-S crossed-up on the cobbles for them too.

This new Jaguar really couldn't have been a better companion for our 1000-mile blast around Italy: cosseting enough to let us survive, brutally fast enough to execute the hundreds of overtakes as swiftly as possible, raucous enough to put a smile on everyone's faces, good looking enough to reach places other press cars couldn't and engaging enough to really enjoy on the mountain passes. An RS from Porsche is ultimately a more focused driving tool, but the greater useability of this R-S is something that gives it its own very appealing draw.

It should almost be an anti-climax when we reach Brescia at 3am and our press sticker doesn't let us drive up to the finish ramp, but the end of any journey as epic as the Mille Miglia could never be seen as anti anything. I'm sure someone has won, but it honestly doesn't seem to matter – in the modern Mille Miglia it really is the taking part that counts.

As the BA flight touches down at Heathrow the following morning I realise that I've had just ten hours' sleep in three days. No wonder it feels like a dream. Must remember to stop at any red traffic lights on the way home… *End*

JAGUAR
PROTOTYPES

World-renowned Jaguar historian **Philip Porter** presents
a selection of prototypes from the marque's archives:
some of them famous, a few never seen before

1 SS Jaguar 100 Coupé

APART FROM THE production range of SS Jaguar models displayed on Stand 126 at Earls Court in 1938, there was a striking closed coupé of the familiar SS Jaguar 100 sports car. This Lyons-designed body was an interesting precursor of things to come, and one can see hints of XK120 fixed-head and maybe a little Bugatti influence in the tightly furled cabin. The show car, which had the 3 1/2-litre engine, was priced at £595, and a 2 1/2-litre was listed (although never built) at £545. This unique prototype was fitted with an all-synchromesh gearbox.

The first owner, who received it as a 21st birthday present, found the car to be rather impractical; modifications had to be made to the interior to make it driveable. Apparently the doors dropped, too, and the red colouring on the steering wheel rubbed off on the driver's trousers! Such are prototypes...

2 XL

Little is known of the XL, but it is undoubtedly the step between the pre-war SS100 sports cars and the sensational XK120 of 1948. Lyons liked to work with full-size mock-ups, and this styling exercise was built in 1946-47. It is certainly confusing that L comes after K in the alphabet but, in fact, the name of the production 120 was taken from the engine designation: XK.

3 Bubble-top C-type

Legendary aerodynamicist Malcolm Sayer designed the XK120C, or C-type as it came to be known unofficially, in 1950-51 and it famously won Le Mans in '51. During March the following year he drew a number of alternative body shapes, all variations on the theme, and this closed version was among them.

Assuming drag of the 1951 C-type to be 100 %, he calculated that drag for this configuration would be 84.5%. If you were to cut the roof off this design, you would be left with the head fairing behind the driver – just as it appeared on the D-type in 1954.

4/5 Light alloy car

The 'light alloy car' has to be one of the most significant Jaguar prototypes ever built. This model introduces the familiar elliptical mouth that is still a hallmark to this day. It is very much like the E-type but, built in 1953, was way ahead of its time and startlingly modern – one can see similarities with Alfa Romeo's fabulous Disco Volante (flying saucer) designs.

The other significant aspect of this car is that it was Jaguar's first monocoque sports racer and was the link between the C-type and the D-type. It was variously named the C/D, the prototype D-type, XK120C Series II, XP11, XKC 054 and XKC 201 but, at the factory, was generally referred to simply as the 'light alloy car'.

6 Brontosaurus

The Brontosaurus served to prove that even styling genius William Lyons was human. It was a very curious machine that he had built, possibly with some record-breaking in mind, and it did very little other than hurtling around the factory perimeter with Lyons at the wheel.

Its other purpose was probably as a 'wake-up' call to Jaguar's designers, whom Lyons – possibly with some justification – was always urging to hurry up and complete their designs. Lyons had his own small team of designers for creating prototypes and produced this to show things could be done quickly. The Bronco, as it became known, was not one of his better efforts. →

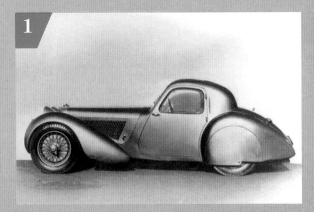

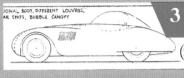

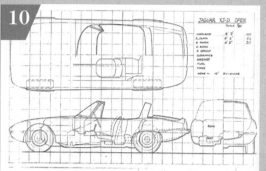

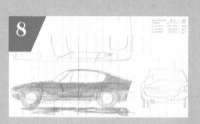

Shortened 2+2 E-type

For several years after the launch of the two-seater E-type in 1961, Williams Lyons and Heynes had dithered over producing a larger, four-seater version. They had built longer examples, wider variations and changed their minds to such an extent that the Experimental Department built a mock-up with telescopic tubes so it could be widened or lengthened at will.

Eventually, the 2+2 appeared, and in production form was simply a modified fixed-head coupé. However, the alternative thinking continued and there was a view at Jag that the E-type, particularly the 2+2, was too long for European markets. In May 1966 Sayer drew this shortened 2+2.

XJ 3-litre GT

Among the design and development of the sports and saloon cars, projects overlapped, converged or diverted. The XJ saloon, for example, started life as a large sporting GT. This mid-1960s design, which was based on the E-type, was described as a 'four-seater sports sedan'.

It was variously seen as a supplement to the sports car range or a replacement for the small Mk2 saloons for which Jaguar disastrously never produced a successor. One can see the fashionable Kamm tail treatment and the beginnings of the

XJ-S front wing and headlamp treatment that would appear about 10 years later.

XJ21 by Winterbottom

In the latter half of the 1960s the manufacturer's ageing management agonised over the E-type's successor, and a plethora of designs was produced – at least on paper. The debate raged on, and one contributor was a young designer by the name of Oliver Winterbottom, who would later work for TVR and Lotus. This design went as far as a quarter-scale clay model, with details such as aluminium wheels made in the Daimler toolroom.

XJ-21 convertible

A number of XJ-21 designs were done by Sayer in 1967/68 but one appeared to find favour and actually progressed quite far down the line, as one internal memo confirms: 'The bodies are styled and arrangements are being made with PSF [Pressed Steel Co] for the tooling.' Open and closed versions were drawn and both were 2+2s. However, someone got cold feet; or maybe it was a casualty of the fatal British Leyland debacle that had commenced in 1968. The model was cancelled. Mistake!

XJ-S by Sayer

The XJ-S was something of an amalgam of

thoughts by Lyons and Sayer, but it was actually Sayer who, in September 1968, proposed building 'a 2+2 sports based on XJ4 parts'. (Confusingly, XJ4 was the internal name for the production XJ6 that would be launched that year.) 'The image sought after is of a low, wide, high-speed car at least as eye-catching as those the Italians will produce...'

In arriving at the final shape, which was constrained by increasingly influential US federal safety regulations and, in particular, the belief that open cars would be outlawed, Sayer produced a sheaf of designs, including this one.

F-type

Another car, shown at the Detroit Motor Show in early 2000, that Jaguar should have produced. The F-type concept oozed the sheer sculptural, sensuous beauty of the 120 and E-type, and would have been a worthy successor. It would also have had a 'halo effect' on the whole range, giving Jaguar that sense of vibrant excitement again. In fairness, current and forthcoming regulations might well have made the actual execution challengingly difficult.

Jaguar directed its limited funds to developing diesels instead. Deposits had been taken, though, and harm was done because the firm has always been famous for fabulous sports cars – and its survival will always depend on them. **End**

MOTORS EUROPE

ZWAKMAN

CARS IN STOCK

Jaguar

1948	Jaguar MK4 3.5 ltr. DHC LHD
	Jaguar XK120 *light weight works car*
1952	Jaguar C-Type *replica*
1955	Jaguar MK7 M RHD
1958	Jaguar XK150 Coupe *by Bertone* LHD
1959	Jaguar MK2 2.4 ltr. RHD
	Jaguar MK9 LHD
1960	Jaguar MK9 RHD
1964	Jaguar MK2 3.8 ltr. manual LHD
1966	Jaguar MK2 3.8 ltr. LHD
	Jaguar XKE 4.2 ltr. S1 2+2 Coupe LHD
	New York show car
1971	Jaguar XJ6 4.2 ltr. S1 manual LHD
1973	Jaguar E-Type V12 S3 OTS RHD *concours*
	Jaguar XJ12 *prototype* RHD
1976	Jaguar XJ12 Coupe RHD
1984	Jaguar XJS Spider *by Lynx Motors* LHD
1989	Jaguar XJS V12 Coupe LHD
1991	Jaguar XJR15 RHD

SS

1934	SS1 20HP period café racer
	SS2 12HP Tourer
1935	SS90
	SS1 20HP DHC *#001*
	SS1 20HP Tourer
1936	SS2 12HP *four-light* Saloon
	SS100 2.5 ltr.
1937	SS Tüscher DHC 2.5 ltr.
1938	SS100 FHC

Aston Martin

1937	Aston Martin 4 seat DHC
1938	Aston Martin 2 seat DHC
1953	Aston Martin DB2 DHC LHD
1955	Aston Martin DB2/4 DHC LHD
1960	Aston Martin DB4C GT LHD
1994	Aston Martin DB7 TWR *one-off prototype* RHD
2006	Aston Martin Vantage Coupe *#001* LHD

Daimler

1961	Daimler SP250 Dart RHD
1962	Daimler Majestic RHD
1968	Daimler 250 V8 RHD
1973	Daimler Sovereign 2.8 ltr. RHD

Other brands

1937	A7 Opal Roadster
1964	MG Ashley RHD
1978	Bentley T2 RHD
1990	VM Lotus Seven LHD
1998	Bentley Continental T LHD

WWW.ZWAKMANMOTORS.COM

SUPER.
CAT.

This is the most intriguing vision yet of the supercar of the future, powered by electricity and gas turbines. And perhaps most remarkably of all, it's a Jaguar. **Harry Metcalfe** gets a private audience with the stunning C-X75

IT APPEARS IN YOUR mirrors as a speck on the shimmering horizon. As it eats up the distance, you watch, mesmerised. Slowly the shape takes definition – unfamiliar but utterly captivating. You drop your window, straining for aural clues. Nothing. As it gets closer, there's just the roar of tyre on tarmac. Then it's suddenly upon you and flashing past, a low, exotic sliver of silver. The sound now is like nothing you've ever heard before, a seductive hum overlaid with a keening, turbine-like whine and above it all an aircraft-like whistle…

It sounds like the future, but this is late-summer 2010, and if you had been lucky enough you would have seen Jaguar's concept supercar being put through its paces in the Spanish countryside. Forget everything you thought you knew about the British marque. The future starts here.

'Jaguar should be all about fast, beautiful cars.' Design director Ian Callum is showing me around C-X75 just days before it departs for its world premiere at the Paris Motor Show. C-X75 might be a rather clumsy name, but as far as the looks go – and let's not beat around the bush here – this is one →

'Under the stunning
skin is a combination
of electric motors and
gas turbines quite unlike
anything we've seen before'

JAGUAR C-X75

ENGINE
Four electric motors,
two 'switched reluctance'
generators, two gas
micro-turbines
MAX POWER
Total of 780bhp from
electric motors; additional
188bhp from turbines
MAX TORQUE
1180lb ft
CO2
28g/km
TRANSMISSION
Single-speed
BRAKES
Regenerative braking.
Ventilated discs, 380mm
front, 345mm rear, ABS, EBD
WHEELS
21in diameter front,
22in rear, aluminium alloy
TYRES
265/30 ZR21 front, 365/25
ZR22 rear, hand-cut Pirelli
KERBWEIGHT
1350kg
POWER-TO-WEIGHT
587bhp/ton (electric
motors only)
PERFORMANCE
0-62mph 3.4sec (claimed)
0-100mph 5.5sec (claimed)
0-186mph 15.7sec (claimed)
Top speed 205mph (claimed)
EV range 68 miles
(extended range 560 miles)
BASIC PRICE
n/a
ON SALE
2020?

'We wanted to pull the same emotional heartstrings that classic Jaguars like the XJ13 and D-type did'

absolutely gorgeous Jaguar, one whose exquisitely judged curves have left me almost speechless.

'We wanted to mark 75 years of Jaguar by creating a really special concept car,' continues Callum, 'but also to think about where the company goes next in terms of design and technology. You should always learn something from doing a car like this.' And there's no question that what's under the stunning skin is every bit as breathtaking as the bodywork above, boasting a combination of electric motors and gas turbines that is quite unlike anything we have ever seen from a mainstream manufacturer.

Yet it's the looks that grab your attention first, of course. I've had only a few moments to drink it all in, but as far as I can tell the C-X75 looks stunning from almost any angle you care to choose. So, I ask Callum, where did the inspiration for the car come from?

'This model is a vision of what's to come from Jaguar,' he says, 'but having said that, for me, the XJ13 is possibly the most beautiful Jaguar ever made. Together with the D-type, it was something we wanted to pay homage to.

'I don't like unnecessary lines on a car, and you won't find any on the C-X75. We've managed to keep it exceptionally clean by using mechanical aerodynamic aids working under the car, rather than having them on the bodywork. This has really helped to keep its appearance as clean as possible.'

Callum's assistant design director Julian Thomson was closely involved in this project and reinforces the point. 'We wanted the C-X75 to pull at the same emotional heartstrings that classic Jaguars like the XJ13 and D-type did in the past,' he says.

Not that the C-X75 is in any way 'retro'. The 'mouth' of the car is a further development of the

Clockwise from opposite page
Interior leaves you in no doubt that the C-X75 is a concept (for now, at least). Doors and rear bulkhead are clothed in nano-technology speaker panels for the hi-fi; seats are fixed, so the wheel, instruments and pedal box are all electrically adjustable. Detailing throughout the car is just exquisite.

grille first seen on the XF and made even more prominent on the XJ. The C-X75 takes the design one step further, elongating the opening to give a sportier face. Gone is the oval mouth of Jaguars from the past – this is the way Callum wants the face of the marque to develop. Expect to see something similar on the next-generation XK and the rumoured two-seater sports car.

It is an exceptionally low nose, yet Callum assures me that, if Jaguar wanted to build the car today, it could. Only a minor tweak to the chin spoiler would be required to meet all current, stringent pedestrian crash regulations. Indeed, the

depth of engineering throughout is impressive. To keep drag to a minimum, the front grille (there to serve the radiators that keep the batteries cool) and the front brake vents open solely when they are actually needed, while discreet vertical spoilers on the rear corners of the bodywork come into play only as speed rises, directing airflow around the rear wheels to help stability and reduce drag. The end result is a Cd figure of 0.32, which is remarkably good for a supercar.

But then, this isn't just another Veyron rival. 'From the outset I wanted this car to have a hybrid drivetrain,' says Callum, 'because this offers far →

more freedom for the design team to experiment with the packaging, which is very different on a hybrid than it is on a machine which has a conventional engine.

'We also have to think what a future, greener world might want from a supercar, and this is our answer. The C-X75 is a confident, beautiful and fast Jaguar.'

How fast? Extremely, according to all the computations. Perhaps the least impressive stat is the projected 0-62mph time of 3.4 seconds; from that point on the C-X75 really gets into its stride, hitting 100mph in a claimed 5.5sec, passing 186mph in 15.7sec and covering the quarter-mile in just 10.3sec (with a terminal speed of 156mph) before topping out at a claimed 205mph.

But it's the way the C-X75 would achieve those figures that's the really remarkable thing. For a start, each wheel is powered by its own dedicated 195bhp, 295lb ft electric motor, each weighing 50kg and mounted inboard of the suspension, keeping the unsprung weight to a minimum. Effectively, this gives the car 4WD as well as useful 'torque-vectoring' properties, thanks to a central computer that distributes power independently to each electric motor to suit the conditions – in effect a form of super-advanced traction and stability control for maximum performance.

Added together, the four electric motors give the all-aluminium, 1350kg C-X75 a maximum power output of 780bhp and 1180lb ft of torque, which equates to 587bhp/ton. That's Veyron-beating power-to-weight, and the C-X75 still has another trick up its sleeve…

The electric motors draw their power from a bank of lithium-ion batteries (with a total capacity of 19.6kWh) installed down the spine of the car, helping to keep the model's centre of gravity as low as possible. These can be charged up from the domestic grid in six hours (via a standard domestic plug) to give a range of up to 68 miles in electric-only mode. But here comes the really interesting bit – they can also be charged via the onboard gas turbines.

Peer through the canopy behind the driver cockpit and you will spot two dinky little turbines resting just below the glass in what I'd like to call the engine bay but probably shouldn't. Each of these beautifully finished, aluminium jet engines weighs just 3kg and produces 94bhp once they're spinning at their heady maximum of 80,000rpm. Each gas turbine is linked directly to its own dedicated 'switched-resistance' generator, the latest super-efficient unit and compact enough to give a total combined weight for both turbine and generator of 35kg. The driver can choose either to use the turbines to supplement the electric motors' power (in track mode) or to recharge the batteries on the move (in normal mode).

The turbines are fed fuel from twin tanks with a total capacity of 60 litres (they can run on a variety of fuels including diesel, biofuels and liquid petroleum gas). Combined with a fully charged battery, the C-X75 is capable of travelling for up to 560 miles between fill-ups, which works out at the equivalent of 42mpg.

Much work has gone into controlling the underbody airflow to create plenty of downforce as speed rises. There's a prominent venturi visible ➔

From opposite left
Jaguar design supremos Thomson (left) and Callum. Wheels are 21in front, 22in rear, fitted with custom-made Pirellis featuring a green F1-style wear indicator around their circumference. Twin dials show speed on a rotating drum (on the left) and power being used (on the right). Around the edge of each dial is a rev-counter for each turbine, rising to 80,000rpm. Gear selector is modelled on an aircraft's engine controls. The button on the side of the lever offers the driver an override function to fire up the turbines for maximum acceleration.

'With full fuel tanks and a fully charged battery, the C-X75 would travel up to 560 miles between fill-ups'

JAGUAR DREAM CAR

GAS TURBINES EXPLAINED

The gas micro-turbines fitted to the C-X75 are the
latest, multi-stage axial-flow compressors, just
like those fitted to commercial jets but in miniature.
They offer massively increased compression and
efficiency compared with previous-generation
micro-turbines, but can they be viewed as
a realistic car power source of the future?

Jaguar teamed up with Bladon Jets, based
in the UK, to investigate developing viable gas
turbine-driven generators for automotive use
under a government-sponsored project. Tony
Harper (head of Jaguar Land Rover research)
is the man in charge of the project, and he
reckons gas turbines show real potential.

'Using a conventional engine to power
generators in a range-extender vehicle is a
very heavy solution,' he says. 'These gas turbines
produce a huge amount of power yet weigh
only 3kg each. The tricky part is connecting them
to a generator – they spin at 80,000rpm, which

is too fast for a generator to operate at – but we
are finding ways around this that I cannot discuss
at the moment.'

These are not 'thrust'-type turbines, so we
won't be seeing after-burners on future Jaguars!
Instead, they work in a similar way to those
turbines used for generating electricity in power
stations. What Harper likes most about gas
turbines is that they will offer a relatively small
weight penalty while providing genuine range-
extending properties to cars in the future. So
when might we see them in a production vehicle?

'The C-X75 is a vision of what a 2020 supercar
might be like, but we could see turbines in
automotive use before this date,' says Harper.
'We'll just have to wait and see.'

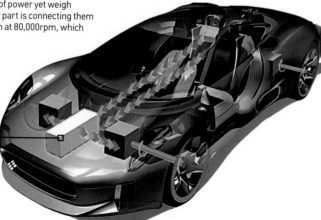

C-X75 has an electric
motor for each wheel and
lithium-ion batteries. Twin
turbines mounted behind
the cockpit can recharge
the batteries – or provide
an extra surge of power.

from the rear of the car, finished off with a moveable
carbon fibre rear diffuser. This is effectively an
active aerofoil that automatically lowers as the
speed increases, giving more downforce as it does
so. There is an added twist in all of this aero
technology, too – once the twin turbines have
kicked in, their exhaust gases are channelled into
the venturi to further boost downforce.

Feeding sufficient air to the gas turbines was
another critical aspect of the design, and Callum
and his team settled on two sill-mounted aluminium
intakes together with a roof-mounted vent. Turbines
have a very different 'air requirement' to that of a
conventional engine. Because they spin at such
enormously high speeds, they swallow a huge
amount of air – when both turbines on the
C-X75 are spinning at 80,000rpm and producing
maximum power, they consume a total of 70,000

'It's the most thorough rethink of where the supercar might be heading in the future'

litres of air a minute. Compare that with the 7500 litres of air needed by a 5-litre engine producing its maximum power at 6000rpm and you can see just how greedy these turbines are. At full bore, they are literally sucking the car forward.

This hunger for air partly dictated the cabin architecture. The seats are fixed to the bulkhead, as in a single-seater race-car, with the air to feed the turbines passing smoothly around them through channels in the structure of the body. Because the seats are fixed, the steering wheel, controls, main instrument binnacle and pedals can all be electrically adjusted towards the driver via switches on the steering wheel and the dash itself.

The interior is typically concept-car-wacky. LED lights glow from inside the doors and bulkheads, exposing the frankly weird nano-technology speaker panels that hide behind a cool, micromesh

fabric covering. These use dozens of tiny moving coil transducers in an ultra-thin honeycomb pattern to literally surround the driver and passenger with an all-enveloping sound. This could be from whatever music source you care to choose or, alternatively, they could be used as active sound-cancelling speakers, to isolate the cabin from the whistling generated by the turbines.

But a Jaguar without its growl? Callum admits that the team did think about adding some sort of engine soundtrack, but decided against it as driving the car was enough of an event in itself. As for the noise it generates, jet engines do make a whistling sound but apparently it wouldn't dominate the driving experience. According to the engineers, you get more of a sense of the volume of air being sucked in than the noise of the turbines themselves.

We'll have to hope we get the opportunity to

find out for ourselves. Callum has driven the car in Spain but the gas turbines weren't hooked up. For the moment the C-X75 is purely electrically powered. So how close is it to being a production possibility? Realistically, nothing quite like this will appear until 2020 at the earliest. But there's much to get excited about here.

I can't get over the amount of free thinking that has gone into this car. Thanks to its all-aluminium construction it weighs about the same as today's hatchbacks, despite packing a heavy battery pack and four electric motors. It has the potential to out-drag a Veyron Super Sport yet would emit only 28g/km on the official cycle, or it could drive 68 miles on electric-only power when needed. The C-X75 is the most thorough rethink of where the supercar might be heading in the future – and it's a Jaguar. Who'd have thought it? *End*

Back to the future

*Fifty years since Jaguar
last launched a sports car,
we reveal what follows
in the wake of the trailblazing
SS100, XK120 and E-type*

WORDS Glen Waddington // PHOTOGRAPHY John Wycherley

'IWANT JAGS** to make people smile. The world is too serious.' These are the words of Jaguar design director Ian Callum, just a few weeks before the world gazes for the first time upon the C-X16 'production concept'. A new Jaguar sports car, for the first time in 50 years? You bet. Reckon on it being a reality in 2013. For now, this is the show machine that is to make its international debut at the 2011 Frankfurt International Motor Show.

'It's a lovely balance of modernity and classic looks,' says Ian. 'I'm probably more pleased with this car than any other I've been involved with.' This is the man responsible for the current range of XK, XJ and XF – but consider the lineage that led to it and you'd have to be pretty bullish about what you're going to follow all that heritage with.

Jaguar launched the E-type in 1961, at the very least matching the stir that had been caused in 1948 by the XK120, which innovated with its twin-overhead-camshaft XK engine – in production right up to 1992 – and bowled the world over with gorgeous looks that set the marque's flowing style for years to follow. And Jaguar might never have been considered a sports car manufacturer at all, had it not been for the SS100 announced in 1935.

The new C-X16 follows an extremely illustrious past. This is the tale of how we got from there to here. →

Above and right
SS100 features traditional British
sports car styling inside and out –
yet it's still recognisably a Jaguar.
A good thing, too, as this was one
of the first cars to wear the name.

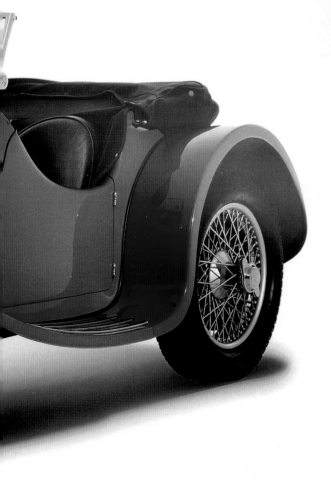

'Those proportions, the rounded rear haunches, those soulful headlamps. You've seen their like since, but you saw them here first'

1938 SS JAGUAR 100
ENGINE 2663cc straight-six, OHV, twin SU carburettors
POWER 104bhp@4600rpm **TORQUE** n/a **TRANSMISSION** Four-speed manual,
rear-wheel drive **STEERING** Worm and nut **SUSPENSION** Front: beam axle,
semi-elliptic leaf springs, friction dampers. Rear: live axle, semi-elliptic leaf
springs, hydraulic dampers **BRAKES** Drums **WEIGHT** 1143kg
PERFORMANCE Top speed 96mph. 0-60mph 12.8sec

JAGUAR'S SPORTS CAR STORY begins with paired innovations: the company's first bespoke chassis meeting its first bespoke engine – but we need to understand a little history before we go much further. The firm's origins as a coachbuilder (in fact, it became known as Jaguar only after World War Two, and the uncomfortable connotations of Swallow Sidecars' initials) meant it had always worked with the chassis, engine and running gear of other manufacturers.

The Austin Seven Swallow was launched in 1927; a year later the firm moved from Blackpool to a new 40,000sq ft factory in Foleshill, West Midlands, and began building 50 models per week. Its relationship with the Standard Car Company grew, and the first SS vehicles emerged on modified Standard chassis in 1931. Billed as 'The dream cars with the £1000 look', the 2.0-litre SS1 and 1.0-litre SS2 sold for less than a third of that, establishing the Jaguar tradition of value for money. But they also established a sleek, sexy and sporting style, one company co-founder William Walmsley was uncomfortable with. His partner William Lyons, in effect, bought him out in 1934, shortly after SS Cars Ltd had been floated as a public concern.

The shortlived SS90 roadster arrived in 1935, only 23 being made on a shortened chassis (fully 1ft 3in chopped out of the SS1's Standard underpinnings) and with a 70bhp 2663cc twin-carb version of Standard's sidevalve straight-six. But for September of that year, along came the SS100, using the 90's chassis and also a totally re-engineered engine, with an overhead-valve crossflow cylinder head and twin SU carburettors to give a 104bhp output – all designed by consultant Harry Weslake. That power figure is significant: Weslake had negotiated a contract that earned him extra money for every horsepower he found above the 95bhp stipulated by William Lyons!

That name? Well, the car was said to crack 100mph – but, more importantly, it wore a winged badge at the top of the grille bearing the legend 'SS Jaguar'. Lyons had been on the look-out for a new brand name, having hoped to take over the Sunbeam marque before being pipped by the Rootes brothers. He selected 'Jaguar' from a list of animal-inspired epithets provided by Nelson Advertising. The first Jaguar sports car had arrived.

And with it came much fanfare. *Motor* magazine road tested the SS100, achieving a genuine 96mph and 0-60mph in 12.8 seconds. *The Autocar* drove the same model, and its writer was moved to say: 'With its rapid acceleration and hill climbing, it is a vivid car not easily equalled from point to point when suitably handled.' Quite so.

Even now, there's something in the SS100's forms – a word that Ian Callum is fond of using – that marks it out as a true Jaguar: those long-nose proportions, the roundedness about the rear haunches, the soulfulness of those huge, expressive headlamps. You've seen their like since, but you saw them here (well, in the SS90) first. It's a surprisingly compact car, one that suddenly feels all the more so as you flip back the rear-hinged door and insinuate yourself behind the wheel. Or, rather, under it: getting your thighs in is a squeeze and would be made much easier with double-jointed knees.

Once in, you sit with legs straight ahead, barely feeling contained by the scant bodywork and fold-flat windscreen, to survey a full set of ivory-faced Smiths instruments. They're scattered all the way across the dashboard, and your view of the road ahead is focused by the gunsight of the line along the bonnet. Gorgeous.

And it's a real entertainer. Not fast by today's standards, but with a generous spread of torque that's underpinned by the fat burble of the exhaust and the mechanical threshings ahead of you. Plenty of vintage-style gear whine, too, and a gearshift that feels precise yet stiff. But the steering isn't too vague and the slightly hoppity ride cushions you from the very worst road imperfections yet keeps you perfectly →

well-informed of exactly what the tarmac is doing – and how well you're attached to it.

The SS100 enjoyed the same new Burman Douglas steering box, Girling rod brakes and enlarged drums as the Jaguar saloons that were launched alongside it, and in 1937 Jaguar's own Bill Heynes (founder of its engineering department) enlarged the engine to a 3485cc version that would sell above the 2.5-litre. Its new bore, stroke and multi-branch exhaust manifold not only guaranteed better performance (thanks to its 125bhp power output), they also took the SS100 further along the path from its Standard origins – as did all-steel coachwork and a new, stiffer chassis. A total of 309 SS100s (118 of them with the larger engine) were built before World War Two saw production cease in 1939.

Ah, the war. Jaguar did not intend to remain idle throughout those years but, while company executives were not discouraged from planning for what would happen after, no actual *engineering* could be seen to be taking place that was not sanctioned by the Government. So, on paper, work began on the next generation of cars during the early 1940s, centring around a new engine – in fact a whole series of engines.

We all think of Jaguar as a luxury car manufacturer today, and it was certainly a cut above the likes of Austin back then. Yet still its most popular cars had four-cylinder engines. And so what was launched as a twin-cam straight-six began as a family of in-line fours and sixes in a report laid out by Jaguar's Walter Hassan in October 1943. A 1.8-litre four-cylinder twin-overhead-camshaft engine was tested two years later but by 1947 the XK was being developed solely as a six, with a 3.4-litre capacity and a cylinder head inspired by that of the BMW 328.

What is far more audacious is the way this engine was announced to the public. At the 1948 British Motor Show, held at London's Earls Court, Jaguar stunned visitors with its beautiful new XK120. This was developed as a prototype on which work was being carried out for a new flagship saloon. The show car was handmade on shortened MkVII saloon underpinnings, including its independent front suspension. And powering it was the new XK: a 160bhp 3.4-litre tour de force with twin overhead camshafts, an aluminium cylinder head, hemispherical combustion chambers, inclined valves and central spark plugs – and a hugely strong seven-bearing crankshaft that could trace its origins back to the Standard engine of SS's past. The XK was truly the kind of motor you might expect to find powering an Italian thoroughbred.

Initial demand was overwhelming – and caught Jaguar napping. The works could handbuild the car only in limited numbers, each with an alloy body; 200 were finished this way before Pressed Steel tooled up for volume production, which began in 1950. At £995 for the roadster, Jaguar convincingly slammed the value nail squarely on the head again. A fixed-head coupé joined it in 1951, and a luxurious drophead coupé arrived in 1953.

It is worlds ahead of the SS100, with an unadorned, all-enveloping body, its grille in-unit with the bonnet and with sleek spats covering the rear wheels. That feline-like line that flows over the front wings, down to a waist ahead of the rear wheels and then up and over is more sharply defined on this car than on any other Jaguar – yet you can clearly see its origins in the SS100, and follow it into place on the E-type and C-X16.

But we're getting ahead of ourselves. Clambering in the XK120 is a little easier than it was with the SS100, but that wheel is still thigh-squeezingly huge. The seats are generous, the dashboard a simple slab of modernism, almost aircraft-like in its modest efficiency. And the XK engine – its voice, its generosity, its character – dominates every aspect of the drive.

At the other end of the scale, Earls Court was also the scene of the Morris Minor's launch in 1948. The Jag is utterly decadent by →

Right
That curvaceous (dare we say cat-like?) Jaguar style really established itself with the XK120, but car was even more remarkable for its advanced twin-cam engine.

'That feline-like line is more sharply defined on this car than on any other Jaguar'

1953 JAGUAR XK120

ENGINE
3442cc straight-six, DOHC,
twin SU carburettors

POWER
160bhp@5000rpm

TORQUE
195lb ft@2500rpm

TRANSMISSION
Four-speed manual,
rear-wheel drive

STEERING
Recirculating ball

SUSPENSION
Front: wishbones, torsion bars,
telescopic dampers, anti-roll bar.
Rear: live axle, semi-elliptic leaf
springs, hydraulic dampers

BRAKES
Drums

WEIGHT
1295kg

PERFORMANCE
Top speed 122mph.
0-60mph 11.7sec

1963 JAGUAR E-TYPE 3.8 FHC
ENGINE 3781cc straight-six, DOHC, triple SU carburettors
POWER 265bhp@5500rpm **TORQUE** 260lb ft@4000rpm
TRANSMISSION Four-speed manual, rear-wheel drive
STEERING Rack and pinion **SUSPENSION** Front: wishbones, torsion bars,
telescopic dampers, anti-roll bar. Rear: lower wishbones, fixed-length
driveshafts, twinned coil springs and telescopic dampers **BRAKES** Discs
WEIGHT 1219kg **PERFORMANCE** Top speed 150mph. 0-60mph 7.4sec

comparison and, if its performance feels satisfyingly strong today, imagine the impact its claimed top speed beyond 120mph (yep, hence the name – it had been tested on Belgium's Jabbeke highway minus windscreen, making it the world's fastest production car) and its 0-60mph time of 11.7sec would have had on sensible British dads who fancied a Minor in all its 27.5bhp, 919cc sidevalve glory.

The XK120 woofles into life, settling to a smooth and steady beat, chuffing through twinned tailpipes. There's similar gear whine to accompany forward progress as there was in the SS100, though it's overcome here by greater stridency from that magnificent engine. You need a firm hand on the gearlever, especially to coax it into second from first (for which the stick lies almost prone on the transmission tunnel), and getting used to the combination of a long throw with an extremely narrow gate takes a little time. Open roads are the car's real forte, once you're rolling and free of the city confines that serve to magnify the heaviness of the steering at low speeds. That torquey strength manifests itself in increasing confidence as speeds rise, but Jaguar's success with chassis tuning also plays a huge part. Despite its live rear axle the XK120 rides with grace and poise, yet corners with precision. It feels far more modern than its wartime origins would suggest.

It even informs the new C-X16 in character; you can certainly imagine a warm response for the new car at Frankfurt. And the XK didn't seek favour among the 1940s equivalent of the lambswool sweater types perceived as today's Jag drivers. Says Ian Callum: 'Were the XK120 and E-type targeting golfers? No.'

And the road testers of the time were effusive, too. In April 1950 *The Autocar* said: 'Nothing like the XK120, and at its price, has been previously achieved – a car of tremendous performance yet displaying the flexibility, and even the silkiness and smoothness, of a mild-mannered saloon.' Oh, it scored its first race victory at Silverstone in 1949, and Ian Appleyard's road-registered NUB 120 won the Alpine Rally in 1950. Quite a car.

But even the XK120 dated. As it was developed into 1954's XK140 and 1957's XK150, its character morphed into that of a more luxurious GT, and the wartime origins of its styling and construction methods weren't exactly hip come 1961.

Enter the E-type to a rapturous reception. If any car captured the spirit of the Swinging Sixties and then held it to ransom, this was it. And *this* is the Jag whose character the C-X16 is trying hardest to evoke. As Ian says: 'We're going for a more spirited, more youthful market. It's more about the Kings Road than the golf club. That was *the* place for E-type owners.'

All Jaguar fans will be well aware that 2011 marks the 50th anniversary of the E-type's historic Geneva launch, so we won't bang on here about the epic drives by Bob Berry and Norman Dewis to get the demonstration cars there on time. Nor will we spend long recounting the E-type's motorsport success (Graham Hill scored a victory on its first outing; in Lightweight form it kept the Ferrari 250GTO at bay). But we will dwell a little on the design and engineering aspects that not only made the E-type a success in terms of sales and popularity, but also established key Jaguar ethos for decades.

It's powered by the XK engine (still so modern in 1961), launched with the XK150S's 165bhp 3.8-litre version and the same Moss four-speed manual gearbox strapped to it. The torsion bar front suspension is similar in layout, too, but gone is the live rear axle, replaced by an ingenious subframe-mounted independent system that employs fixed-length driveshafts as the upper links, with twinned coil springs and telescopic dampers. You saw it here first, but it followed in the 420G saloon, the XJ6, XJ-S, XJ40 and even the XK8 of the 1990s. It's responsible for the gliding sensation for which Jaguars became →

'If Jaguar is going to look anywhere in its back catalogue for inspiration, it's just got to be here'

Above and below
The E-type is the archetypal Jaguar sports car, as much a legend now as it was when launched in 1961. Fifty years on, it's the obvious inspiration for Jaguar's new C-X16 concept car.

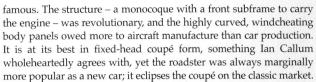

Above and below
The design language might be new, and the supercharged hybrid petrol-electric drivetrain a bold step into the future, but you'd know what it is even if it didn't wear a badge.

famous. The structure – a monocoque with a front subframe to carry the engine – was revolutionary, and the highly curved, windcheating body panels owed more to aircraft manufacture than car production. It is at its best in fixed-head coupé form, something Ian Callum wholeheartedly agrees with, yet the roadster was always marginally more popular as a new car; it eclipses the coupé on the classic market.

Just over two grand got you a 150mph sports car back in 1961 – about half the price of an Aston Martin DB4 (the C-X16 aims to perform a similar trick). And the E-type is still utterly beguiling today. The cockpit is snug, like the other two, but you feel more in tune with the road and, frankly, closer to it. The XK still snarls and it's quick to rev in 3.8-litre form; the Moss gearbox feels as recalcitrant as ever, though it offers satisfaction if you persevere. What's really special is the way the E-type rides, with a gracefulness denied many a luxury saloon. There's motion over the road surface but bumps are beautifully rounded off rather than pummelled into submission, and it comes at no cost of slackness in the handling. Yes, if Jaguar is going to look anywhere in its back catalogue for inspiration, it's just got to be here.

WE WALK into the studio to see the C-X16 for the first time. It reminds me of how I felt when I first laid eyes on the Aston DB9: it's exactly how a Jaguar sports car for 2011 (okay, 2013) should look. Beautiful.

There's a whole load of tech blurb from Jaguar that describes the potential of the production model: just like the trio of sports cars that precede it, it's heavy on innovation, promising a petrol/electric hybrid drivetrain that combines electrical assistance with a twin-scroll supercharged 3.0-litre V6 that will pump out 375bhp for performance of 0-62mph in 4.4sec and a top speed *limited* to 186mph. Quick, but also green: 41mpg and 165g/km of carbon dioxide emissions are projected. The structure will be aluminium and we'd be disappointed if it were to be anything less: the XJ saloon has employed alloys for two generations now. Here it promises to keep weight down to 1600kg.

All that's in the future, though, because this show car is based on cut-down XK8 underpinnings and runs with that model's V8. Its bodywork, all put together in carbonfibre over four months, is an exquisite blend of curves and edginess; this is Jaguar's first sports car since the E-type, and its first two-seater since then, too (if you forget a few XJS convertibles).

No coincidence that we're looking at the C-X16 in the E-type's 50th anniversary year, nor that there are clear E-type visual cues. Check out those tail lamps: bigger and better integrated, certainly, but they're the same shape as an early E's. 'If people get the reference then that's great. If not, it doesn't matter,' says Ian Callum. 'No aspect of the design can be a style reference for the sake of it, they all have to stand up on their own. But if people recognise something, then that makes me smile.'

Those same people might recognise the side-mounted tailgate, too, though it rises electrically on a giant motorised hinge. The idea is that, on production versions, you'll simply touch the Jaguar 'leaper' badge on the back to be rewarded with the theatricals.

'The tailgate is a little tongue-in-cheek. Feasible? Not sure. The mechanics certainly work but the access is limited. It's a good bit of fun though, and we like that,' says Ian. 'We're not trying to replace the E-type. This model is more grounded in reality. I wanted to do something people would like but within the realms of modern car →

'It couldn't be anything other than a Jaguar, yet the grille is a new shape, and so are the headlamps'

Right
Jaguar design director Ian Callum had fun leading the team that designed the C-X16. It's most obviously playful at the rear, with those E-type-aping tail lamps and the side-hinged tailgate.

packaging. We couldn't possibly pass current regulations with a vehicle the size of the E-type and with those proportions. That was a straightforward act of perfection.'

Praise indeed, but there is absolutely no need to make excuses for this car. Take a look at it face-on. It couldn't be anything other than a Jaguar even from here, yet the grille is a new shape, and so are the headlamps. How does it work, then? 'It was inspired by the XF, but elongated and reproportioned. The lamps are modern, they follow the graphic of the car very carefully. There's a lot of lovely lead-in to the apertures, and a very obvious power bulge – all our cars have that, it's a subconscious and deliberate symbol of Jaguar. The face registers quite naturally.

'Otherwise it's a form language; there are creases and edges but the forms leading into them are deliberately delicate. For instance, the front three-quarter, where the wing flows into the lower bumper, that's very rounded, very Jaguar.'

If I have a favourite aspect of the C-X16, it's the view along the flanks from the front three-quarter, watching the crease that begins aft of the headlamp rise, then drops and melts in the door as another one takes over above it and kicks up over the rear wheelarch. Very Jaguar. Ian's best bit is further back, somewhere that is even more recognisably E-type. 'My favourite element is the rear three-quarter, the way the roof sweeps back in profile,' he says. 'The character of the glass leading into the rear is something I have always wanted to do.' And, just

as with Jaguars past, stance is key. 'I believe in absorbing a car when you look at it – you need to get the proportions and stance right, or you have lost people's attention straight away. This has a totality about it.' Inside, like its forebears, the C-X16 is intimate: the windscreen header and cant rails feel shrink-wrapped around you. The facia is clearly driver-oriented; there's no wood anywhere (again, like the old cars) and the shapes are new for a Jaguar – though the dashtop looks a bit Aston Martin and the binnacle flows into the centre console in a manner redolent of the Audi R8's.

You'll recognise some XF switchgear, naturally enough, but its cylindrical gear selector is absent, replaced by a jet fighter-style joystick. Tellingly, the air vents are bespoke even in this prototype. Manufacturers do not go to those lengths if production isn't a certainty.

As this show car does the rounds, it's accompanied by a minder with a very important toolkit: it has all the bits necessary to keep the C-X16 alive. In it is a 'growler' – you know, the badge that bears the Jaguar face in full snarl – except this one has been customised so it wears a pair of shades. The car isn't carrying it today; there's a decision to be made about whether or not it will at Frankfurt.

'The growler badge may go on the show car,' smiles Ian. 'Cool cat. That's what this car is all about.' He may be laughing, but Jaguar will be taking this new car very seriously indeed. Everybody else better had, too. *End*

2011 JAGUAR C-X16

ENGINE
2995cc supercharged V6 plus 70kW electric
'Hy-Performance Boost System'
POWER
375bhp (plus 94bhp)
TORQUE
332lb ft (plus 173lb ft)
TRANSMISSION
Eight-speed automatic,
rear-wheel drive
STEERING
Rack and pinion,
electrically assisted
SUSPENSION
Front and rear: wishbones,
coil springs, telescopic dampers,
anti-roll bar
BRAKES
Discs
WEIGHT
1600kg
PERFORMANCE
Top speed 186mph (limited).
0-62mph 4.4sec

Coventry climax

In the summer of 2005 car making came to an end at Jaguar's Browns Lane after
more than 50 years. But there's more to the marque than a Coventry address

WORDS: Mark Dixon // PHOTOGRAPHY: Mark Dixon/Jaguar Daimler Heritage Trust

Quality is vital to us all

Above and left
Mk2 saloons being built in
Browns Lane's main assembly
hall in 1964; new XKs and XJs
get the bright-light treatment
during final inspection.

LOOK TO YOUR LEFT as you make the final
approach to the site of Jaguar's old car plant at
Browns Lane, and you might well see sheep
grazing in the fields. They're a reminder that the
factory was a comparatively recent addition to
Coventry's rich industrial heritage: it wasn't built
until 1939, which is why it was located on the fringes of suburbia
rather than close to the city's red-brick Victorian heartland.

Nearly all the great Jaguar models, from XK120 onwards,
were made here and, although the company had other sites over
the decades, Browns Lane was its headquarters for as long as
most people could remember. All that changed in the summer of
2005, when Jaguar production was transferred from Browns
Lane to Castle Bromwich in Birmingham, as part of then-owner
Ford's plans for improved efficiency.

Browns Lane wasn't built as a car factory, although ironically →

Above
Aerial view of Browns Lane in 1995: circled is the admin and reception building, with the main assembly hall – the WW2 shadow factory – running front to back.

it was occupied during WW2 by one of Jaguar's later acquisitions, Daimler. In the mid-1930s the Air Ministry – belatedly realising that Hitler wasn't such a decent chap after all – drew up a plan to involve several of Britain's big car makers in producing aircraft components. The Ministry would stump up the capital for new factories and pay the auto companies to set up shop in them.

Daimler, Rover, Austin, Standard and The Rootes Group all signed up to the scheme, by which it was intended that each factory would monitor, or 'shadow', the others' progress to co-ordinate production. The new plants were consequently known as shadow factories, and Browns Lane was officially Daimler Shadow Factory No 2. Well into the 21st century, traces of camouflage paint could still be seen on some of the older buildings.

This first career as a wartime assembly plant explains why Jaguar had the luxury of one of the longest continuous assembly lines in Britain. The main assembly hall, also known as No 1 Factory, was where sports and saloon models were put together, entering as painted bodyshells and exiting as fully functioning cars. Its spaciousness was the attraction to William Lyons when he was seeking to expand Jaguar after the war.

Since 1928 Jaguar had occupied a site at Swallow Road, Coventry – another wartime factory, a munitions plant dating from WW1 – but the authorities refused Lyons permission to develop it further after WW2. Fortunately, he was on first-name terms with the permanent secretary to the Ministry of

Supply, which controlled all those recently-built shadow factories. The contact brokered a deal whereby Lyons could lease the million-square-foot Browns Lane plant.

Transferring production from Swallow Road to Browns Lane was a mammoth task. It took more than a year to complete the move, using lorries that had been commandeered from all around the Midlands at weekends, but the operation was carried out so efficiently that a machine operative could leave work at Swallow Road on a Friday and start on the same machine at Browns Lane on the Monday. On 28 November, 1952, Lyons was able to officially show off the completed plant to his dealers and suppliers.

The 1950s were good years for Jaguar, as the company launched a slew of new models, including saloons both large – MkVII – and small (MkI). But it so nearly all went disastrously wrong on the night of 12 February, 1957, when a fire that had started in the woodworking shop spread to the main factory building. By the time the fire brigade arrived, they were facing an inferno not seen in Coventry since the Blitz.

More than 270 cars, most of them completed MkVIII and MkI 3.4 models that were awaiting despatch, were destroyed by the blaze. Several XKSS sports racers, perhaps as many as nine that were in the process of being converted from D-types, literally melted into puddles of liquid alloy as the fire obliterated a devastating quarter of the factory. But the wartime spirit had not yet evaporated, and more than 130 companies offered Jaguar material assistance, including some of the firm's closest

'By 1996 Jaguar was winning industry awards for quality – which came as quite a surprise to anyone who remembered the 1970s'

competitors. Incredibly, limited production was resumed just 36 hours later and within six weeks it was back up to normal levels. As it turned out, 1957 would be Jaguar's best year yet for numbers of vehicles built.

In the following decade, Jaguar became Coventry's largest employer, thanks in part to the acquisition of Daimler and its plant at Radford. Both factories received some modernisation, but the 1970s marked the beginning of a period of stagnation for the marque after it was subsumed into the vastly inefficient British Leyland empire. Sales improved again in the 1980s, yet then boom turned to bust and Jaguar's future looked precarious once again. In December 1990 the cavalry finally arrived in the shape of a takeover by US giant Ford.

At the time, of course, there was much teeth-gnashing about yet another prestige British manufacturer passing into foreign hands, especially since one of Ford's first actions was to cut the 12,000-strong workforce by one-third in order to improve efficiency. However, 15 years of ownership proved Ford to be a relatively benevolent parent. In 1993 a new £8.5m overhead-mounted assembly line was installed at Browns Lane, and by 1996 Jaguar was winning industry awards for its manufacturing quality – which came as quite a surprise to anybody who remembered some of the cars that were produced under the Leyland regime in the mid-1970s.

Unfortunately, having the best product in the world is no good if you cannot find enough buyers for them, and the falling strength of the pound in the early 2000s hurt Jaguar sales badly. Even so, it came as a severe shock when Ford announced in September 2004 that it was transferring car production from Browns Lane to Castle Bromwich in Birmingham and shedding more jobs in the process. The collapse of MG Rover helped put this news into perspective. Browns Lane would survive, albeit in a much-reduced state, with the Jaguar Daimler Heritage Trust continuing to occupy the fine new building it moved into in 1998.

Obviously this was a difficult time for Jaguar, but when *Octane* toured the plant in April 2005 there was little sense of resentment in the air. The irreverent banter that characterises British car factories still competed with the whirr of power tools and the hum of forklift trucks, and despite recent media intrusion, no-one objected to having their photograph taken. Ironically, because many Jaguar workers had been with the company a long time, they were at an age where the prospect of early retirement was starting to look quite attractive.

Jaguar enthusiasts shouldn't get too misty eyed about the relocation, either. In his day, Sir William Lyons wouldn't have hesitated to move from Browns Lane if it had become economically necessary. Tradition is all very well but, as those MG Rover events at Longbridge proved, staying in business is more important. **End**

Right
The contented smiles of a happy workforce; sewing seat trim on what looks like a pre-war Singer; losses suffered in 1957 fire did not hold firm back for long.

SIX-CYLINDER
Jaguar E-type

At least as beautiful as a contemporary Ferrari
or Aston, the E-type is still a relative bargain
– but prices for good cars are rising as more
and more buyers jump on the bandwagon

WORDS: RICHARD DREDGE

NINE OUT OF TEN COOL CATS who expressed a preference reckon this is the most glamorous, sensual car of all time. And is that any wonder? There aren't enough superlatives in the dictionary to do the E-type justice; if grown men had car posters on their bedroom walls, this Jag would grace most of them. All those clichés about setting the world alight are true; the E-type really did rewrite the rulebook.

Besides having looks, pace, power, engineering and heritage, the Jag also offered an extra quality over its rivals – relative affordability. While Aston Martin, Ferrari, Porsche et al boasted worthy rivals, they were all much more costly. That price differential has remained; a superb E-type may be a valuable piece of kit, but an equivalent DB4 or 250GT will cost you rather more.

The mythology of the E-type started early, thanks to an infamous road test in *The Autocar* that (just) proved Jaguar's

claim of a 150mph top speed. In fact, the model tested had almost certainly been fitted with a specially prepared and blueprinted engine, and a more realistic top speed for production cars is round about 140mph. That's still plenty fast enough for most people, although hard-chargers may want to consider a modern five-speed gearbox conversion – oddly, the E-type was not offered with overdrive, unlike its XK predecessors.

Jaguar historian Philip Porter runs the E-type Club. He owns several examples of the breed himself, and comments: 'There is a massive spread of values from £7000 to hundreds of thousands – or £1m-plus for a genuine Lightweight. At the one extreme you can buy a 2+2 project car and at the other a superbly restored, heavily upgraded Series One roadster.'

Fixed-heads used to be around half the price of roadsters but, quite rightly, that gap has narrowed considerably in

recent years. Series One FHC restoration projects are still £10,500-17,500; roadsters are in the £14,000-26,000 bracket.

Porter says: 'Many factors influence car values, including structural integrity, completeness, powerplant displacement (unless a very early model, the 4.2s are worth a shade more at present), whether it's a 'matching numbers' machine and whether it's left- or right-hand drive.'

For a useable car that hasn't been fully restored or upgraded, expect to pay £18,000-30,000 for a coupé and £26,000-46,000 for an open car. Really excellent original or restored examples start at £42,000 for coupés and £67,000 for roadsters. Some reputable dealers charge considerably more – and with good reason, as a proper professional resto costs at least £80,000 and upgrades can add far more.

Derek Hood runs JD Classics, one of the UK's largest E-type specialists. He,

'Fixed-heads used to be half the price of roadsters but, quite rightly, that gap has narrowed considerably in the last year or two'

along with Henry Pearman of Eagle E-types, is responsible for some of the most exacting E-type restorations in the UK. The companies also offer a wide range of upgrades to make the cars more useable in modern conditions.

Says Hood: 'Early E-types always looked better than they drove, which is why buyers will pay a premium for cars that have been sympathetically upgraded. Improved braking, cooling and suspension systems are valued highly, as are five-speed gearboxes, fuel injection and discreet installations for stereo or phone.'

You might assume that it's the earliest E-types that are the most sought after, especially the flat-floor models that were produced for just a year. This isn't the case, though; the relative lack of usability of these early cars means it's the 4.2-litre editions that everyone wants, thanks to their better seats, nicer gearbox, stronger

brakes and torquier engine. Hood continues: 'We're now seeing the very best 4.2-litre Roadsters at £200,000-plus but, to command such a price, it will have had everything done, including a list of upgrades; a 3.8-litre model is worth around 15% less. It is no surprise that the best cars can attract such sums of money, as a properly executed full restoration can be £160,000 and then there's the value of the project vehicle to be taken into account.'

ENGINE
The XK powerplant that lives under the E-type's bonnet is renowned for its durability as long as it is looked after. Easily capable of giving 150,000 miles between rebuilds, the straight-six isn't especially stressed unless the car is regularly thrashed – and few owners use their E-types very hard.

Get the engine up to temperature

before taking the model for a test drive; listen for any knocks or rattles as it gets warm. Do the usual checks for oil leaks as well as smoke from the exhaust; you can expect to see a few wisps when starting from cold but things should quickly settle. Once fully warm, look for at least 40psi on the oil pressure gauge, with the motor turning over at 3000rpm.

Allow the engine to tick over for a few minutes and make sure that the electric cooling fan cuts in; they often don't. If the needle on the temperature gauge just keeps climbing, the powerplant may well have overheated at some point – so make sure there's no evidence of the head gasket having blown, by looking for white 'mayonnaise' (the result of oil and water mixing) on the underside of the filler cap.

If the engine is smoking badly or it's very rattly, a complete rebuild is clearly on the cards – but don't get too hung up →

Above
Even American safety regs – side repeater lights, uncowled headlights and wraparound bumpers – couldn't ruin the E-type's sex appeal.

'Frankly, if all is well with the body, the car is unlikely to give any insurmountable problems elsewhere'

about this. You can rebuild an XK engine at home from around £2000, or pay £6000 or more to get it done professionally to a high quality.

However, if you take the DIY route, be warned that the XK unit isn't as easy to revive as some others. If the last motor you overhauled was a Ford Crossflow unit, expect the E-type to be more of a challenge.

TRANSMISSION

With a fairly bullet-proof transmission, there is little to worry about where the E-type's drivetrain is concerned. It doesn't last forever, though, so listen for clonks which signify worn universal joints or whining that betrays a worn differential. Fixing the former is straightforward; the latter is less easy to put right and rather more costly, with a replacement costing £750.

Gearboxes are also strong, but the recalcitrance of the Moss unit fitted to 3.8-litre cars is legendary. It's also noisier than the later version, so don't expect a gearbox that's especially easy or pleasant to use, particularly when selecting first or reverse. If things are really noisy, anticipate paying £900 for a rebuilt transmission, whether it's a Moss unit or a later one.

SUSPENSION, STEERING & BRAKES

Ideally you should jack up each wheel and rock it diagonally to feel for wear in the bushes and bearings. Expect to feel some play at the rear wheels; if there isn't any, the bearings have been set too tight and will probably overheat and fail. There are bearings in the hub as well as the lower fulcrum; a little play in each of these can lead to what feels like an alarming amount of movement at the wheel, but it should be no more than an eighth of an inch or so.

At the front there shouldn't be nearly as much play in the wheels, although don't be surprised if you can detect a small amount. If it is bearing wear that's easy to sort, but it might be that the lower wishbone balljoints have worn. These act directly on the wishbone, which can be shimmed only so much before it has to be replaced at a little over £100 per side.

Remove the rear wheels and look at the axle cage mountings, which can perish or break. If you've already driven the car by this stage, and it feels rather lively at the back, it could be because the rear-wheel steering is coming into effect as a result of the wear. While you're under there, ensure there's no oil leaking from the diff onto the inboard rear brakes. Any signs of trouble and it's an axle-out job to put things right.

BODYWORK, ELECTRICS & TRIM

Those glamorous E-type looks can hide a multitude of sins, and it's easy to view potential purchases through rose-tinted

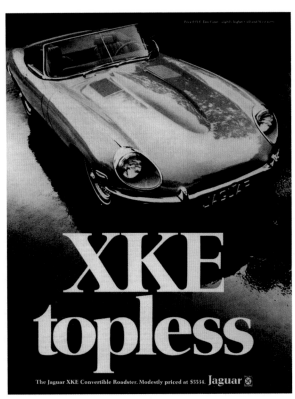

XKE topless

The Jaguar XKE Convertible Roadster. Modestly priced at $5534. **Jaguar**

eyewear. Don't let your heart drown out your head, though; buying an overpriced dressed-up shed could leave you out of pocket to the tune of tens of thousands of pounds. Properly restoring an E-type is a hell of an undertaking, and many people get it wrong.

Frankly, if all is well in the body department, the car is unlikely to give any insurmountable problems elsewhere – but check all is what it seems.

If an example has been restored, poor bodywork repairs are one thing you'll possibly have to contend with. If the car hasn't been revived, E-types can rot just about anywhere, so check every square inch of metal – twice over. Lift the fuel filler flap and see what's lurking beneath: if it's a mess, other bits will have been missed as the car was clearly restored with no attention to detail.

Panel gaps should be tight and even, especially where the bonnet butts up against the bulkhead. With the bonnet accounting for nearly half the length of the car, it's tricky getting things to line up properly – which is why they often don't. Also check all the seams as well as the front valance, which frequently harbours rot.

Coupé tailgates rarely rust but boot lids do, along with door bottoms. In the case of the latter there should be a polythene sheet inside the door casing;

it's usually missing. The door fills up with water as a result, and with the drain holes often blocked up, the water has nowhere to go.

Don't overlook the frame ahead of the front bulkhead, which supports the engine, steering and suspension. The tubes that make up this frame can crack as well as corrode, and it's not easy to check that all is well because it's rather overcrowded in there. If any work needs doing, everything ahead of the bulkhead will have to be removed for access.

Door locks can give problems so try locking, unlocking and opening each door from inside as well as out; don't underestimate the hassle you could have getting everything to work properly.

'We regularly spend 200-300 hours on this type of seemingly minor work on perfect-looking E-types whilst preparing them for our showrooms,' agrees Eagle's Henry Pearman.

Electrics give few problems, and there is really nothing to worry about trim-wise because everything is available. It will soon get costly if everything needs doing though.

CONCLUSION

It is easy to overlook the differences between the various E-type iterations, but you can't afford to do this because those differences are very significant. Put simply, →

JAGUAR E-TYPE 3.8 COUPÉ

ENGINE
3781cc straight-six, twin overhead camshafts, 12 valves. Alloy head, cast-iron block. Three SU HD8 carburettors
POWER
265bhp@5500rpm
TORQUE
260lb ft@4000rpm
TRANSMISSION
Four-speed manual, rear-wheel drive
SUSPENSION
Front: independent via transverse wishbones, torsion bars and telescopic dampers, anti-roll bar. Rear: independent via lower transverse tubular links, twin coil springs each side, telescopic dampers
BRAKES
Servo-assisted discs all round, in-board at rear
WEIGHT
1202kg (2644lb)
PERFORMANCE
0-60mph 7.1sec
Top speed 149mph
COST NEW
£2160

CLUBS

E-type Club. +44 (0)1584 781588,
www.e-typeclub.com

Jaguar Drivers' Club. +44 (0)1582
419332, http://jaguardriver.co.uk

Jaguar Enthusiasts' Club. +44
(0)1179 698 186, www.jec.org.uk

Jaguar Clubs of North America
(umbrella organisation),
www.jcna.com

BOOKS

E-type, End of an Era
by Chris Harvey. Haynes,
ISBN 0 946609 16 0

Jaguar E-type (Great Cars)
by Nigel Thorley. Haynes,
ISBN 0 1 85960 813 2

*Jaguar E-type, the Definitive
History* by Philip Porter. Haynes,
0 85429 580 1

*Jaguar E-type,
the Complete Story*
by Jonathan Wood. Crowood,
ISBN 0 1 86126 147 0

*Jaguar E-type 3.8 & 4.2-litre,
Essential Buyer's Guide*
by Peter Crespin. Veloce,
ISBN 0 1 904788 85 8

Original Jaguar E-type
by Philip Porter. Bay View,
ISBN 1 870979 12 5

'Few cars at any price are as rewarding to own or drive as a properly restored E-type'

Above
Without doubt, the Series One fixed-head coupé is the cleanest-looking Jaguar E-type of them all.

if you get the wrong E-type for your needs you'll wonder what all the fuss is about. Also, don't get taken in by the glamour of the roadster when the coupé is more affordable and every bit as good to drive – and better looking too in the eyes of many. However, bear in mind that with many coupés scrapped or converted to roadsters, fixed-heads are now rarer than open-topped examples – which is why their values are on the up.

If you're after an original right-hand-drive car, they're far rarer than you might think. Around 85% of E-type production was exported, which is why many right-hand-drive E-types have been converted from left-hand drive at some point (this barely affects value though).

The bottom line is that you must ensure the car you buy is what it claims to be. Check the correct powerplant is fitted and that it's not a roadster which left the factory as a coupé (or ensure the price is much-reduced). The Jaguar Daimler Heritage Trust is invaluable in being able to provide you with details of the model's original specification. However, you should also invest in a copy of Philip Porter's book *Original Jaguar E-type* (see

panel, right), which will highlight any inconsistencies in the car's specification.

If the model does need any work, there's no need to fret about any problems with parts availability, because absolutely everything is available to revive an E-type, no matter how tired. The cost of all the parts and necessary labour is another matter, but a competent home mechanic can tackle just about any job.

We'll let Derek Hood wrap up: 'There is no such thing as a bargain where the E-type is concerned. We frequently encounter people who buy a car that's priced at £20,000 below what would be expected. Then the new owner starts delving and discovers that to get the Jag up to the standard they were expecting, it needs £50,000 spent on it.

'Few models at any price are as rewarding to own or drive as a properly restored E-type. And there's the rub: the car must be properly restored if any pleasure is to be derived from it – and there's a huge amount of enjoyment to be gained from E-type ownership.' *End*

THANKS TO Henry Pearman, Derek Hood and Philip Porter.

TIMELINE

1961: E-type launched at Geneva Motor Show in coupé and roadster guises, with 3.8-litre XK engine.

1962: Heelwells incorporated into front floors; earlier editions are known as 'flat-floor' cars.

1964: Engine now displaces 4.2 litres, while an all-synchromesh gearbox is fitted. There are also improvements to brakes, servo and seats.

1966: 2+2 E-type available, with longer wheelbase and higher roofline.

1967: Series 11/2 model arrives, with headlamp fairings deleted and engine modified for US emissions regulations.

1968: Series 2 goes on sale, designed to meet US safety regs. Wraparound bumpers, bigger sidelights (now below bumper) and different carburettors. However, brakes are improved and windscreen rake is increased on 2+2.

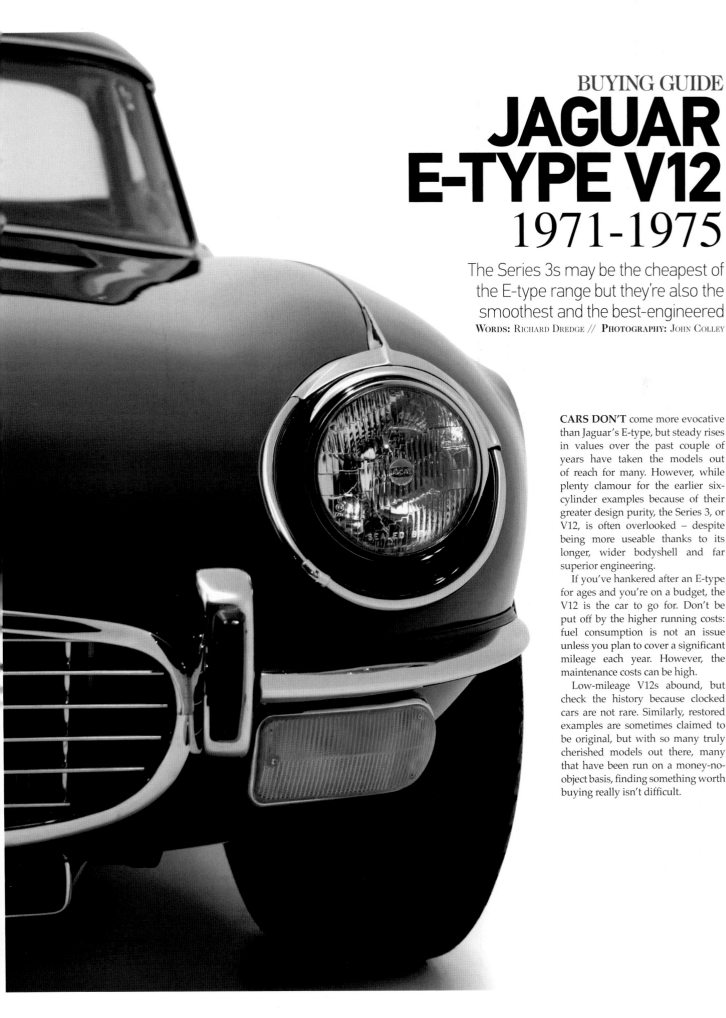

JAGUAR E-TYPE V12
1971-1975

The Series 3s may be the cheapest of the E-type range but they're also the smoothest and the best-engineered

WORDS: RICHARD DREDGE // **PHOTOGRAPHY:** JOHN COLLEY

CARS DON'T come more evocative than Jaguar's E-type, but steady rises in values over the past couple of years have taken the models out of reach for many. However, while plenty clamour for the earlier six-cylinder examples because of their greater design purity, the Series 3, or V12, is often overlooked – despite being more useable thanks to its longer, wider bodyshell and far superior engineering.

If you've hankered after an E-type for ages and you're on a budget, the V12 is the car to go for. Don't be put off by the higher running costs: fuel consumption is not an issue unless you plan to cover a significant mileage each year. However, the maintenance costs can be high.

Low-mileage V12s abound, but check the history because clocked cars are not rare. Similarly, restored examples are sometimes claimed to be original, but with so many truly cherished models out there, many that have been run on a money-no-object basis, finding something worth buying really isn't difficult. →

JAGUAR E-TYPE V12

ENGINE
5343cc all-alloy V12,
sohc per bank, 24 valves,
Four Zenith-Stromberg
carburettors
POWER
272bhp@5850rpm
TORQUE
304lb.ft@5600rpm
TRANSMISSION
Four-speed manual or
three-speed auto
SUSPENSION
Front: independent via
wishbones, torsion bars,
telescopic dampers, anti-roll
bar. Rear: independent via
fixed-length driveshafts,
lower transverse links,
radius arms, twin coil spring
and telescopic damper units,
anti-roll bar
BRAKES
Servo-assisted discs
WEIGHT
1527kg (3361lb)
PERFORMANCE
0-60mph 6.4sec
Top speed 146mph
COST NEW
£3387 (1971)

BODY

Look for poor panel fit, corrosion and kinked chassis tubes that have been caused by low-speed knocks. Bonnet misalignment occurs through the latter: because this section is so huge, check for even panel gaps and make sure the bonnet isn't distorted. Also ensure that the car hasn't been jacked up where it should not have been; the radiator support is sometimes wrecked because of this, with the radiator potentially pushed into the bonnet. All body panels are available new from specialists.

Most E-types have been restored, so ask who did the work and what was done, and find out if there's a photo record. Be wary of cars that have had major home renovations – without the proper jigs the bodyshell may have distorted. Lifting the fuel filler flap may reveal bare metal and even rust, suggesting a superficial restoration and likely problems.

Under the bonnet check for bulkhead corrosion, especially around the battery tray. The scuttle sides contain box sections, which rust from the inside out. By the time corrosion is visible outside, the inside is rotten, which means costly repairs.

The rear of the monocoque also rots, especially the B-posts and chassis strengthening rails; sills are durable but check for filler. Get underneath and look for corrosion around the rear radius arm and anti-roll bar mountings. Finish by checking the double-skinned rear wings for rust, along with the wheelarch lips, plus the top and bottom of each door.

Beware of left-hand-drive cars changed to right-hand steering and 2+2s converted to roadsters. Most conversions are fine, but values are lower. RHD chassis numbers start IS.10001 (roadster) and IS.50001 (2+2); LHD cars are numbered IS.20001 (roadster) and IS.70001 (2+2).

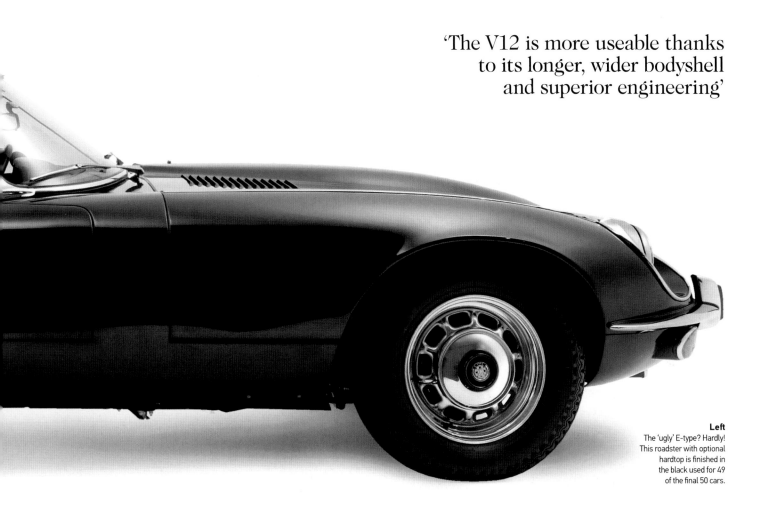

'The V12 is more useable thanks
to its longer, wider bodyshell
and superior engineering'

Left
The 'ugly' E-type? Hardly!
This roadster with optional
hardtop is finished in
the black used for 49
of the final 50 cars.

ENGINE

Properly looked after, the V12 powerplant will cover 200,000 miles with ease. However, poor general maintenance can lead to overheating, so idle the engine for several minutes and watch the temperature gauge.

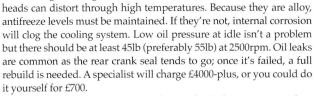

Harshness points to previous overheating; the long block and heads can distort through high temperatures. Because they are alloy, antifreeze levels must be maintained. If they're not, internal corrosion will clog the cooling system. Low oil pressure at idle isn't a problem but there should be at least 45lb (preferably 55lb) at 2500rpm. Oil leaks are common as the rear crank seal tends to go; once it's failed, a full rebuild is needed. A specialist will charge £4000-plus, or you could do it yourself for £700.

The V12 has 20 rubber coolant hoses; check they're not perished because replacement can be involved and they need to be to correct specification – the coolant system runs at 15lb (earlier E-types are just 4lb) so the hoses have to be reinforced. A full set is £150.

Original rubber fuel lines will need replacing and the Zenith-Stromberg carbs go out of tune when their diaphragms perish. Rebuilt carbs are the best solution; there are four at £350 each. Incidentally, the V12 is happy to run on unleaded in standard form.

TRANSMISSION

Most V12s have a three-speed Borg Warner Model 12 automatic transmission, but the Jaguar four-speed manual is more sought after. They're both durable units, yet the latter can suffer from weak synchromesh on second and third; check for difficulty selecting gears when the 'box is cold. If a revived manual is needed, expect to pay £450 for an exchange one.

If ratio changes are jerky on the auto or there's any slipping, the unit needs a service, involving fresh fluid, filters and adjustment of the bands. If things are really bad an overhaul will be required; budget £1500 for a rebuilt 'box. Clutches, differentials and driveshafts are durable, but check for vibrations, clonks or whining.

STEERING & SUSPENSION

The rack-and-pinion steering is reliable, but wear in the column universal joints is normal. Replacement is easy and they're less than £100 for the pair. If there are creaks from the rear suspension, it will be because the lower hub pivots have corroded; if not greased regularly they wear rapidly or seize. Don't be surprised if there's detectable play in the rear wheelbearings; if there's none at all they've been overtightened, and will overheat as a result.

At the front, be wary of too many shims between the wishbone and ball joint – two or three is okay, but any more and there is a danger of the suspension collapsing. Fitting exchange wishbones is the easiest solution; it's a cheap and easy exercise.   →

Below
Independent rear
suspension, just visible
here, will suffer if not
greased properly.

'Values are going up, if rather steadily, and the cars are surprisingly useable'

BRAKES & WHEELS

The brakes should feel very strong, but imbalance isn't unusual – it's frequently caused by oil on the in-board rear discs which has leaked from the differential. Fixing this is involved, as the diff has to come out. Contrarily, the self-adjusting handbrake often seizes through lack of greasing; try to roll the car on a level surface and see if it quickly grinds to a halt.

Steel disc wheels were standard but chromed wires are now more common – check for damaged spokes and worn splines, which get a hard time because of the V12's torque.

MARKET

High fuel prices and steep running costs have put many people off buying the V12 E-type, to the point where you can now get a useable 2+2 for £11,500 – but it won't be all that good under the shiny paint. Even the nicest 2+2s rarely fetch more than £30,000, while you can typically add around 50% to purchase an equivalent roadster.

Transmissions don't generally affect values, but while most buyers of fixed-heads don't mind an automatic, it's the stick shift that roadster fans usually want. Commemorative cars rarely surface for sale, and mint examples have been known to touch six figures.

ELECTRICS & TRIM

Unrestored cars often have poor earths or brittle wiring – fix with emery paper (cheap) or a fresh loom (more expensive). The heater motor suffers from failed circuitry or seizure through lack of use, but access is easy as it's next to the battery under the bonnet. Check that the radiator's thermostatic cooling fan cuts in, because failure can lead to major bills.

Brightwork can be replaced: mazak door handles, tail-lamp housings etc tend to be pitted. A fresh mohair roadster roof is £800, add the same again for fitting it.

CONCLUSION

Just 7990 roadsters and 7297 coupés were built, but survival rates are high and those that have lasted this far are generally cherished examples. With great specialist and club support, the Series 3 E-type makes huge sense on many levels: values are only going up, if rather steadily, and the cars are surprisingly useable, even on the longest journeys.

Perhaps the only problem is the size and complexity of that V12. In fine fettle it makes the car, but if you get a bad one the costs will quickly add up. And, unlike with the six-cylinder models, you're unlikely to get your money back. *End*

THANKS TO Gordon Yardley at Woodmanton Classics.

JAGUAR DAIMLER XJ
1968-1992

Considered one of the best saloons in the world when new,
the Jaguar and Daimler XJs are now something of a bargain.
Choose wisely, and they can still be utterly rewarding

WORDS: RICHARD DREDGE // **PHOTOGRAPHS:** MAGIC CAR PICS

CHEAP LUXURY IS EASY TO FIND, but the value offered by Jaguar's XJ is spectacular. Six-and-a-half grand buys a mint XJ6 and a thousand more doubles the cylinder count; choose either and you'll have one of the most comfortable models ever made.

Pronounced Car of the Year in 1969, the XJ marked the start of a new era for Jaguar. Offered in three series with a choice of wheelbases, transmissions and engines, it could also be ordered in coupé form. Working out what to go for can be a challenge, but you should always buy on condition and treat the specification as secondary.

Both Jaguar and Daimler versions are worth the same amount, and what series you buy makes little difference. Condition is all, yet coupés are worth slightly more than saloons. A worthy XJ6 is £2000-plus, £4000 bags a nice one, and £6000 gets you something really special. Add 20% for an XJ12 and the same again for a coupé.
→

Right
Jaguar purists consider
the Series I to be the
most desirable of all XJs.

JAGUAR XJ6 SERIES III 4.2

ENGINE
4235cc in-line six, DOHC, 12
valves. Alloy head, cast-iron
block. Lucas/Bosch
L-Jetronic injection
POWER
205bhp@5000rpm
TORQUE
236lb ft@3700rpm
TRANSMISSION
BW three-speed auto,
rear-wheel drive
SUSPENSION
Front: double wishbones,
coils and telescopic dampers,
anti-roll bar. Rear: lower
wishbones with fixed-length
drive shafts, coil springs and
telescopic dampers
BRAKES
Discs all round,
servo assisted
WEIGHT
1760kg
PERFORMANCE
0-60mph 10sec
Top speed 127mph
COST NEW
£14,609 (1980)

'Few unrestored cars remain in good condition, while many renovations aren't very well done, so be careful'

BODY

Due to inadequate rustproofing, poor quality and low values, bodged XJs abound. Few unrestored cars remain in a good condition, while many renovations aren't very well done. Rot areas include the bottoms of the A-, B- and C-posts, the sills, rear arches and valances. Check these, and the wheel well and door bottoms. Less obvious are the rear suspension radius arms and mounts and the front and rear screen surrounds, especially on the Series III. If there's any corrosion around either screen, repair involves taking out the glass. Once removed, the repairs aren't too difficult.

Bonnet hinge mounts also corrode, and can break altogether. The bonnet can rust, as can the bootlid, wings around the headlights, plus the jacking points; check these areas very carefully for filler by taking a magnet with you.

The rad support frame dissolves, which is an MoT failure; if left to fester, rust then eats into the front chassis structure. Repairs are a big job on the XJ6 and even worse on the XJ12 due to poor access. Finally check the front subframe, which can rot, especially on Series IIIs and some Series IIs. Expect to pay £1800-plus for a specialist to supply and fit a used subframe.

ENGINE

Look for a service history, make sure the motor sounds right and ensure the oil is clean. A rebuild is needed at the first sign of wear; delay things and the bills will quickly mount.

The straight-six has an alloy head, so antifreeze must be maintained. Even a cared-for engine will need a fresh radiator every 5-10 years, at £220 plus fitting. Expect oil pressure of 40psi when cruising – but senders and gauges can be unreliable. Smoking on the overrun or when the throttle is blipped points to hardened valve stem seals or worn guides, a £1500-plus fix. A greasy underside suggests a failed rear crankshaft oil seal, which requires an engine rebuild. Specialists charge £4000-plus for the full Monty, or you could do it yourself for upwards of £600 – but it's an involved job.

SU carbs suffer from worn automatic chokes. Rebuilt units are approximately £420, an electric system is £300, or a manual conversion is £85.

The V12 is costly to rebuild, so ensure the oil has been changed frequently and that antifreeze has been maintained. This unit is long-lived if looked after, but the key is to search for signs of previous overheating – which can scrap an engine.

TRANSMISSION

The autos had a Borg Warner trans until 1977, then XJ12s got a GM400. Some Series I autos were clunky when new, but later cars should be smooth. Even if all seems well it's worth inspecting the fluid for colour, level and condition. If it's black and smells foul, a rebuild is on the cards, at £900-plus. The manual is strong and usually fitted with overdrive. If this is slow to engage, the oil probably needs changing or topping up; wear is unusual. Diffs are tough but can leak oil over the inboard rear discs. Repairs are at least £1200; the seal often leaks because the brakes have overheated, so a full rebuild might be needed.

STEERING & SUSPENSION

All XJs have power steering, which is generally reliable, but check for leaks. If the fluid isn't topped up, the car probably isn't cherished. Worn suspension and rear subframe bushes are usual so ensure they've not split; worn front tyres point to perished suspension bushes, knocking out the geometry. There are a huge number of bushes and renewal is costly and involved. Inspect the dampers as they can leak, which is an MoT failure. Replacements cost £45 upwards apiece, so do a bounce test and make sure the car quickly settles. →

TIMELINE

1968
XJ6 introduced to replace S-type, 420,
420G and Mk2
1969
Daimler Sovereign goes on sale
1972
XJ12 and Daimler Double-Six join range
1973
Production of SWB models ceases
1974
Series II XJ arrives and XJ coupé reaches
showrooms. Final 2.8-litre cars are built
1975
XJ6 3.4 and Daimler Vanden Plas 4.2 arrive
1977
Final coupés are built
1979
Series III arrives and six-cylinder cars
gain a five-speed option
1981
V12s are now in HE (High Efficiency) spec
1982
Six-cylinder cars get a BW66 auto
1987
Final XJ6 is built
1989
V12s can now officially use unleaded
1990
Anti-lock brakes now standard
1991
Last XJ12 is built
1992
Last Daimler Double-Six is produced

SPECIALISTS

David Marks
www.davidmarksgarages.co.uk
Alan Lloyd
www.jaguar-specialists.com
Aldridge Trimming
www.aldridge.co.uk
David Manners
www.jagspares.co.uk
Knowles-Wilkins Engineering
www.kwejaguar.co.uk
Martin Robey
www.martinrobey.com
SNG Barratt
www.sngbarratt.com

CLUBS

Jaguar Enthusiasts' Club
www.jec.org.uk
Jaguar Drivers' Club
http://jaguardriver.co.uk

BOOKS

Original Jaguar XJ
by Nigel Thorley. Bay View Books
ISBN 1 901432 11 4
Jaguar XJ, the Complete Companion
by Nigel Thorley. Bay View Books
ISBN 1 870979 22 2

Below
Series II models like
this had similar rear
styling to the Series I.

'Mint examples are cheap – but they can be hard to find, so you'll have to search to find the car that's right for you'

BRAKES & WHEELS

The rear brake discs are mounted inboard and as a result they often get neglected or covered in oil from a leaking differential. They also sometimes rust, so check their condition as replacing the various bits is fiddly and time consuming – although at least it's all work that you can do yourself, without any special skills.

The handbrake is frequently poorly maintained as it isn't very accessible; it has its own calipers and pads, which can seize up. Make sure the car can be held on a hill using just the handbrake, as fixing this can be a pain.

TRIM

Much of the XJ's appeal lies in its cabin, which is as luxurious as you'll find. Most XJs have leather trim, but the 3.4 was introduced for the fleet market so it often came with cloth. Any interior that's seen better days could cost big money to fix – as much as £3500 if all the trim needs TLC.

Then there are the carpets and maybe the wood, too; the potential for serious expenditure should not be underestimated. Also make sure all the exterior brightwork is there and in good condition; most XJs came with lots of bodywork trim and some of it is hard to revive.

ELECTRICS

Series II XJs suffered all sorts of electrical gremlins; Series Is and IIIs are generally better but you still must check everything carefully. Switchgear on early cars could be unreliable and the powered window buttons are usually the first thing to pack up. Everything is available to put things right, but some bits are costly so be prepared for big bills if there are lots of problems.

XJ looms tend to be quite complex and faults can be tricky to pin down, so look for evidence of bodgery such as modern stereos and alarms being spliced in; sorting these can be a nightmare.

CONCLUSION

Nowhere are Grace, Space and Pace more readily available than here; all three are offered in abundance. Even better, mint examples are cheap – but they can be hard to find, so you'll have to search to find the car that's right for you. Tread carefully if you are considering a restoration project, because costs can quickly escalate.

There is a surprising amount you can do yourself yet these cars are complex in places and experts will be essential for some jobs. That's why you need to weigh up just what's needed if you're buying a model that needs work of any kind. ◼

THANKS TO David Marks of David Marks Garages for his help with this feature.

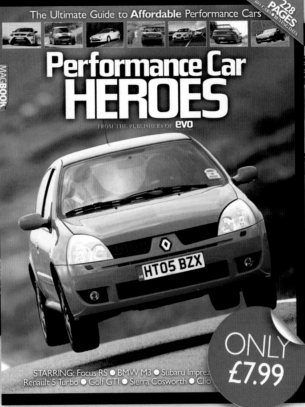
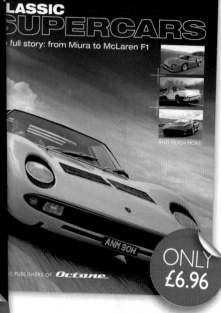

JAGUAR XJ-S

With a 21-year production run, there are plenty of XJ-S models to choose from. Consider your choice carefully, buy the right one and you won't regret it

WORDS: SIMON GOLDSWORTHY

GO ON, TREAT YOURSELF. You know you deserve it. For the cost of a service on a Ferrari, you could go out and buy the kind of power that you can't even begin to justify with a straight face, packaged with such sensual grace that it leaves a deliciously-guilty feeling every time you run a hand over the panels. Yes, the XJ-S has the lot. But can you make a case for using one as a daily driver?

In part, that comes down to what kind of driving you do every day. The XJ-S was originally conceived as a true Grand Tourer, capable of devouring huge distances while cocooning the occupants in the utmost luxury. Which, to be quite honest, couldn't be more different from the average school run or office commute.

But stay with it for a moment. Just because the run to work is dull, that doesn't mean you want it to be uncomfortable. Surely borrowing a little glamour from an imaginary cross-continental jaunt can only leave your energy levels higher when Monday morning rolls around? And if the school run is an integral part of your day, then it stands to reason that most of your passengers will be rather short in stature and so ideal for the pint-sized plus-two seating out back.

Yet every indulgence comes at a price, and there is no getting away from that dreaded Jaguar curse of prodigious thirst. The XJ-S was more aerodynamic than the E-type, but the very first cars struggled to get into double figures under all but the gentlest of use. That's hardly surprising when you consider the long, wide and extremely sturdy bodywork sitting on a modified version of the XJ6C floorpan. Combine this with a lusty 5.3-litre V12 engine and – although driving a car with so much torque that it can accelerate to over 140mph from rest in top gear alone may get addictive – paying for the privilege at the pumps on a daily basis will always be painful.

Fortunately, there are various ways of mitigating this problem. The most obvious is to buy a post-1981 car with a 5.3HE tag on the back. That stands for High Efficiency, and refers to the adaptation of Michael May's head design for the combustion chambers. Combine this with the fuel injection

Above
XJ-S's styling was controversial but it followed the seminal E-type and opinions have since mellowed.

'Buy one that is sound and has been regularly serviced. Leave some money over for the occasional hefty repair bill, then relax and enjoy the experience. You deserve it!'

and you get the same power, a torque curve that comes in usefully lower down the rev range and a 20% improvement in economy. Heck, with that you can even push towards 16mpg.

Or, if you are confident enough in your own abilities not to need the reassurance of 12 cylinders, then go for the 3590cc AJ6-engined models that arrived in 1983. They'll still do 142mph thanks in part to the five-speed Getrag gearbox, but can squeeze up to the psychological 20mpg barrier.

With either of these later machines, you will also get facelifted interiors with the wood paneling that these cars'

elegance somehow seems to demand. There were subtle but fairly extensive changes to the panelwork in 1991, but those distinctive flying buttresses at the rear remained.

If you really cannot live with them, there is always the Convertible option available from 1988. But whichever you choose, don't think about trying to run an XJ-S on just loose change – it takes all the fun out of the experience. Buy one that is sound and has been regularly serviced. Leave some money over for the occasional hefty repair bill, then relax and enjoy the experience.

As we said, you deserve it! `End`

Octane

CLASSIC & PERFORMANCE CARS WEBSITE

JAGUAR: THE FAMILY TREE

Your ultimate guide to Jaguars, classic and modern. From the earliest SS to the svelte new XJ, they're all here for your enjoyment...

WORDS: MATTHEW HAYWARD

SS1 1931-1936

This is where it all started. The SS1 was William Lyons' first car built on a purpose-made chassis, rather than borrowing someone else's. The Standard Motor Co supplied the underpinnings and six-cylinder engine, and the model was created especially for SS Cars. Despite its sporting styling, the SS1 was not fast by 1931 standards, although its good looks and low price made up for this.
Power: 55bhp Top speed: 72mph

SS2 1931–1936

The SS2 was not a replacement for the SS1, but a smaller and cheaper counterpart which was sold alongside the original model and widened the appeal of Lyons' cars. It was considerably smaller than the SS1, due to its use of the Standard four-cylinder side-valve engine, but it was well proportioned and looked equally as good as its bigger brother.
Power: 27bhp Top speed: 60mph

SS90 1935

Based on a shortened version of the SS1 chassis, the SS90 was an open-topped sports car powered by the Standard side-valve engine but with an uprated alloy cylinder head and twin carburettors. Even with these modifications, the SS90 remained a leisurely drive and a mere 23 were built before the company switched to the SS100 in 1936.
Power: 70bhp Top speed: 90mph

SS100 Jaguar 2½-litre 1936–1941

The SS100 was the car the SS90 should always have been, and was a landmark in the growth of the marque. Its engine was a development of the SS90's, and featured the same upgrades as the 2½-litre saloon's – power output rose from 70bhp to 102bhp, and performance was significantly improved. The SS100 Jaguar was conceived as an image-building exercise, with Lyons expecting it to do well in competition circles. In the end, 308 were sold – most to road-going enthusiasts.
Power: 102bhp Top speed: 94mph

SS Jaguar 1½/2/3½-litre saloon 1936-1940

This was the first Jaguar saloon that had the power to match its looks, paving the way for the company's subsequent legendary big, fast cars. Performance was impressive for the class of 1936, thanks in no small part to the Standard engine getting a boost from twin SU carburettors and an overhead-valve set-up in the range-topping 2½-litre version. From 1938, the bodies were formed from pressed steel rather than hand-beaten aluminium, because demand for the cars had outgrown supply and production volumes needed to rise significantly. **Power: 102bhp Top speed: 88mph**

Jaguar 2½/3½-litre saloon 1946-1949

After production of the SS cars ceased in 1940, the assembly line was turned over to military use until 1945. Now known by the marque name Jaguar, the firm's first post-war model was the handsome 2½-litre saloon. This was basically a light update of the pre-war car, but powered by Jaguar's own engine. In 1947, the company launched the drophead coupé, designed very much with the export drive and American market in mind. **Power: 102bhp Top speed: 87mph**

Jaguar Mark V 1948–1951

Designed as a replacement for the 2½-litre saloon, the Mark V was the first Jaguar to feature independent front suspension. This was the last model powered by the six-cylinder Standard-derived engine that had served the company so well for over 20 years.

Power: 125bhp Top speed: 91mph

Jaguar XK120 1948–1954

Originally planned to raise marque identity through competition, the XK120 proved such a hit that Lyons put it into mainstream production. The first 240 examples were aluminium-bodied, but to meet with demand Jaguar switched to pressed-steel panels in 1950. The remarkable new twin-cam six-cylinder XK engine was a major motivating factor behind the car's success. In 1951 a fixed-head coupé XK120 was launched, extending appeal.

Power: 180bhp Top speed: 125mph

Jaguar MkVII/VIIM 1951–1957

The firm enlisted the help of the Pressed Steel Company to mass-produce body panels for its newest saloon. The elegant MkVII was powered by the XK engine, which was lauded for its responsiveness in the XK120 and gave this car an impressive turn of speed, too. In 1954 the VIIM was launched, with a new high-compression XK motor boosting power from 160bhp to 190bhp.
Power: 160bhp Top speed: 105mph

Jaguar C-type 1951–1953

Only 53 XK120Cs were ever produced, partially due to delays in moving to the Browns Lane factory in Coventry. The tubular chassis and aluminium body helped the car drop 450kg compared with the standard XK120 roadster, but mechanically the models were similar although the engine was upgraded and performance suitably uplifted. The C-type won at its first Le Mans attempt in 1951.
Power: 200bhp Top speed: 144mph

Jaguar D-type 1954–1957

The D-type was perhaps *the* competition car of its day; it was never actually designed as a road vehicle. The alloy monocoque body and highly efficient aerodynamic shape resulted in a machine that took Le Mans by storm from 1954-57. The car's designer, Malcolm Sayer, moved to Jaguar from Bristol Aeroplanes after World War Two, and brought with him considerable aeronautical experience to aid high-speed stability.
Power: 250bhp Top speed: 170mph

Jaguar XK140 1954–1957

Replacing the XK120 was never going to be easy, and many existing customers were left feeling disappointed by the XK140. Although more powerful, it was bigger and heavier, and so less of an out-and-out sports car. However, the driving experience was blunter and more relaxed, resulting in a long-distance cruiser which was perfect for the impending motorway age.

Power: 190bhp Top speed: 123mph

Jaguar 2.4/3.4 1955–1959

Just like the D-type racer, the 2.4 saloon featured unitary construction; the first road-going Jaguar to do so. The new model's swooping, low-roofed styling set the trend for its successors for years to come, and proved a big hit with buyers. Initially the car was offered with the detuned, short-stroke 2.4-litre XK engine, but a larger 3.4-litre version was added to the range to satisfy demand in the USA.

Power: 112bhp Top speed: 101mph

Jaguar XKSS 1957

When Jaguar gave up racing the D-type, it was left with a handful of unused, lightweight monocoque chassis. A vestigial windscreen and fabric roof were added, and the road-going XKSS was born. Lyons planned to sell the car in the USA, to people who wanted to compete in Class C production racing. However, only 16 found homes before the factory fire of 1957 destroyed the remaining cars.

Power: 250bhp Top speed: 144mph

Jaguar MkVIII/IX 1957–1961

As with the VII before it, the MkVIII featured independent front suspension. It resembled the VII in many ways, but was much more luxurious and chrome-laden – and these features divided opinions. Despite its bulkiness, however, the MkVIII was agile and fun to drive, even more so in 220bhp MkIX form. Race-proven disc brakes were standard on the later cars, a Jaguar first.

Power: 210bhp Top speed: 106mph

Jaguar XK150 1957–1961

At 1364kg, the XK150 wasn't exactly a lightweight. Aluminium panels were added to the exterior in an attempt to rein in the overall bulk, but still it tipped the scales at 50kg more than the XK140. The XK150 was the first Jaguar available with all-round disc brakes, and it proved an excellent stopper. In 1959 the XK150S was launched, and boasted an impressive 265bhp and a limited-slip differential to handle the extra power.

Power: 190bhp Top speed: 125mph

Jaguar Mk2 2.4/3.4/3.8 1959-1967

For many, the Mk2 is the definitive classic Jaguar. When new, it was roomy, fast and affordable, and leagues ahead of the opposition. Unsurprisingly, the Mk2 was a massive success in both the UK and USA, with a total of 83,976 examples produced. Dynamically it was spot-on, too: thanks to various suspension and cosmetic upgrades, it felt so much more than a revised 2.4/3.4 'Mk1'.
Power: 120bhp Top speed: 96mph

Jaguar E-type 1961-1975

Another landmark Jaguar – and although it's debatable that the first models were really capable of a genuine 150mph, there's no denying it was the fastest car you could buy for the money. As it grew older, it also became fatter due to American safety and emissions regulations. All E-types had independent suspension and all-round discs. The Series IIIs, introduced in 1971, ushered in the remarkable new V12 engine, but visually the larger bumpers and wide chrome grille jarred.
Power: 265bhp Top speed: 151mph

Jaguar 420 1966-1969

The marque created its 420 by facelifting the S-type and shoehorning the 4.2-litre XK engine under the bonnet. In doing so, the ultimate expression of the Mk2 family emerged, although the new front-end styling was less elegant. New features such as the MkX's variable-ratio power-steering made it a very pleasant driving experience indeed.
Power: 245bhp Top speed: 122mph

Jaguar MkX 3.8/4.2/420G 1961-1970

Serving as the marque's flagship for nine years, the MkX was a technological tour de force. The firm threw in everything it could – unitary body, independent rear suspension and an all-round disc brake set-up. As Jaguars went, this one was hard to beat in terms of value for money – and for years it was in the *Guinness Book of Records* for being the widest production car available in the UK.
Power: 265bhp Top speed: 120mph

Jaguar S-type 3.4/3.8 1963-1968

The S-type was designed as an intermediate model to plug the gap between the Mk2 and MkX. Using the smaller car as a starting point, it was created by rummaging through the parts bin. It used the MkX's independent rear suspension, plus had an extended back end and an improved interior. The result was a luxury sports saloon that extended the life of the Mk2 usefully, and which today is cruelly undervalued compared with its illustrious brother.
Power: 210bhp Top speed: 114mph

Jaguar 240/340 1967-1969

Bestowing the 2.4 engine with a modified cylinder head and improved inlet manifold meant that the Mk2-based 240 could finally top 100mph. The same motor in this car's predecessor never had enough power to push it past the magic ton; a fact that caused Jaguar embarrassment. Production continued long after the arrival of the XJ6, and it proved a useful money-spinner for the firm.
Power: 133bhp Top speed: 105mph

Jaguar XJ6/XJ12 S1 1968-1973

This was the first generation of the very successful XJ model line-up, and introduced a new platform strategy that saw a single range replace the mixed bag of previous cars. The Series I XJ6 was not entirely new yet it was designed to reinvent the Jaguar brand, echoing the important values of previous models but moving the marque forwards. The XJ boasted all-round independent suspension for a world-beating set-up, as well as the well travelled XK engine.

Power: 245bhp Top speed: 124mph

Jaguar XJ-C 1975-1977

The two-door XJ-C was prematurely announced in the summer of 1973, yet due to delays in development and production engineering the car wouldn't go on sale for a further two years. It was worth the wait, though, thanks to successful styling and world-class dynamics. All models got a vinyl roof, but the frameless windows that had caused so much trouble during development were noisy at speed and often leaked. A total of 8373 XJ-Cs were manufactured.

Power: 167bhp Top speed: 116mph

Jaguar XJ6/XJ12 SII 1973-1979

Many detail improvements were made to the XJ when creating the Series II. The new heating and ventilation system was welcome, as were the further tweaks to the XK engine which boosted fuel economy. The interior received an upgrade, but the only external differences were the smaller grille and raised front bumpers to help the XJ meet USA safety regulations. Unfortunately the Series II was plagued with poor build quality and reliability issues – a sign of the times.

Power: 167bhp Top speed: 124mph

Jaguar XJ-S 1975-1996

Based on a shortened XJ6 chassis, the XJ-S was the long-awaited replacement for the E-type – yet it ended up missing the mark with buyers. It wasn't a sporting drive in the way the early E-types were, but a Grand Tourer cast in the Series III mold. The XJ-S was in production for over 20 years, and it eventually became a financial success for Jaguar after blooming late in life.

Power: 285bhp Top speed: 150mph

Jaguar XJ6/XJ12 SIII 1979-1992

With a little help from Pininfarina, the XJ's subtle but effective late-life facelift kept it fresh enough to make it desirable for a further 13 years. In 1981, the V12 version received HE cylinder heads, pushing fuel consumption from the realms of scandalous to merely excessive. The XJ's continuing commercial success was helped by continually improving quality standards during the 1980s.

Power: 285bhp Top speed: 146mph

→

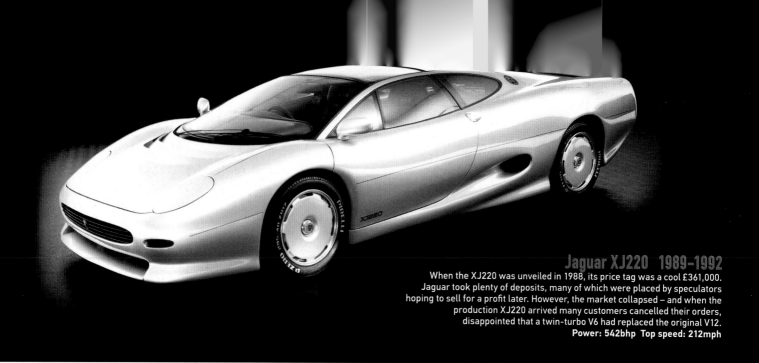

Jaguar XJ220 1989–1992

When the XJ220 was unveiled in 1988, its price tag was a cool £361,000. Jaguar took plenty of deposits, many of which were placed by speculators hoping to sell for a profit later. However, the market collapsed – and when the production XJ220 arrived many customers cancelled their orders, disappointed that a twin-turbo V6 had replaced the original V12.
Power: 542bhp Top speed: 212mph

Jaguar XJ6/12 (XJ40/XJ81) 1986–1994

Development work on the XJ40 started back in 1972, but it dragged on so long because of a lack of funding and management direction from BL. When the car arrived, it embodied the best and worst of contemporary Jaguar – it was technologically ahead of the previous XJ and its rivals, but quality was woefully lacking. The V12's four-year delay also limited the model's appeal.
Power: 223bhp Top speed: 140mph

Jaguar XJR-15 1990

Built by Tom Walkinshaw Racing (TWR) for Jaguar, the XJR-15 was little more than an XJR-9 Le Mans car with an all-new Peter Stevens-designed Kevlar and carbon-fibre body. Unlike the XJ220, it was powered by a normally aspirated V12 engine producing 450bhp. The XJR-15 remains a very raw, unrefined, street-legal race car, which does little to hide its competition roots.
Power: 450bhp Top speed: 185mph

Jaguar XJ6/XJ8/XJ12 (X300/X305/X308) 1994–2003

Mechanically similar to the XJ40, this car's more curvaceous frontal styling harked back to the earlier XJ models. The X300 also signalled the entrance of higher-quality Jaguars overseen by Ford. The limited visual upgrades made a huge difference to the X300's overall desirability, and because Jaguar insisted that it didn't want to share any components with cars from its parent company, the temptation to dip into Uncle Henry's parts bin was successfully resisted.
Power: 216bhp Top speed: 137mph

Jaguar XK8/XKR 1996–2006

The XK8 was styled with the E-type very much in mind, although Jaguar didn't want it to seem too retro. Designed in-house at Whitley in Coventry, the AJV8 engine was completely new and claimed to be one of the most technically advanced motors of its day. However, there was little else in the way of ground-breaking technology to mark out the rest of the car, which shared its underpinnings with the XJ-S. Despite that, the XK8 became the best-selling Jaguar sports car to date.
Power: 290bhp Top speed: 155mph

→

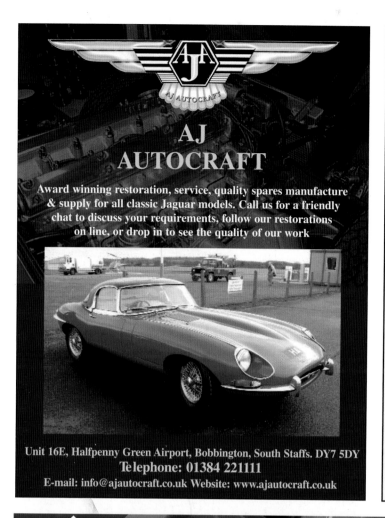
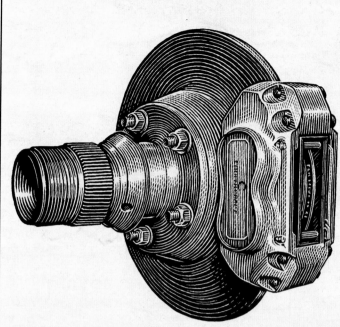

Jaguar S-type 1998-2008

Sharing its platform with the Lincoln LS, the early S-type wasn't blessed with great handling but it did offer fine value for money. Jaguar worked some of its magic into the later cars with an improved dynamics package that transformed the drive. Retro styling split opinions, but this was the company's first model in this sector for over 30 years, making Jag ownership a more affordable proposition. **Power: 240bhp Top speed: 146mph**

Jaguar XJ/XJ6/XJ8/XJR 2003-2009

On the surface this XJ looked just like the old one, but it was actually new from the ground up. It featured an aluminium monocoque, stiffer and lighter than the steel equivalent, and this was complemented by lightweight aluminium outer body panels. This lightness was the main reason for the XJ's excellent performance, handling and economy compared with its more conventionally engineered rivals. **Power: 240bhp Top speed: 145mph**

Jaguar XF 2008-date

Based on the show-stopping 2007 C-XF concept, the production XF represents a new direction for Jaguar design, and is a more forward-thinking model than any car produced by the company since the original XJ. The XF was introduced as a direct replacement for the S-type, and actually uses that vehicle's platform. But substantial structural changes have been made, improving safety, stiffness and space efficiency, and the overall result is a vast improvement for the driver. **Power: 235bhp Top speed: 147mph**

Jaguar X-type 2001-2009

The big cat's baby completed the four-model strategy devised by Ford to take the luxury-car fight to BMW. Originally available in 4WD form, the X-type struggled in the marketplace and picked up only with the introduction of the 2- and 2.2-litre diesels. It initially sold well in the USA, but a combination of strong competition and a poor exchange rate saw Jaguar pull the model from that market in 2007. **Power: 194bhp Top speed: 135mph**

Jaguar XK8/XKR 2007-date

The all-aluminium XK shares virtually nothing with its XK predecessor, apart from its AJV8 engine. Although the car is no more powerful, its lower kerbweight and improved body stiffness have radically improved this generation. The XKR version, which features a supercharged V8 motor producing an impressive 420bhp, is now considered a genuine supercar. **Power: 300bhp Top speed: 155mph**

Jaguar XJ 2009-date

'The new XJ is truly beautiful, exhilarating to drive and, with its bold, enlightened design, meets the challenges of our fast-changing world. It re-imagines the ultimate sporting luxury car.' So says Jaguar of the latest incarnation of its four-door flagship, available in standard and long-wheelbase form. Range-topping spec, an aluminium body and an emphasis on economy and emissions as well as muscle give this model everything it needs to take the marque into the future. **Power: 271bhp Top speed: 155mph**